CO 1 50 15

CW00594867

MURTON
5|97

SH

5015127   1329-973

DURHAM COUNTY COUNCIL
Arts, Libraries and Museums Department

Please return or renew this item by the last date shown.
Fines will be charged if the book is kept after this date.
Thank you for using *your* library.

 100% recycled paper

American political parties

Do the major American political parties fight over patronage rather than over issues involving public policy or principle? The lack of ideological depth and clarity of US parties is often remarked on by observers. This book argues that appearances can deceive and seeks to introduce the complexity of the American party system to an international student audience.

The text has been organized to examine the historical evolution of the party system and the forces that have shaped and re-shaped it. With this background established, the contemporary situation and scenarios for the future are closely examined. McSweeney and Zvesper focus their discussion on party policies and interests, development, realignment, organization, elections and the electorate, parties in government and the debate over the decline and reform of the party system in the US. Essential reference information is included on the 1988 and 1990 congressional and presidential elections and parties under the Bush presidency.

An accessible introduction for students of American politics as well as an interpretation of interests to other scholars, this book will appeal to students and lecturers of American and comparative politics on both sides of the Atlantic.

Dean McSweeney is Senior Lecturer in the Department of Economics and Social Science at Bristol Polytechnic. **John Zvesper** is a Lecturer in Politics at the University of East Anglia.

American political parties

The formation, decline and reform of the
American party system

Dean McSweeney and John Zvesper

London and New York

DURHAM COUNTY LIBRARY

ACC No. 5015127

CLASS No. 329. 973

First published 1991
by Routledge
11 New Fetter Lane, London EC4P 4EE

Simultaneously published in the USA and Canada
by Routledge
a division of Routledge, Chapman and Hall, Inc.
29 West 35th Street, New York, NY 10001

© 1991 Dean McSweeney and John Zvesper

Typeset in Times by Michael Mepham, Frome, Somerset
Printed and bound in Great Britain by
Biddles Ltd, Guildford and King's Lynn

All rights reserved. No part of this book may be reprinted or reproduced
or utilized in any form or by any electronic, mechanical, or other means,
now known or hereafter invented including photocopying and recording,
or in any information storage or retrieval system, without permission in
writing from the publishers.

British Library Cataloguing in Publication Data
McSweeney, Dean, *1951 –*
   American Political Parties: the formation, decline and
   reform of the American party system.
   1. United States. Political parties
   I. Title   II. Zvesper, John, *1948 –*
   324. 273
   ISBN 0-415-01169-8
   ISBN 0-415-01170-1 (pbk)

Library of Congress Cataloging in Publication Data
McSweeney, Dean, 1951 –
   American political parties: the formation, decline, and reform of
   the American party system / Dean McSweeney, John Zvesper.
   p.   cm.
   Includes bibliographical references (p.) and index.
   ISBN 0-415-01169-8
   ISBN 0-415-01170-1 (pbk)
   1. Political parties—United States—History. I. Zvesper, John,
   1948–. II. Title.
JK2261.M42   1991
324.273'09—dc20
90–19553
                                                            CIP

Contents

Figures and tables

Preface

The celebrations of the bicentenary of the framing of the American Constitution in 1987–89 will not be matched by comparable celebrations of the bicentenary of the founding of the American party system in 1991–92. Nevertheless, observers of the workings of American politics will rightly continue to focus at least as much of their attention on the party system as on the more formal institutions of government set up by the Constitution. It is true in the USA as elsewhere that extra-constitutional devices such as modern bureaucracy and twentieth-century communications media, devices dating from more recent times than the party system, are also now rivals for observers' attention. However, although the political decline of the party system – traceable in part to the flourishing of those newer political devices – makes the party system less important than it once was, that decline itself has come to be both a topic and a worry to political scientists. Therefore the undeniable decline in the importance of the party system does not – at least not yet – warrant a proportionate decline in the study of that system. That at any rate has been our assumption in writing this book, in which we describe the historical development and the basic features of the party system, and the continuing importance of parties in the political system, as well as the causes and the extent of the decline in that importance. The last quarter century has been a period of remarkable fluidity in the party system. We think it is now necessary and possible to put into clearer perspective its much-discussed decline, and to see why the system is neither withering away nor being reformed out of existence.

As residents of Europe, we have naturally written with the intention of making American political parties more intelligible to observers outside the USA. But our study is addressed equally to American-based observers. One of our concerns has been to explain the distinctive qualities of American parties, as contrasted to parties in other countries. Such an explanation may be even more useful to Americans than it is to foreigners, who already sense this distinctiveness even if they do not fully understand it. An increased awareness and understanding of the distinctiveness of their party system should deepen Americans' understanding of both their own and others' political systems. In this effort we have been assisted by materials supplied by the US Information Service at the American Embassy in London and by Pippa Norris. Joan Patrick and Ceri McSweeney, Angela Thomas, Jonathan and Louise Zvesper provided a mix of forbearance and diversion.

We are co-authors of the whole book, but it will probably not surprise anyone to reveal that the primary responsibility for Chapters One to Four was Zvesper's, while that for Chapters Five to Ten was McSweeney's. The separation of our powers was less distinct in the composition of the more speculative final chapter, so primary responsibility there cannot be so easily attributed. If there are errors of fact or interpretation they are *his* responsibility.

DM and JZ

1 Introduction: the debate over party in America

'I am not a member of an organized political party. I am a Democrat.' Will Rogers' witticism applied to a particular American political party at a particular time: the Democratic party in the 1920s, a coalition of incongruously diverse interests, with a tendency to reflect that diversity in very public displays of internal disagreements and in a chaotic kind of organization. But his point might well be made about all of the major American parties throughout the two hundred years of these parties' history. Especially from a European point of view, but also from the point of view of many American observers – admirers as well as critics – American political parties are such diverse coalitions, and so loosely organized and so weakly disciplined, that they seem scarcely to qualify for the label 'political party'.

Related to this internal diversity and loose organization, and equally remarkable – again, both to some native as well as many foreign observers – is the lack of ideological depth and clarity of the major parties. These parties often seem to be fighting merely over patronage rather than over issues involving any public policy or principle. Theodore Roosevelt once complained that the average New York party boss was 'quite willing to allow you to do what you want in such trivial matters as war and the acquisition of Puerto Rico and Hawaii, provided you don't interfere with the really vital questions, such as giving out contracts for cartage in the Custom House and interfering with the appointment of street sweepers' (Letter to Henry Cabot Lodge, 1898, cited in Garrity 1984: 231). American political parties seem somehow to be *highly* and *broadly* competitive – between as well as within themselves – without being very *deeply* competitive: politicians and ordinary citizens become highly excited about partisan contests along a broad range of issues, but the ideological range of the major parties seems generally so narrow that one is hard pressed to see any deep differences between the parties or to say why the partisan feelings run so high.

Appearances can deceive. We shall be arguing that to some extent these common perceptions are misperceptions. In the first place, one needs to remember that there are many places other than the USA where the classic English model of tightly disciplined, highly programmatic parties does not apply: for example, one finds rather amorphous parties in Ireland, factionalized dominant parties in Italy and Japan, parties as personal followings in France. It is useful and necessary to distinguish American political parties from political parties in European and other countries, but they are not totally dissimilar. Moreover, it is precisely the distinctive qualities of American political parties that make it inappropriate always to measure or to judge them by Eurocentric – or, as is perhaps more common, by Anglocentric – standards.

Briefly stated, on the question of organization, we shall notice that the American universe of party organizational types is diverse, and has included some impressively tight and effective structures, penetrating into government to an extent that would be enviable by most European parties. On the question of ideological depth, we shall argue that the conventional wisdom is unwise, and that interesting and deep issues of principle have been essential ingredients in American party battles, even though these battles have not been as broadly ideological as European ones. Finally, as for the oddity of some of the interest group coalitions comprising the major American parties, while not denying that the genius of the politician as a broker of the demands of interest groups has been highly prized and sometimes severely taxed in American politics, we shall remember that it is not only in America that politics makes strange bedfellows, and we shall suggest that there has usually been an intelligible relationship between the combinations of interests assembled by the parties and the ideological and policy positions of those parties.

However, we begin by accepting that there is some truth in the common perception that American parties are different. In this introductory chapter we focus first on the cultural and political environment of party development in the United States. The anti-party attitudes encouraged and expressed by this environment from the very beginning of American political party history help explain many of the distinctive features of the American party system. We note that the constitutional and legal environment of parties continues today to embody these attitudes – often in a cruder and more hostile form than the originals – and to hamper or at least to direct in heavy-handed fashion the operation of parties as organizations and as governing bodies. We conclude this introductory chapter with some reflections on the implications of the umbrella nature of the major parties.

THE NOVELTY AND QUESTIONABLENESS OF PARTY SYSTEMS

Students of party systems should begin by reflecting on the relative novelty of their subject. Thoughtless acceptance of party government is as unedifying as thoughtless denunciation of it. Of course, political *parties*, as distinct from party *systems*, are inherent in and as old as political life itself. Political theorists who would suppress the conflict of partisans generally end up proposing the suppression of politics itself, whether by means of a Leviathan state or by means of transition to a stateless, politics-free society. However, to accept the role of partisan conflict in politics is not necessarily to accept either the inevitability or the desirability of a party *system*, in which one, two or several parties become informal institutions of government. In a party system, one or more political parties is accepted as an important part of the public constitution – of the way that politics is seen and expected to work – and partisanship itself is accepted as a more or less publicly respectable practice.

In the last two centuries, party systems have been established in all modern governments. This is a great and remarkable change. Students of the American party system, which currently sometimes appears to be declining to extinction, may want to ask whether that change is irreversible. But we draw attention to that change here in order to point out that it has been everywhere incomplete. The questionable character of political parties persists. Even in countries, and in those individual American states, where the constitution accommodates political parties more readily than does the American federal Constitution, party government is not identical to constitutional government. Even in one-party regimes, the party is distinct from the government. Parties and partisanship, as the words themselves indicate, are and are seen to be partial. They do not directly represent everyone, and therefore their claims to advance the public good are suspect. Partisanship is much more respectable than it used to be, but it is still not completely respectable – in public opinion, that is, whatever may be the opinions expressed in political science textbooks. Even in Britain, for so long the model party government country in the textbooks, public opinion harbours doubts that anything that is 'party political' can be wholly respectable.

The anti-partisan attitudes expressed by Americans are therefore not unique. However, in the United States these attitudes have probably been more effective than elsewhere in shaping constitutional, legal and moral restraints and constraints on political parties.

THE RANGE OF ATTITUDES TOWARDS PARTISANSHIP

Because of the importance of attitudes towards political parties in establishing and maintaining party systems, it is important to study with some care the possible and actual range of attitudes in any given country. Three basic attitudes towards political parties are possible, once it is accepted that they are an inevitable part of political life. All three of these attitudes were expressed during the formative period of the American regime, from the Revolution in the 1770s to the rise of a mature party system in the 1840s. None of the three attitudes has completely disappeared today.

Parties as unrespectable elements with selfish purposes

The traditional view of parties, which goes back at least as far as Aristotle's *Politics*, tries to moderate partisan conflict with rational arguments about the common good, to which all parties are encouraged to contribute. In this view, parties do not merit elevation into respectable public institutions, although it is admitted that they often do control public policy, if only from behind the scenes. Parties unmoderated by rational statesmen are selfish interests, too private-spirited to be regarded as parts of the public constitution. Parties are inevitable and tolerable, but in their raw, unrefined state not particularly desirable or useful elements in a political regime, because they are embodiments of class interests, not the public interest. Parties are expressions of economic class interest that are at best – and only rarely – transformable (by statesmanship, not by party government) into forces supporting a constitution and policies serving the public good.

Parties as unrespectable organizations with public purposes

Compatible with the traditional attitude of toleration accompanied by suspicion and attempts to moderate is this rather different view of parties as the secret weapons of statesmen, to be deployed less in public than in private, but nevertheless for public purposes not otherwise attainable. This second view is for obvious reasons less prominently expressed than the first one; secret weapons lose much of their value if they are too explicitly discussed. But it can be seen, for example, in the attitudes taken by the first American partisans, the Jeffersonian Republicans, before they went public with their partisanship in 1791. In this view, parties are not motivated merely by private interests, but by public purposes. They are not interest groups or personal cliques. Instead they are, or at least on occasion can be, associations of citizens or politicians motivated by a desire to serve the public interest, and informed by a view of what the public interest requires in the circumstances.

The conspiratorial manner of this public service is necessary both for the immediate reason that publicity might ruin the scheme at hand, and for the more indirect reason that partisans of this kind do not want to set a precedent and encourage the general public respectability of partisanship, because it is difficult if not impossible reliably to distinguish this good, public-spirited partisanship from the bad, selfish kind, from which it is rarely entirely separable. Parties are emergency devices, to be used in the dark as much as possible and only as a last resort; they are not everyday instruments of government, to be employed frequently and in broad daylight.

Publicly respectable parties

The traditional attitude was expressed more in ancient political theory than in practice in the governments of the ancient republics of Greece and Rome, and in any case it had to be modified when political partisanship became associated with the cosmopolitan principles of Christianity. This association – unknown, of course, to pagan political theory – created new and great difficulties for the strategy of moderating partisan conflict in order to direct it towards the public good. The modification of the traditional attitude resulted partly from the attempt to pursue this strategy in the context of this important new circumstance. Pursuing this strategy in this context seemed to require reversing the traditional attitude towards party, and produced the attitude essential to modern party systems: partisanship is to be accepted as a publicly respectable political practice. This modern attitude has been based on three very different arguments.

Respectability for one party of principle

Partisanship must be accepted because the pursuit of the public interest needs to be maintained by a (single) party dedicated to it (however much this party may incidentally involve the promotion of particular private interests as well). This argument in effect replaces the second view (parties as emergency devices, to be kept private and infrequent) with the view that principled partisanship needs to be continuous because the emergency is continuous: that is, either private interests are too strong to be subordinated to the party's view of the public interest without the use of partisanship, or – worse – private interests have already organized a party working against the public interest, so they need to be counterbalanced and defeated by the public-spirited party. This view informed the Jeffersonian Republicans after they went public with their partisanship, and it has reappeared whenever an American party has seen itself as the saviour of the republic, lined up against the enemies of the republic.

Respectability for two or more parties of principle

Partisanship must be accepted because legitimately competing views of the public interest need to be represented and promoted, in a system of (two or more) parties. Most commonly, this argument sees the need both for a party of progress and change, and for a party of conservatism and stability. The assumption of both attitudes towards respectability is that parties (or, in the first attitude, *a* party) motivated by secular, this-worldly principles can be less of a challenge to moderate politics than are religious parties, and that they may even be necessary in order to help suppress these latter disruptive forces.

Respectability for parties of private interest

Finally, the most sophisticated (not to say accurate) view is that partisanship must be accepted because an impartial, public interest simply does not exist. Once this truth is acknowledged, and especially after the parties of principle associated with the supra-political claims of revealed religion have been suppressed, there is no reason not to allow or even to encourage the open pursuit of private interests – perhaps preferably in a two-party system, which offers more incentives for conflicting interest groups to make deals with each other than are offered in a multi-party system. Parties, even if they are merely private-spirited interest groups, or at most log-rolling coalitions of such interests, are not only inevitable and tolerable, but also desirable. Parties are essentially private and selfish, but making them operate more in the open makes their competition less extreme and more honest. This third variation on the third attitude may seem more recognizably American, but in fact all three variants of this attitude have made important contributions to the shape of the American party system.

PARTIES AND THE ORIGINAL INTENTIONS OF THE FOUNDERS

It can be seen from our sketches of these attitudes (and it is obvious anyway) that one's attitude towards parties depends partly on how one defines parties. Are parties just selfish private interests, or are they principled political groups? Are they 'parties of interest' or 'parties of principle'? Failure to keep in mind this obvious distinction can cause confusion about the attitudes towards party expressed by American politicians in the early days of the Republic. It is somewhat misleading, for example, to think of the Constitution of 1787 as 'A Constitution Against Parties' (*pace* Hofstadter 1969). What the framers of the Constitution had in mind when they condemned political 'parties' were 'factions'. According to James Madison, the 'Father of the Constitution' and one of the co-authors of *The Federalist* (the classic commentary on and defence of the Constitution), a 'faction' is

> a number of citizens, whether amounting to a majority or minority of the whole, who are united and actuated by some common impulse of passion, or of interest, adverse to the rights of other citizens, or to the permanent and aggregate interests of the community.

> (*The Federalist* 10)

In *The Federalist*, as well as in other contemporary statements, 'parties' and 'factions' are often interchangeable terms, and when they are, parties are of course looked on with a traditional attitude of suspicion. But it is 'parties of interest' rather than 'parties of principle' that are suspected. American political parties as we know them today, which are (as we shall see) in important ways 'parties of principle', would not be subject to the same suspicion.

Not even 'factions' ('parties of interest') are totally condemned by the framers' views. The development of interest groups is accepted as inevitable in a free (republican) political life. And in the modern world, it is acknowledged that a great diversity of economic interests – 'a landed interest, a manufacturing interest, a mercantile interest, a moneyed interest, with many lesser interests, grow up of necessity....' (*The Federalist* 10). We shall see shortly how important this fact and the acknowledgement of it have been to the style of American party politics.

Although the American founders adopted much of the traditional attitude towards political parties, their own political thought was much more optimistic than that of the ancients. They had great hopes that their experiment in republicanism would be more successful than those in the ancient world, where the political philosophers' call for moderation of partisan warfare had gone unheeded. They thought that the middle-class character of American society (relatively free from the extreme social divisions that poisoned both ancient republics and modern European politics), the spread of enlightened, liberal education in the modern world, and their own advances in the science of politics, would all help make the American republic less mired in faction – and therefore more durable – than ancient republics had been (Zvesper 1989). They did not think parties as interests could be avoided, but they did think – optimistically, it turned out:

1 that the distance between interest groups and the new political institutions being set up by the new Constitution could be great enough to allow ample space for deliberation by politicians, relatively free from 'the spirit of party and faction' (*The Federalist* 10), and

2 that although 'a zeal for different opinions... concerning government' has been known to produce partisan conflict (*The Federalist* 10), parties of principle would no longer be needed in America, where everyone agreed on the principles of government.

In other words, they assumed that parties of interest would thrive in American society, but parties of principle would not (because they would not be needed), and that the operations of government, at least at the national level, could be kept fairly insulated from the parties of interest. Theirs was to be not a Constitution *against* parties (whether of interest or of principle), but a Constitution *above* parties of interest, and *untroubled by* parties of principle.

Both of these expectations of the founders were to be thwarted within a few years of their Constitution being put into operation. The first administration under this Constitution took office in 1789; by the elections of 1792, open party warfare was evident (Hoadley 1986:189-90; Zvesper 1977:68–81). The doubts of the founders about the need for publicly respectable partisanship have never disappeared from American politics. However, they have been intensified – and distorted – by reaction against the parties in various reform movements, stemming mainly from the progressive reform era of the early twentieth century. It is important to distinguish the founders' distrust of parties of interest and their failure to foresee the recurring need for parties of principle, from the progressives' reaction against the kind of parties that American parties had become a century later, in the latter part of the nineteenth century. As we shall see when we look at the development of the party system in Chapter Three, the founders' views were relatively easily converted (in the first half of the nineteenth century) into support for a party system. The ease of this conversion is due to the fact that their views were actually less generally hostile to partisanship than the progressives' views (which themselves were primarily concerned with purifying rather than abolishing the parties). Lumping together the anti-party views of the founders with those of the progressives is a very common mistake that hinders the attempt to understand how anti-party attitudes have affected American politics.

We shall return to the development of American attitudes towards parties when we look at the development of the party system in Chapter Three, and when we consider the barriers to party realignment in Chapter Four, the difficulties of party organization in Chapter Six and the obstacles to party government in Chapter Nine. Here we merely note that this old question of the propriety of partisanship is still today a contentious political and legal issue in the United States, in a way that it is not anywhere else. The current debate over the extent to which parties should be legally regulated stems in part from this continuing questionableness of political partisanship (Lawson 1985, Epstein 1989).

PARTY COALITIONS AND RHETORIC IN A LARGE REPUBLIC

One of the best-known advances in political science made by the founders, and a feature of their political thought that has often fascinated and some-times instructed political scientists in the twentieth century, is Madison's case for the possibility and even the necessity of a large territory and a large and diverse population, for the successful structuring and functioning of politics in a republic – that is, in a regime not based upon a monarchical or aristocratic 'will... independent of the majority' (*The Federalist* 51). Madison argued, contrary to the traditional view that republics were appropriate only in small countries, that the use of federalism and representation made republican politics possible in a large country, and – more importantly – that a large territory made republican politics less likely to succumb to 'the mischiefs of faction' – that is, less likely to be dominated by a majority party acting unjustly towards minorities or unwisely with regard to the long-term interests of the community at large. As for the latter danger, representation can 'refine and enlarge the public views by passing them through the medium of a chosen body of citizens, whose wisdom may best discern the true interest of their country' (*The Federalist* 10); and as for the former danger (oppression of minorities), a heterogeneous population 'spread over an extensive region' is less likely to 'be subject to the infection of violent passions or to the danger of combining in pursuit of unjust measures' (*The Federalist* 63): with an enlarged territory, 'you take in a greater variety of parties and interests; you make it less probable that a majority of the whole will have a common motive to invade the rights of other citizens [because no one party will be 'able to outnumber and oppress the rest']; or if such a common motive exists, it will be more difficult for all who feel it to discover their own strength and to act in unison with each other' (*The Federalist* 10; see also *The Federalist* 51).

Madison's case for an enlarged territory and diverse population has been taken by later generations of political scientists as a classic statement of the necessity of broad coalition-building in American party politics. In a large and diverse country, only parties that are broad coalitions of various interests, and only politicians who are builders or at least beneficiaries of such coalitions, can expect to succeed. Madison himself and his colleagues did not think quite in these terms, because (as we have seen) they hoped that parties of interest (factions) would not be so intimately involved in the political deliberations of the representatives elected to govern the new nation. Their views are far from the principles of those twentieth-century political scientists (e. g. Arthur Bentley or David Truman) who see in all party politics only the interplay of group interests, and who tend to adopt the third non-traditional attitude described above (parties of private interests to be granted public respectability, the public interest being a phantom). Nevertheless, the adjective 'Madisonian' is now frequently used to describe the process of broad coalition-building that successful American party politicians have to engage in. And this usage is not wholly inaccurate, because in that process the moderation of diverse groups' demands through mutual concessions arranged by politicians acting as brokers can have a similar effect to one sought by Madison and the other founders, even though it reaches that end by different means. That end is the avoidance of extreme class conflict between rich and poor: the avoidance of the oppression of the poor by the rich, and of the rich by the poor. As noted above, the divisions between rich and poor were expected to be less extreme in America than in the Old World. But that in itself might sooner exacerbate than moderate class warfare and oppression, since classes more within sight of each other might well contend more rather than less. Madison's observations about the internal diversity of the classes of the rich and the poor – a diversity greater in a large and economically developed republic than in a small and undeveloped one – provide an additional and perhaps greater reason for the founders' hopes that partisan conflict between socio-economic classes would be less of a problem in their modern republic than it had been in the ancient ones. In Chapter Five, we shall be looking in some detail at the explanations offered for the relatively small success of socialist parties in the USA. But we note here that from the outset the socio-economic diversity of the large republic was relied upon to prevent class consciousness from dominating party conflict. When the rich *and* poor members of each economic sector are pitted against the rich *and* poor of several others, the division between rich and poor becomes less politically salient, and the resulting patterns of alliances among the 'various and interfering interests' (*The Federalist* 10) is likely to be quite intricate, even internally contradictory.

The necessity of rather Byzantine coalition-building has been accompanied by a higher regard being accorded by many Americans to party politicians who have been able to build such coalitions, than to those who have appealed to straightforward class divisions. They are celebrated as 'artists in group diplomacy' (Binkley 1947: 338). Their artistry often requires them to be less clear in their public statements and policy positions than they might otherwise be. The fictional Mr Dooley's famous caricature of President Theodore Roosevelt's position on the 'trusts' (monopolies) serves to encapsulate the public rhetorical style as well as something of the strategy of the successful American group diplomat:

The trusts are heijious monsthers built up by the inlightened intherprise ov th' men that have done so much to advance progress in our beloved counthry. On wan hand I wud stamp thim undher fut; on th' other hand, not so fast. What I want more thin th' bustin' iv th' trusts is to see me fellow counthrymen happy an' continted. I wudden't have thim hate th' thrusts. Th' haggard face, th' droopin' eye, th' pallid complexion that marks th' inimy iv thrusts is not to me taste. Lave us be merry about it an' jovial an' affectionate. Lave us laugh an' sing th'octopus out iv ixistence.

(Quoted in Binkley 1947: 339)

As Mr Dooley intimates, at its worst, this coalition strategy and rhetorical style can serve only to mask an opportunism barren of any real ambition or result beyond merely staying in political business, and avoiding harsh partisan choices and fights. Even at its best, it is a strategy and style calculated to annoy the lovers of clear and simple partisan divisions (such as is found in open class warfare), or of uncluttered statements of purpose and ideological purity.

Nevertheless, building diverse, difficult-to-manage coalitions, cross-sections of society rather than sections, has always been an imperative of party politics in the large American republic, and has often required in coalition managers a rhetorical tactfulness that can seem like wilful blandness. There are other reasons for the lack of clarity in the ideological and policy positions of the most successful American parties and party politicians; as we shall see in Chapter Three, there has even been a principled argument against too easy and frequent an appeal to high principle in the American party system. But the simple necessity of difficult, imaginative coalition-building goes a long way to explain the issue fuzziness of the most successful American party politicians. Because coalition-building and coalition-maintaining is a gradual and incessant process, the policy positions of the major parties, even when the differences between them are deep, are only painfully and gradually defined. Even relatively strong partisan presidents like Andrew Jackson and Franklin Roosevelt have been elected in the first place without tightly defining what they would do in office; and after they are elected, presidents and Congressmen go on bargaining with each other and with interest groups, so their policy positions are subject to amendment as they go along. Government by consent in the USA is a continuous process, not a matter for elections and party government to settle at a stroke.

In the next chapter, we briefly and selectively survey the history of American parties, paying particular attention to differences between the interest coalitions and policy positions of the major parties, in order to show that American parties have not lacked such differences, however differently they may have manifested them in comparison to parties elsewhere. In

Chapter Three we examine the establishment and development of the party system by looking at historical changes in its purposes and techniques, and at its problematic relationship to the federal Constitution. In this survey, as in Chapter Two, we emphasize the dual nature of the party system, its functioning as an instrument both for policy conflicts and for interest coalitions. Chapter Four focuses on critical party realignment, the means by which the party system has moved on from one set of conflicts and coalitions to another. In Chapter Five we explore the causes and consequences of the dominance of American politics by two parties, looking at the state as well as the federal level, and paying particular attention to the weakness of American socialist parties. The principal structures and activities of modern party organizations – both formal and informal – are dissected in Chapter Six; in Chapter Seven we examine in greater detail their activities in elections; and in Chapter Eight we review relations between parties and the electorate. An account of the influence of parties on government (and the lack of it) completes our study of the structures and functions of the party system, but in Chapter Ten we summarize and assess the importance of the decline of that system, and pinpoint the reasons for the rather drastic decline that occurred in the 1960s and 1970s. In a final chapter we speculate about ways in which the party system might change in the near future.

2 Party policies and interests

In this chapter we survey the history of American political parties, to see what the major party battles have been about, and to emphasize the fact that successful major parties have been parties both of interests and of principle. They have owed their success not only to the comprehensiveness of their group coalitions but also to the rhetorical or ideological banners that they have waved. This is especially clear at the presidential level, since presidents (and vice presidents) are the only elected representatives of the whole of the large republic. In presidential contests, the most successful 'artists in group diplomacy' have been not those (like Henry Clay, the losing candidate in 1836 and 1844, Thomas Dewey, the loser in 1944 and 1948, or Walter Mondale, the loser in 1984) who have demonstrated only a cool calculation of the current logic of group diplomacy in the large republic, but those who have combined that calculation with 'the heart-warming message of a crusader for a living cause' (Binkley 1947: 394). The trick has been to lead a crusade to save the republic, without saying anything that would alienate the support of any group essential to electoral victory. Building broad coalitions of interests need not mean avoiding ideology, but if the power of ideology is to be used, it must be used deftly. It is no mean feat of statesmanship for an American politician to find a common political principle that is acceptable to a sufficient number of groups to add up to an electoral majority.

One can trace certain continuities between the interests, personnel and rhetorical themes of the first major parties – the Federalists and the Jeffersonian Republicans – and later ones. The Federalists, who disappeared from the scene during the second decade of the nineteenth century, were in some of these ways replaced by the Whigs (from the 1830s to the 1850s) and then by the Republican party of today (which traces its history to the 1850s). (However, it must be added that the Republican party of the 1850s traced the antislavery policies that were its *raison d'être* to Jefferson, not to Federalists or Whigs.) From the Jeffersonian Republicans can be traced a line of continuity through the Jacksonian Democratic party of the 1830s right up through to the New Deal Democrats and the Democratic party of today. Thomas Jefferson and Andrew Jackson are still the patron saints of the Democratic party. In spite of the continuities, the historical breaks are significant. Historians and political scientists generally present the history of American political parties in terms of five distinct 'party systems' – that is, five historical periods in each of which two major parties have contended. The periods of transition between the historical 'systems' are periods of 'critical elections', during which party loyalties and agendas are established for several subsequent decades – for the duration of that 'system'. (The concept of critical party realignment has become so important in discussions of the American party system that we devote all of Chapter Four to this topic.) The two major parties of each system display interesting and significant divisions within themselves, but we concentrate here on the divisions between the parties, which are deepest during the system-forming periods of critical elections.

THE FIRST PARTY SYSTEM (1790s–1820s)

James Madison and Alexander Hamilton, the major co-authors of *The Federalist* and two of the leading figures in the campaign to get the Constitution ratified, were optimistic about their experiment in republican government in the modern world. But in fact in private they both expressed doubts about the probable success of the new framework of government, thinking that in spite of the new government's being an improvement on the altogether too flimsy government set up by the Articles of Confederation (the previous constitution), it would still prove to be too weak to overcome the clashing interests and loyalties of the individual states. Hamilton, who was appointed secretary of the treasury in the new administration, set about to cure this defect by means of policies that would attach certain powerful economic groups to the success of the newly constituted central government. These policies soon met with considerable opposition, first within Congress and then (starting in 1792) in elections to Congress and (starting in 1796) the presidency. Madison led the opposition in Congress, and Thomas Jefferson assisted from his position as secretary of state. The opposition to Hamilton's Federalist party called itself the Republican party, because it portrayed itself as the saviour of the republic, which Hamilton's policies were threatening to turn into a monarchical government, on the English model, and with an English tilt in its foreign policy, too. The Republican party was stronger in terms of the popular appeal of its policies and in terms of the number and size of the interest groups that it assembled, but the involvement of American loyalties in the French Revolution and the wars following that revolution prevented this superiority from resulting in a decisive victory for the Republicans until 1800, when Jefferson was elected president. The presidency, House of Representatives and Senate then all remained in Republican hands for the duration of the first party system.

The interests that Hamilton hoped to join to the fate of the union of the states under the new government proved to be too narrow and too static to provide sufficient support after the Republican party challenged Federalist control. Hamilton's policies, set out in 1790 and 1791 in a series of cogent reports to Congress (which wrote most of them into law), were designed to make a political asset out of the financial debts that the government had inherited from the American Revolution. The government owed $12 million to foreigners and over $40 million to American creditors. Everyone agreed that the foreign debt should be repaid in full, but the new secretary of the treasury proposed as well that the federal government not only repay fully (instead of in part, as was generally expected) the domestic portion, but also that it take over the remaining war debts of the individual states (about $21 million). The idea was to give public creditors not only abroad but also at home a strong interest in the survival and flourishing of the central government, and to wean them away from interdependence with and loyalty to the state governments. Hamilton's policies naturally attracted the support of many rich and influential groups, especially merchant shipowners and financiers along the eastern seaboard. The Federalist coalition also included many groups of workers in industries that received the benefit of protective tariffs under the new government. However, Federalist policies – for the purposes of broad coalition-building – over-rewarded these interests, piling benefit on top of benefit, and therefore failed to broaden the party's support by spreading benefits in a way that attracts new recruits. They also alienated the support of some groups, most importantly large plantation owners in the south, who had supported the Federalist movement for a stronger central government in the years before it was revealed how that government was to be used against agrarian interests.

Ultimately, Hamilton and other Federalist leaders hoped their policies of funding the war debts, setting up a national bank to help establish sound money, and promoting manufactures by positive governmental patronage, would encourage a development of the American economy that would benefit all interest groups, although temporarily it favoured some interests (the non-agricultural ones) over others. So their vision was a moral, publicly defensible one, not simply a narrow, selfish economic vision.

However, the Federalists' ideology – the image of an enterprising society that they presented to Americans as their future – was an excessively cool and calculating vision, when compared to the Republicans' alternative. The Republicans' ideal was a society of virtuous farmers, whose economic independence made them morally and politically independent, and who needed to be presided over by a simple, frugal, low-profile, *laissez-faire* government, rather than by the energetic administrative Hamiltonian state. The warmer moral vision of the Republicans was more appealing in part simply because it was presented to a country in which ninety per cent of the population earned their living by farming. But Republicans did not restrict their coalition or their ideological attraction to agrarian interests. They stretched their ideal to include virtuous commercial and manufacturing interests as well. Jefferson once spoke of 'those who labor in the earth' as God's 'chosen people' ('if ever he had a chosen people'), but later he allowed that in the United States, with the safety valve of the land in the west to which urban labourers could repair when oppression threatened to turn them into a dependent, immoral urban proletariat, manufacturers could be 'as much at their ease, as independent, and moral as our agricultural inhabitants'- (Jefferson 1903–5 [1805], 11: 55). In fact, the Republican party was if anything more receptive than the Federalists to the full range of economic enterprise in the United States; the Federalists, for all that they favoured equality of economic opportunity in principle, were slow and indirect in expanding such equality. The social elitism and the narrow economic policies pursued by Federalists led to a gradual defection from the party by those members of the business community who saw greater opportunities opening up under the Republicans.

Thus the partisan division between Republicans and Federalists was much more complicated than a simple division between agrarian interests and non-agrarian interests. Republican candidates were supported most in areas where the established elites were being challenged by 'new men' taking more advantage of America's economic opportunities than Federalists really liked. However, the relation between these interests supporting and supported by the Republican party and the ideology of that party is also less than straight-forward. The Republicans did not content themselves with appealing to the Federalist principles of equality of opportunity, and pointing out that this principle was not being applied as well as it might be. This would have been to admit that the Federalist moral vision of an enterprising society accurately captured their true desires. Republicans chose rather to advance their desire for ungoverned enterprise by appealing to the virtues of the American people that made them much less readily transformable into politically neutral economic maximizers than Federalist policies seemed to assume. If they wanted what the Federalists were offering (bigger pieces of a growing economic cake), they wanted it faster and more widely than Federalists were prepared to deliver it, and – crucially for the substance of the party's ideology – they did not want to admit that they wanted it at all (Fischer 1965: 203–18; Zvesper 1977: 81–4, 123–31). They were a party of democratic capitalists, but they denied 'the spirit of capitalism'. They did not want to confess that their economic ambitions were perhaps great enough to make their independence somewhat precarious, and to warrant some economic regulation and direction by an energetic central government.

Because of their much wider and deeper ideological appeal, the Jeffersonian Republicans are properly regarded as the first true American political party, the first to campaign effectively to take power in order to save the republic from a set of policies that was threatening its ruin. In office, although they were able to consolidate their power by avoiding the most extreme measures that their opponents had feared, they consistently pursued policies in keeping with their ideological position, policies which sharply distinguished their administrations from those of the Federalists.

1 They scaled down the taxation of the central government, and nevertheless were able to enjoy revenue surpluses that enabled them to reduce the national debt (which they, unlike the Federalists, did not regard as a national blessing), by drastically reducing governmental expenditures, especially on the armed forces.

2 When war between France and England began to hurt American liberty and property, by the seizure of neutral vessels and the impressment of American sailors, the Republican administrations responded for several years with an ineffectual embargo, which hurt American interests much more than foreign ones; the reasoning behind this policy was the same as that behind the domestic policy of low-profile government. The Republicans' rather utopian ideal of free international trade matched their policy of domestic *laissez-faire*.

3 Tariffs on imports were kept relatively low; the Hamiltonian policy of using this device to encourage the growth of domestic manufactures was rejected.

4 The Federalist policy of trying to control state banks' unco-ordinated issues of credit was not pursued, not only because state banks were often closer to Republican interests, but also because Hamilton's scheme of planning and stabilizing the expansion of the money supply from the vantage point of the central government seemed to Republicans to smack of governmental 'consolidation' (collapsing the American federal system into a unitary government) and a British monarchical policy rather than an American republican one. It seemed to them that American government was being distorted into a unitary (rather than federal) and monarchical (rather than republican) system by Hamilton's policies. As explained by a Republican campaign pamphlet in 1800, Hamilton's 'funding system begets and perpetualizes debt; debt begets intrigue, offices, and corruption; those beget taxation,... a standing army,... monarchy, and... an enslaved and impoverished people' ('Marcus Brutus' 1800: 4).

THE SECOND PARTY SYSTEM (1820s–1850s)

The Republican administration, in spite of its pacific ideology, was eventually driven to fight another war against Britain (1812–15), both to defend American property and liberty, and to feed the land hunger of the Republican party by making a bid to seize some of the remaining British American territory. Neither of these aims was accomplished. Instead, the war increased the embargo's un-Jeffersonian tendency to encourage domestic manufactures (foreign markets and supplies being interrupted), and inspired a rather un-Jeffersonian nationalism that gave the *coup de grace* to the remnants of the Federalist party (whose opposition to conflict with Britain had made them adopt an antiunionist stance) but also gave a large part of the Republican party – who called themselves National Republicans – a Federalist-type agenda of central government promotion of domestic economic development. When President John Quincy Adams (the son of the last Federalist president, but who took office as a National Republican) presented this agenda to Congress in 1825, the immediate and effective opposition to it led to the rebirth of the two-party system, Andrew Jackson's election in 1828 signalling the arrival of a new majority party, the Jacksonian Democrats. By 1836 the National Republican opposition to Jackson, based in New England and the Ohio Valley (the then northwest), had allied themselves with those southern planters who were dissatisfied with Jackson's acceptance of a rather high level of protective tariffs. But this alliance dictated a new name for the anti-Jackson party. States' rights southerners could not call themselves *National* Republicans. To emphasize their opposition to Jackson's energetic exercise of executive power (especially in his crushing their attempts to 'nullify' federal tariff laws), they called themselves Whigs, and this name was then adopted by National Republicans in the north as well. The Whig party became the second of the two heterogeneous major parties in this system, rivalling the Democrats in all sections of the country. In voting in congressional elections, Whigs were much stronger, and Democrats much weaker, in New England than elsewhere (Ladd 1970: 100–2), but especially at the presidential level this was a period of real two-party competition, until the late 1840s and 1850s, when southerners deserted the Whigs and returned to the Democratic party, turning it into an instrument to defend slavery.

The Jacksonian Democrats defined themselves by a crusade against the Bank of the United States (which had been rechartered by the Republicans in the days of post-war nationalism in 1816). The Democratic party also opposed federal patronage of business enterprise and internal improvements (such as roads and canals). Jacksonian Democracy was thus an updated and westernized version of the Jeffersonian Republican crusade against Hamiltonian Federalism. The Whigs inherited Federalist policies. They were more successful electorally than the Federalists had been, partly because they were better at mimicking the Jacksonians than the Federalists had been at imitating the Jeffersonians. As their name indicates, the Whigs engaged more fully in the popular rhetoric of American party politics than had their Federalist precursors. When they won the presidency, they did so by nominating military heroes as presidential candidates, rather than party regulars who might emphasize too much the Whig party platform (manifesto) and policies, which were politically less marketable. In short, the Whigs learned better than the Federalists the role of the lesser of the two major parties in each successive American 'party system': the role of moon to sun. We shall elucidate more fully in Chapter Four how each historical 'party system' – with the possible exception of the current one – has had a dominant party, a natural party of government, whose glory must be reflected 'me too' fashion by the subordinate party if it is to survive and to prosper at all. In the first system the dominant party was clearly the Republicans, and in the second it was clearly the Democrats. Whig presidents were elected (in 1840 and 1848) only during economically hard times (and, in the latter case, when the Democrats were deeply divided over the slavery question, which was to be the basic issue of the third party system).

In principle, the Whigs, like their Federalist predecessors, were the party of sound finance and protected commerce and manufactures; the Democrats, like the Jeffersonian Republicans, were the party of the plain farmer (and therefore of westward expansion, cheap sales of public land, and aggressiveness towards Britain and Amerindians). The Whigs' principles were calculating rather than heartwarming. Only one Whig platform that dared to specify the party's 'great principles' was ever issued. In that platform (in 1844), the party's principles were 'summed as comprising' (in addition to anti-executive reforms) 'a well-regulated currency; a tariff... discriminating with special reference to the protection of the domestic labor of the country; [and] the distribution of the proceeds of the sales of the public lands...' to individual states. (This land revenue distribution policy resembled Hamilton's assumption of state debts, and had been carefully designed by Henry Clay for the Hamiltonian purpose of making public creditors grateful to the federal government, but also to reassure protectionists that the federal treasury surplus would not be used as an excuse to reduce tariffs, and to allow certain states to carry on with internal improvements without alarming states' rights opponents of the use of federal funds for these purposes [Johnson and Porter 1973: 8–9].) The Democratic platforms from 1840 (the first one issued) to 1856 contained a list (almost identical in all five) of opposite and more eloquent principles. These mainly concerned limitations on the federal government. Democrats denied that the federal government had the power to embark on 'a general system of internal improvements', to assume 'the debts of the several states, contracted for local internal improvements', 'to foster one branch of industry to the detriment of another', or 'to charter a national bank' – nor (reflecting abolitionist agitation, and anticipating the transition to the third party system) 'to interfere with or control the domestic institutions of the several states' (Johnson and Porter 1973: 2–4, 10–12, 16–18, 23–7). From 1844, the Democrats' platforms also contained statements against the Whigs' land revenue distribution policy, and in favour of territorial expansion (into Oregon and Texas).

In spite of the tendency of the Democrats towards agrarian interests and that of the Whigs towards everyone else, even more than in the first party system, the parties in the second system shared interest groups quite promiscuously. There were some elements of every major economic sector in both parties. What seems ultimately to have distinguished these parties is the same thing that distinguished the heterogeneous parties of Hamilton and Jefferson. Whigs expressed a 'special concern for endless progress under democratic capitalism, stimulated by the state'; whereas Democrats would 'insist that the changing world is full of terrors, and hint at least that once there was a better, even as [they help] perfect the instruments of change' (Meyers 1957: 237). Like the Jeffersonians, Jacksonians were ambivalent and fretful, and Whigs, like Federalists, were more open, calculating, comfortable and comforting, about the commitment of the United States to economic development, which all of the parties were actually advancing. In their rhetoric against credit systems and expensive, complicated economic works, Jacksonians, like Jeffersonians before them, 'were in some degree censuring their own economic attitudes and actions'; they were both 'the judges and the judged' (Meyers 1957: 121).

In addition to the westernization and democratization of party politics in the second system, relative to the first, and besides the innovative organizational and attitudinal developments to be discussed in Chapter Three, one further distinction between the first and second party systems is noteworthy: the growing saliency of immigration and ethnicity. Immigration grew from 128,502 in the 1820s to 2,814,554 in the 1850s (Ladd 1970: 76). The anti-British sentiments of the Democratic party were boosted by the large numbers of non-Anglo-Saxon ethnic groups who were associated with the Democrats. The Whigs, on the other hand, as the party of the economically more secure, were identified with English-Americans. Whig labour groups resented the rivalry of immigrant labourers. They resented the declining economic importance of native artisan crafts, as opposed to the less skilled industrial work undertaken by the immigrants. They pushed the Whig party towards anti-Catholicism and nativism (opposition to immigration and immigrants, to the 'foreign born' and their foreign cultures). Much Whig nativism was directed against the large numbers of Irish immigrants, who therefore found their political home in the Democratic party. One of the basic principles declared in the Democratic platforms from 1844 to 1856, alongside the increasingly insistent statements denying that slavery was a federal matter, was an invocation of 'the liberal principles embodied by Jefferson in the Declaration of Independence... which makes ours the land of liberty and the asylum of the oppressed of every nation', and which makes it wrong to 'attempt to abridge the privilege of becoming citizens and the owners of soil among us'. In 1856, when nativism was represented by a nationally competitive third party (the American or 'Know Nothing' party), the Democrats added to their platform a specific denunciation of the 'political crusade... against Catholic and foreign-born' (Johnson and Porter 1973: 2, 4, 9, 17, 24–5). The Whigs did not officially embrace nativism, but neither could they officially repudiate it, since they relied on it for electoral support. Their vice presidential candidates in 1844 and 1848 were nativists; Millard Fillmore, who was elected as Zachary Taylor's running mate in 1848, and became president on Taylor's death, was to be nominated for president by the American party in 1856. Ethnicity and race were from this time onwards to play an important role in defining the differences between the two major parties.

THE CIVIL WAR PARTY SYSTEM (1850s–1890s)

Although the 1830s and 1840s were a period when the two major parties, Democrats and Whigs, dominated party competition nationally, these parties' determination to avoid the disruptive issue of defining a federal policy on the expansion of slavery into US territories (to be organized into new states) led to a series of third-party movements. Antislavery forces mobilized behind the Liberty party (in 1840 and 1844) and the more comprehensive and more successful Free-Soil party (in 1848 and 1852). The showing of the latter was strong enough in 1848 to persuade elements of both of the major parties to move towards the 'free soil' position, favouring the exclusion of slavery from the territories. This threatened to replace the division between two national parties – Democrats and Whigs – with two sectional parties, northerners and southerners.

Centrist politicians of both parties tried to suppress the slavery question by means of the Compromise of 1850, which gave the south a new, harsh fugitive slave law, as well as federal neutrality on the question of extending slavery to New Mexico and Utah, and gave the north the admission of California as a free state (upsetting the balance between the number of free and slave states), and the abolition of the slave trade (though not slavery) in the District of Columbia. But many northern Whig politicians clung to the free soil position, with the result that the Whig party was split into northern and southern wings, the latter very weak compared to the southern Demo-crats. The Democratic party was not yet so badly split. The American (or 'Know Nothing') party, based on nativist policies, seemed likely to become the new national rival to the Democratic party. However, the Democratic president and Congress then passed the Kansas-Nebraska Act of 1854. This law called for the organization of those territories into states on the same 'popular sovereignty' basis as had been agreed in 1850 (although then as a compromise rather than as a highly principled policy) for Utah and New Mexico, and therefore called for the repeal of the Missouri Compromise of 1820. (This Compromise had admitted Missouri as a slave state, but had forbidden the northern extension of slavery into the other territories acquired as the Louisiana Purchase beyond the latitude that formed the southern boundary of Missouri.) An 'anti-Nebraska' party instantly formed, composed of many northern Democrats as well as Whigs. Anti-Nebraska candidates – soon to adopt the label 'Republican' – won a majority of seats in elections to the House of Representatives in 1854, and although they lost that majority in 1856 (at the same time that they lost their first bid for the presidency), they regained it in 1858, and in 1860 they won both the House and the presidency, an office they were to control until 1884. A new, 'third' party had become the dominant of the two major parties.

This party was organized to support a policy that was widely (although not universally) opposed in the south, and maintained only with difficulty in the north. Many northerners opposed the abolition of slavery for the same reason that they opposed the extension of slavery: they did not want to live and work alongside blacks. Many would have found it much easier to go along with the Democrats' 'popular sovereignty' doctrine, if they had not suspected that the slave power would cheat, and force slavery into territories where it would not naturally have extended itself. The choice of a Republican president in 1860 was a choice, based thus on a mixture of noble and ignoble motives, for a policy that put a stop to decades of temporizing over the slavery issue. It amounted to a rejection of the view held by Stephen Douglas and many other Democrats, as well as many Whigs, that slavery would die a natural death, if only the issue could be removed from the national political arena. This sanguine view, so congenial to nineteenth-century optimism concerning historical progress (in particular, concerning economic progress), is still often held today. In spite of the evidence to the contrary provided by various tyrannical regimes of the twentieth century, it is assumed that 'slavery is impossible in an industrial system' (Ladd 1970: 107), and that the Civil War was an unnecessary war, because there were natural economic limits to slavery expansion, which made taking a political stand against it unnecessary. The debates between these two approaches to the problem of slavery – Douglas's popular sovereignty approach and Abraham Lincoln's political decision approach – constitute a profound political and ideological conflict, wholly within the universe of democratic republicanism, but arguably as deep as any more European-style conflict between aristocracy and democracy, or communism and fascism (Jaffa 1973).

Lincoln, the Republican presidential candidate in 1860, had come into the Republican party from the Whig party. Lincoln and other Republican leaders maintained the old Whig tactic of avoiding any unnecessary offense to nativist sentiments. They also disavowed any intent to make blacks socially equal to whites. Thus they were able to gather into the Republican fold many northern American ('Know-Nothing') voters (especially 'native' labourers), without whose support they could not have become the majority party. Responding to pressure from German-Americans, the Republican party platforms of 1856 and 1860 opposed legislation impairing the security of 'equality of rights among citizens' (1856), specifically of immigrants and naturalized citizens (1860); in 1864, when there was an acute labour shortage caused by the war, the platform even called for the encouragement of immigration 'by a liberal and just policy' (Johnson and Porter 1973: 28, 33, 35–6). However, the party – especially the eastern wing – depended heavily on the support of nativists. Nativism was associated with Puritan and revivalist ('pietist', as opposed to 'liturgical') religious groups, who were the element of many nineteenth-century social and political reform movements. In this element, the abolition of alcohol (the Irish-American's whiskey and the German-American's beer) and the restriction of (non-English) immigration often went hand-in-hand with the abolition of slavery. At least until the Democratic party was captured by its rural, provincial wing in the 1890s (and even then the voters' shifts were mostly temporary deviations from this norm: Ladd 1970: 158–66; Sundquist 1983: 167–8), Catholic Americans and immigrants in general continued to find the Democratic party more welcoming than the Republican party.

In addition to Protestantism and flirtation with nativism, the Whigs brought into the new Republican party their attachment to federal government encouragement of internal improvements (now to include a transcontinental railroad), domestic manufactures and commerce, and hard money. From just after the Civil War (1861–5) down to the present day, the Republican party has been generally known as the party of industrial and financial development, the party of businessmen. This is not a wholly misleading characterization, although the umbrella nature of all major parties is visible in this one as well, especially in the decades during which the party was the dominant of the two major parties (1860-1932). However, it is important to notice that the party did not gain office by presenting itself as the party of business. In its origins, and at least occasionally during its long post-war reign, the Republican party, unlike the Whig party, was a party of conscience and of moral and political reform.

The original tie that bound all of the elements of the party together was opposition to the extension of slavery and of the 'slave power' of the south. The ever-growing population advantage of free over slave states all but guaranteed a succession of Republican presidents all following Lincoln's formula to victory. This threatened to prevent the further extension of slavery; to the slave power, as well as to Lincoln and many other Republicans, this was tantamount to putting the slave system onto a course where it would eventually be extinct. Without expansion, the system would wither. Besides, no more slave states would be created with Republicans controlling the presidency, no matter how tenuous their control of Congress, for Republican presidents would simply veto any bills trying to organize new slave states. After southern states, faced with this prospect, began to 'secede' from the union in 1861, Lincoln managed to enlarge his coalition by emphasizing the defence of the union rather than the opposition to the expansion of slavery. With that emphasis, he was able to keep the northern slave states loyal to the union, and therefore able to win the war against the south. But defence of the union always meant defence of the union with Republicans at the helm, and therefore meant opposition to slavery expansion – and therefore ultimately meant the end of slavery. The near certainty that this Republican policy would bring conflict between north and south actually persuaded many northern business interests to oppose the Republicans in 1856 and 1860 (Binkley 1947: 221, 233–4). War would not generally be good for business. During and after the war, the Republican party attracted, and perhaps could even be said to have been captured by, businessmen. But this was an instance of the old Machiavellian thesis that money follows power. In its origins, the Republican party, like all the other dominant major American parties (Jeffersonians, Jacksonians and New Deal Democrats), was if anything a party of the left, not of the right. (Karl Marx, then the *New York Tribune*'s European correspondent, supported Lincoln.) The platform of 1860 incorporated a Whiggish call for 'an adjustment of... imports... to encourage the development of the industrial interests of the whole country; and... that policy of national exchanges, which secures to the workingmen liberal wages, to agriculture remunerative prices, to mechanics and manufacturers an adequate reward for their skill, labor, and enterprise, and to the nation commercial prosperity and independence' (Johnson and Porter 1973: 33). But the emphasis in the platform, as well as in the campaign rhetoric generally, was on the defence of a true republicanism based on 'the principles promulgated in the Declaration of Independence', against the 'dangerous political heresy' of the slave power, which would carry 'slavery into any or all of the territories of the United States' (Johnson and Porter 1973: 32). Immediately following the platform plank favouring protective tariffs was one demanding passage of the Homestead Act, which had recently been vetoed by Democratic President Buchanan. This Act, which became law soon after Lincoln's election (during the absence of its southern opponents from Congress) made 160-acre parcels of western land available free for settlers to cultivate. Although the census of 1870 was to show that the country now had a majority of workers in the non-agricultural sectors, the Jeffersonian and Jacksonian ideal of a nation of virtuous farmers – free labourers, not slaves – was a powerful element in the Republican party's rhetorical appeal (Foner 1970), and helped the party to replace 'King Cotton' (the dominance of the Democrats, based on southern agriculture) with 'King Corn' (the dominance of the Republicans, based in part on midwestern agriculture). Midwestern farmers were to find their loyalty to the Republican party severely strained in the decades to follow, but they were an essential part of the party coalition; it is worth noting that 'every Republican President originally designated for that high office by the electorate ['Theodore Roosevelt having first entered the White House through the vice-presidency'] came from the corn belt until Herbert Hoover [1928], whose birth in the corn belt was no mean consideration in his nomination' (Binkley 1947: 284–5).

While the Republican party was a party of the north and the west, the Democratic party in this period became a party of the north and the south. The south, after the effort of ruling it from the north was abandoned a few years following the end of the war, entered a century of one-party rule by the Democratic party. In the north the Democratic party came out of the war years having lost most of its reformist, antislavery elements and (an overlapping group) its rural supporters. The northern Democrats became more preponderantly than before the party of the urban immigrant and the professional politician, the 'bosses' of the machines.

After the issue of slavery expansion was settled and the reconstruction of southern politics abandoned, both major parties 'lost their sense of mission' (Sundquist 1983: 106). Ethno-cultural divisions between the parties loom large in this period precisely because division on political issues was lacking. Even on the issue of the tariff the parties' differences were often muted in the platforms, and in practice were diminished even farther. Both parties were receptive to the idea that this was an age when the captains of industry needed to be given space to develop the national economy, and relatively little was required for this purpose in the way of government programmes, once the protective tariff and national banking system were in place, and a hard money regime was maintained. Reform-minded Republicans (such as those who put together a third-party presidential ticket of 'Liberal Republicans' in 1872, which attracted much Democratic party support as well) tended to be entranced by the doctrines of *laissez-faire* economics; they demanded civil service reform and an end to government actions such as grants of land to railroad companies, but they demanded little in the way of positive action by the government (Johnson and Porter 1973: 37–96; Ladd 1970: 115; Sundquist 1983: 124).

THE SYSTEM OF 1896 (1890s–1930s)

Although the party system was highly sectionalized in the 1870s and 1880s, with one-party states the rule rather than the exception, the election results added up to a remarkably even partisan balance. The Democrats won two out of the five presidential elections, and neither Democratic nor Republican presidential candidates won landslide victories. In the House of Representatives, too, the percentages of votes and of seats won by the major parties was very close. All this changed in the 1890s. The congressional election of 1894 produced a healthy Republican majority in Congress, which was thereafter controlled by the Republicans for all but eight of the 36 years down to 1930. The presidential election of 1896 (giving this historical system its textbook name) produced a large Republican majority, and in the 36 years down to 1932, only one Democrat was elected president (Woodrow Wilson, who profited from Republican divisions in 1912 and 1916).

Behind the growing Republican hegemony nationally was an intensification of the already high degree of sectionalization, that is, uncompetitiveness of one of the two major parties in individual states and regions. Republicans consolidated their strength in the north and west, Democrats theirs in the south. If one defines two-party competitiveness as the condition in which the majority party's popular vote averages no higher than 55 per cent of the two-party total in presidential elections, then one finds 74 per cent of the (38) states in this category in the period from 1868 to 1892; but from 1896 to 1928, only 44 per cent of the (48) states were that competitive. Forty-six per cent of the states in the later period – as opposed to only 26 per cent in the earlier one – were highly non-competitive, with the majority party averaging more than 60 per cent of the votes (Ladd 1970: 175–6). Partly as a result of this decline in party competitiveness, voter turnout declined steadily in the period from 1898 to 1928. (The combination of low voter turnout and one-party domination in most states was one of the worrying developments witnessed by those who led the progressive assault on the procedures of American parties and elections in the first two decades of the twentieth century, a subject to which we shall return in later chapters.)

What had happened to shift the national party balance, and to intensify the sectionalized nature of that balance? The basic picture is similar to the one we have just seen in the 1830s to the 1850s: a series of third-party challenges mounted by groups who find too little responsiveness to their concerns within the two major parties, eventually resulting this time not in the replacement of one of the major parties by a third party (as in 1856–60), but in the acceptance by one of the major parties – the Democrats – of the radical demands of the third party – the People's (or Populist) party. The absorption of the Populists by the Democrats amounted to a change in the basic electoral strategy. The Democrats stopped echoing the Republicans and started offering a distinct alternative set of policies. The strategy did not work to the advantage of the Democrats. Rather, it caused a reaction against the Democrats in the electorate sufficiently strong to convert many normally Democratic voters into normally Republican voters. As a result, the Republican party, which was already the dominant party, became even more dominant. The swing to the Republicans in the congressional elections of 1894 can be attributed to the depression of 1893, which struck in one of the rare post-war times that the Democrats had elected the president and both houses of Congress. But the more durable shifts of party loyalty occurred in 1896, and can therefore more reasonably be attributed to the rejection of the policies that the Democrats had embraced along with their nomination of William Jennings Bryan for president in that year (Sundquist 1983: 159–60).

What were the origin and substance of these realigning policies? From the 1870s through the 1890s there were some movements in the United States towards a party of urban manual workers – remarkably little, in view of the exploitation of these workers in these years, but some stirrings, nevertheless, culminating nationally in the ticket of the Union Labor party in 1888. However, most of the protest movements that found their way into third-party politics – and in 1896 into two-party politics – were agrarian rather than urban. The reigning anti-inflationary policies were perceived by the heavily mortgaged farmers to be disadvantageous to their interests, as was the flourishing of railroad and business corporations able to exploit the unorganized farmers both as suppliers of the tools of their trade and as buyers and transporters of their produce. Beginning in the 1870s, independent farmers' parties and clubs operated in many midwestern states, but they avoided fusion with the Democratic parties in their states, because the Democrats were still the party of secession and urban bosses. In Washington, Democratic and Republican Congressmen began polarizing on the issues of railroad regulation and monetary expansion in the 1880s (Sundquist 1983: 125–6), but it was not until 1896 – after several dry years and massive numbers of farm mortgage foreclosures had inspired a Populist presidential candidacy that obtained eight per cent of the popular vote in 1892 – that the Democratic party turned itself into a vehicle for the Populists' policies on the economy. They offered the country the choice of inflation (opposition to the 'un-American', 'British' policy of adherence to the gold standard) and greater federal government regulation of the 'arteries of commerce', which were being run by the 'trusts' in a way that amounted to 'robbery and oppression' (Johnson and Porter 1973: 98–9). The Republican party clung to the opposite pole, favouring deflation and very limited government intervention in the economy. The realignment of the electorate outlined above was a response to this new choice presented to them. In a country becoming more and more urban, agrarian interests, no matter how much their platform rhetoric evoked Jeffersonian ideals and 'that spirit and love of liberty which proclaimed our political independence in 1776' (Johnson and Porter 1973: 98), were now simply too small a single-interest group to meet with national electoral success. The support that the Democrats gained in the agrarian (and silver-mining) west (they already ruled the south) was more than matched by northeastern urban defections to the Republicans.

Bryan was nominated by the Democrats (and defeated by Republicans in the election) again in 1900 and 1908 (a more traditional *laissez-faire* candidate – the last such one ever to be nominated by the Democratic party – having proved no more successful in 1904). The effort of the Democrats in these years to add to their agrarian strength the loyalty of urban labour groups never quite succeeded, although the Republicans were in the process of losing this loyalty by the growing dominance of their anti-labour elements. The American Federation of Labor came out against certain anti-labour Republican congressional candidates as early as 1906 (Binkley 1943: 361), and after 1908 regularly opposed Republican presidents and presidential candidates. A progressive Democrat, Woodrow Wilson, was elected in 1912 because of the division of the Republican vote between Theodore Roosevelt (who ran that year as a candidate of the Progressive party) and the incumbent, William Howard Taft. During Wilson's first administration, social legislation favoured by labour, but hitherto passed only at the state level (and often by progressive Republicans), found its way into federal statutes. The alliance between labour and the Democratic party that was to emerge more clearly in the 1930s has it origins here.

However, the Democratic party was not yet reliably the party of the soldiers of industry. In spite of the slight early twentieth-century *rapprochement* of urban workers and Democrats, who had been separated first by the slavery issue in the 1850s and then by the Democrats' acceptance of Populist policies in 1896, the progressive movements in American politics were in some places dominated by urban, middle-class reformers (including many businessmen). Nor was progressivism, the prevailing mood of American politics in the fifteen years before the First World War, restricted to Democrats. In the cities, Republicans included within their ranks many reform-minded people who had been driven away from the Democrats by the rural emphasis that that party's reformism had taken on in 1896, and in rural areas, many former Populists returned to lead progressive reforms from within the Republican party. Under Theodore Roosevelt's leadership (admittedly accidental, since he first became president as the result of the death of William McKinley), progressivism became a force in Republican politics at the national level. So divisions between progressives and their opponents were not manifested in polarization of the major parties. The progressive era demonstrates the capacity of the American party system to formulate and to produce significant policy changes without consistently presenting a clear choice between the two major parties. Both of the major parties contained progressive and conservative wings, the progressive ones more prominent before the First World War and the conservative ones more assertive during the 1920s, when the mood of the nation was more conservative. Only after the Great Depression began did the two major parties become identifiable as a progressive (or 'liberal') party and a conservative one.

THE NEW DEAL PARTY SYSTEM (1930s–1960s)

Whereas the Republican party won landslide victories in the presidential contests of the 1920s, the Democrats won by landslides in 1932, 1936 and 1940, and they continued regularly to win the presidency until 1968, losing only to Dwight Eisenhower (the military hero of World War II) in 1952 and 1956. The Democrats have won majorities in all but two of the thirty-one elections to the House since 1930, and in all but five of the thirty elections to the Senate since 1932. They have also always been the majority party in national opinion polls measuring party identification since that question was first asked in 1937.

This revolution in the fortunes of the major parties can be traced to the way that party leaders responded to the Great Depression that followed the stock market crash of 1929. The Republicans were led by President Herbert Hoover, who had been elected in 1928 as a moderate progressive, to respond very cautiously, if at all, to popular pressure for federal government action to relieve the misery of the massive numbers of unemployed and other impoverished citizens, and to reshape the structure of the economy to aid its recovery. In 1932 the Republican platform proclaimed that 'The people themselves, by their own courage, their own patient and resolute effort in the readjustments of their own affairs, can and will work out the cure', insisted that 'the relief problem [is] one of State and local responsibility', and chastised the Democrats in Congress for their efforts to provide federal relief (some of which had been vetoed by President Hoover), calling these efforts a 'squandering of public resources and the unbalancing of the budget through pork-barrel appropriations which bear little relation to distress and would tend through delayed business revival to decrease rather than increase employment.' (Johnson and Porter 1973: 339, 341, 350)

The Democrats probably would have won the presidential election of 1932 (when the rate of unemployment was 24 per cent and the majority of Americans had become poor) no matter what they said. So they made few campaign commitments in that year. But as president (from 1933 to his death in 1945), Franklin Roosevelt led the party to the activist policy pole, and presided over a corresponding reshuffling of the major party coalitions. The Democrats' 'New Deal' programme set about 'humanizing the policies of the federal government as they affect the personal, financial, industrial, and agricultural well-being of the American people' (Platform of 1936, Johnson and Porter 1973: 360). (The label 'New Deal' was used by Roosevelt during the campaign of 1932.) The New Deal made the federal government more responsible for relieving economic distress, reviving and maintaining the performance of the economy, and reforming and regulating those economic institutions (such as the stock market) the unregulated behaviour of which seemed to have caused the economy's collapse. It promoted industrial trade unionism and agricultural product price stability. This federal activist position came to be called liberalism, and opposition to it conservatism. In spite of the opponents' protests that they were the true liberals, defending liberty against government, the label stuck. (The situation was similar to the 1780s, when the nationalists had succeeded in stealing the label 'Federalist'.) Although this new liberalism and conservatism were directed toward the issue of governmental intervention in economic life, they were moral points of view, not just different technical judgements about the most efficient organization of the state. Each side thought of the other as fundamentally opposed to the true principles of American republicanism. The Republican platform of 1936 warned that the 'responsibility of this election transcends all previous political divisions' in the country, because Americans' 'political liberty,... individual opportunity, and... character as free citizens,... today for the first time are threatened by Government itself'; while the Democratic platform spoke of the Democrats' 'reestablishment of the American way of living', and charged that 'a Republican administration has and would again regiment' the American people 'in the service of privileged groups'. (Johnson and Porter 1973: 360, 363, 365–6)

The New Deal did not cure the depression (that was done only by the Second World War), but it did endow the federal government with new and significant economic and social responsibilities. It reflected and promoted a shift in the dominant political culture away from regarding the captains of industry as the nation's heroes and custodians, towards regarding government as 'the instrument for bringing in left-out groups, for supervising, policing and managing the complex system which had been developed' (Ladd 1970: 190) under the reign of industrialism since the Civil War. The old nationalism of the industrialists was replaced by a new nationalism of the public administrators. Roosevelt stated this quite clearly in a speech made during the campaign of 1932, calling for 'a re-appraisal of values':

> A mere builder of more industrial plants, a creator of more railroad systems, an organizer of more corporations, is as likely to be a danger as a help. The day of the great promoter or the financial Titan, to whom we granted anything if only he would build, is over. Our task now is not discovery or exploitation of natural resources, or necessarily producing more goods. It is the soberer, less dramatic business of administering resources and plants already in hand, of seeking to reestablish foreign markets for our surplus production, of meeting the problem of underconsumption, of distributing wealth and products more equitably, of adapting existing economic organizations to the service of the people. The day of enlightened administration has come.
>
> (Roosevelt 1932)

As Democratic party leaders moved towards the government activist pole, their group constituency came to include the beneficiaries of that activity. Those farmers whose bad economic years had started before the general economic depression and whose interests were still not being looked after by the Republicans, were more sympathetically treated by New Deal Democrats, whose Agricultural Adjustment Act, Farm Credit Administration and Farm Mortgage Corporation were designed to support farm prices and otherwise to relieve farmers' financial distress. But the most important shift in group support towards the Democratic party occurred in the northern cities. Some of this shift seemed to have been anticipated in 1928, when the presidential candidacy of Al Smith, a New Yorker and an Irish-American Catholic, had drawn northern urban manual workers (at least temporarily and at least at the presidential level) away from their normal Republican loyalty. But this 'Al Smith Revolution' was to do with religion and prohibition (Smith was opposed to prohibition), while the basic issue drawing northern urban manual workers (including 'native' Protestant ones) to the Democrats – and keeping them there – from 1930 onwards was the level and kind of responsibility of the federal government for management of the economy (Sundquist 1983: 191–7, 215–19). (The defections of cultural conservatives in the south *away* from the Democrats in 1928 was perhaps a better indicator of future group movements than was the movement *towards* the Democrats in the north in 1928: Grantham 1988.) Under New Deal leadership the Democratic party and organized labour worked together more closely than ever before. The right of labour to organize for collective bargaining was at last legally enshrined in the National Labor Relations Act in 1935. Although this Act was not vigorously opposed by Republican Congressmen, it was a Democratic measure, and it helped encourage a decade of rapid growth in unionization, reaching 35 per cent of non-agricultural manual workers (the historical peak) in 1945, including more than 80 per cent of the manual workers in the most important industries (including construction, cars, steel and clothing) (Ladd 1970: 190–2). Democrats helped the unions, and the unions helped Democratic candidates. Recognizing the plight of unemployed workers as well as that of employed but unorganized ones, New Deal policies also provided federal unemployment relief, and set up a system of national labour exchanges (which had been vetoed by Hoover) and a number of public works projects to provide employment when private industry failed to do so.

One consequence of the shift of the northern cities to the Democrats was a similar shift of those ethnic minorities who had not hitherto been Democratic identifiers. Jewish-Americans and black Americans steadily (dramatically in the case of southern blacks, in the early 1960s) moved into the Democratic party in the New Deal years, a trend that was strengthened after the Democrats began adding civil rights concerns to their economic concerns in the late 1940s and 1950s, but which began in the 1930s, when federal government activity in economic affairs was the attractive force. Another (overlapping) group that should be included in a summary of the New Deal coalition is the liberal intellectual community. Liberal intellectuals advised government and served as appointed government officials, and intellectuals' interests in free speech, for example, began to be served by the New Deal judiciary's turn away from economic *laissez-faire* towards intellectual or cultural *laissez-faire* and the protection of civil liberties (Shapiro 1978).

One of the most notable effects of these changes in the Democratic coalition was the decline of region and the rise of socio-economic class as a dividing line between the major parties. With the Democrats becoming stronger in the north and west, and Republicans (much more gradually) in the white south, the intra-state and intra-regional competitiveness of the parties rose dramatically. With the Democrats becoming the party favouring programmes financially benefiting the poor, the rich and poor began dividing more noticeably – though never rigidly – into Republicans and Democrats (except in the south, where both rich and poor whites continued to be Democrats for decades after the New Deal, and where blacks began switching to support Democrats only in 1964 and 1965 – and coincidentally began being registered in much larger numbers as a result of the Voting Rights Act of 1965). The socio-economic character of the party division became less marked with the arrival of post-war mass affluence and with the movement by both parties away from the polar policy extremes in the 1950s, but was still visible.

This realignment of the electorate according to the issues and interests affected by the New Deal occurred quickly in some northeastern cities, but only gradually elsewhere, extending the process into several decades, in some places right down to the 1980s and 1990s. Presidential voting was the first to reflect the process, and only gradually did voting for offices lower down the ballot become affected; therefore, persistent split-ticket voting (voting for one party's candidates for some offices, and the other party's candidates for other offices), hitherto a temporary phenomenon when it occurred at all, became widespread. A new generation of state and local political leaders – liberal Democrats in the north, midwest and west, and conservative Republicans in the south – had to appear before this ticket-splitting could decline, and more comprehensive two-party competitiveness grow. Outright conversions of politicians to bring their party labels into line with the New Deal liberal-conservative divide – such as that of Wayne Morse of Oregon from Republican to Democrat in 1955, and Phil Gramm of Texas from Democrat to Republican in 1983 – have been the exception, not the rule.

The process has been slower in the south because of the complication introduced by the issue of race relations and the liberal civil rights policies of the Democrats. Even the mild movement of the national Democratic party toward the integrationist pole in 1948 produced great dissatisfaction among white southern Democrats, but in the deep south this was expressed in a States' Rights party ('Dixiecrat') defection from the Democrats (with Strom Thurmond – then a Democratic governor – as this third party's candidate), rather than in voting for Republicans even at the presidential level. Modern presidential Republicanism began to appear most conspicuously in 1948 and 1952 in the rim south (Virginia, Florida, and Texas), where the racial issue was somewhat less intense and the growth of metropolitan areas had produced economic interests opposed to the New Deal Democrats for the same economic policy reasons as were working for the growth of Republican support in the northern cities and suburbs now experiencing post-war prosperity (Black and Black 1987: Chapter 12; Sundquist 1983: 272–80).

Because of the drawn-out character of the New Deal realignment, the two major parties' internal divisions were (and to a lesser extent still are) particularly salient in this party system. The Democrats' newly rejuvenated liberal northern and western wing (who supplied the presidential candidates until 1976 – with the exception of Lyndon Johnson in 1964, who had ascended to the presidency on John Kennedy's death) clashed with its conservative southern wing (producing a 'conservative coalition' of Republicans and conservative Democrats visible in Congress since Roosevelt's second term). The Republicans' liberal (or 'moderate') eastern wing clashed with its conservative midwestern wing. The eastern wing was more internationalist in foreign policy, midwesterners traditionally more isolationist. Now in addition, midwestern Republicans were becoming more conservative, and eastern ones more liberal, on economic policy. The old midwestern progressive combination of domestic policy liberalism with foreign policy isolationism tended to disappear as a force in American party politics. As the Democrats were gradually becoming the party of midwestern progressivism (liberalism), Republicans were picking up new support among previously Democratic, relatively prosperous conservatives in rural areas in the north and the midwest. Midwest Republicanism was becoming a party of small businessmen rather than of farmers; and it was becoming less discontented with economic conservatism. At the same time, eastern Republicans, more exposed and more responsive to the problems of the industrial economy, were becoming more sympathetic to the liberal New Deal agenda. While midwestern Republicans remained strong in Congress (often in coalition with southern Democrats), eastern Republicans controlled presidential nominations in the 1940s and 1950s, producing candidates who were justly accused of being 'me too' Republicans, those who largely accepted the goals of the interventionist welfare state, and offered simply to prevent its excesses and to make it more efficient.

With both Democrats and Republicans nominating presidential candidates from their liberal wings, the presidential and congressional party systems became so different that commentators began referring to America's 'four-party' system (Burns 1963). During the 1930s, when New Deal issues were fresh and energizing, Congress demonstrated its inherent capacity for partisan solidarity, with Democrats supporting and Republicans opposing liberal policies. But in the 1940s and 1950s, as the New Deal issues were aging, and both parties were retreating towards the centre, the more usual congressional tendency to reflect local and regional differences returned, and the inter-party divisions of Democrats and Republicans were more frequently expressed in congressional debates and voting (Sinclair 1977, 1978).

A SIXTH PARTY SYSTEM? (1960s–1980s)

No event as traumatic for party alignments as was the Great Depression has occurred since the 1930s, and no similar party transformation has occurred. There have been several issues that have polarized the electorate in ways that have cut across the New Deal division, but none has been strong enough, or has been presented powerfully enough, to reshape the major division of the electorate and thus to form a distinct new historical party system. Both a 'new liberalism' and a 'new right' have flourished in the last three decades, both ideological groupings more concerned with social, cultural, and foreign policy issues than with economic policy issues. But neither of these new sets of policy concerns has definitively captured the vast territory that constitutes one of the two major parties. Observers of American parties often comment on their current weakness, but they have proved to be powerfully resistant to the attempts of the new liberals and new conservatives to remake them in their own image.

Admittedly, part of this resistance has consisted in bending to the breeze, both parties in about the same direction and at about the same time. Just as in the progressive era, many important new public policies have been adopted through successful pressure on both major parties. Both parties became more liberal on civil rights issues in the 1950s and 1960s (in platform position-taking, the Republican party was there before the Democrats, in 1944). (However, when it is a question of positive discrimination, Democrats are still – at least officially – more 'liberal' than Republicans). In the late 1970s and 1980s, following the expansion of federal and state government activity and taxation in the 1960s and early 1970s, both parties have responded to calls for 'deregulation', and have exhibited new pessimism about the ability of government to solve social problems. In the early 1970s, both parties adopted a policy of retreating from military commitments in Southeast Asia.

In the decade beginning in 1963 (the first year of 'the sixties'), social and foreign policy issues started taking precedence over economic issues in American public opinion. Civil rights demonstrations, urban riots, campus protests against US participation in the war in Southeast Asia, and counter-cultures of 'alternative' life styles, all drew political attention away from questions concerning economic management and welfare. With the return of hard economic times, around the time of the oil crisis of 1974, the economic issues regained some of their old power to align the major parties, but not all of it; the social issues left their mark, made partisan loyalties more compli-cated, and often weakened them. Traditional, New Deal liberals on economic issues did not necessarily embrace the new liberalism's suspicion of assertive anticommunism in foreign policy; nor (especially in the south) were econ-omic liberals necessarily either traditionally liberal (favouring equal opportunities) or neo-liberal (favouring busing and positive discrimination) on civil rights. Many economic liberals were sympathetic to the new right position on particular social issues such as abortion, women's rights, public school prayer, gun control and rights of criminal defendants. (Note that many of these social issues were propelled into the political arena by the federal judiciary, not by the elected, more obviously partisan branches of govern-ment: a sign of the growing disinclination or incapacity of the party politicians to set the political agenda in these decades.)

Both parties eventually adopted tough, right-wing rhetoric on the 'law-and-order' issue in the late 1960s. After the Soviet invasion of Afghanistan reduced some Democrats' worries about Americans' 'inordinate fear of Communism' (as President Jimmy Carter called it), both parties moved in the late 1970s and early 1980s to support more spending on military weapons (although – in spite of the attempt to establish a 'Reagan Doctrine' favouring the liberation of tyrannies – there was little precision in either party about how or when the weapons should be used, and the spending increases themselves were short-lived).

But in spite of these similar responses to some of the new social issues, the Democratic party still seemed to be the more natural home for the new-issue liberals, and the Republican party for the new-issue conservatives. In 1968 both new liberals and new conservatives deserted the Democratic party in large enough numbers to produce a Republican presidential victory (with many conservative Democrats supporting the segregationist American Independent third-party candidate, George Wallace). In 1972, the Democrats' candidate, George McGovern, presented himself as the candidate of the new liberals, but his candidacy helped produce a landslide for the incumbent Republican president, Richard Nixon, and since 1972, the Democrats have moved back towards the centre ground on the social issues in their presidential candidates – or at least in the way that those candidates have been presented to the voters. In this period, the Republicans have proved to be the natural party of government as far as the presidency is concerned. And for their part, the Republicans have become much more responsive, at least rhetorically, to pressures from the new right, with a new *economic* right (supply-siders and monetarists) adding momentum to the Republicans' rightward movement in the 1970s and 1980s. Ronald Reagan, the symbol of so many new right causes both economic and social, was in the running for the Republican presidential nomination from 1968 onwards. Until 1980, these bids were unsuccessful, but sufficiently encouraging to maintain the effort. Already in 1976, in spite of the incumbent Gerald Ford's winning (with difficulty) the nomination against Reagan's challenge, the Republican platform began to embody new right positions, especially on foreign policy. In 1980, the Republican platform contained a 'right to life' (anti-abortion) plank, and not only called for a strengthening of the individual versus big government – a theme going back to the New Deal – but also, more in tune with the new social issues, called for the encouragement of 'vital communities like the family, the neighborhood, the workplace, and others... between government and the individual' (Johnson 1982: 177, 182). Reagan's nomination signalled that the Republican party had become *the* bearer of the hopes and fears of the new right. Republican moderates did not become extinct, but they became a lot quieter. The electorate did not by any means completely polarize on the lines of the issues of the new liberalism and new conservatism, but the parties, especially in their presidential mode, did so to a remarkable degree (Schneider 1981).

The most important shifts in the group coalitions of the parties in the last three decades have been related to these shifts in the issues and in the different ways that the parties have responded to these issues. The Republican party's movement towards the new right, and especially towards populistic versions of the new right, has been associated with a shift in its base of support (votes and funding) from the northeast to the west and the south. The movement of white southerners away from the Democratic party, which (as we noted above) began on the basis of New Deal economic issues, has been accelerated by southern Democratic conservatism on civil rights, social issues, and foreign policy. Since 1984, a majority of white southerners have identified themselves as Republicans (Black and Black 1987: Chapter 11; Ladd 1989a: 14). The Democratic party's greater resistance to new right social positions, and the Republican party's greater religiosity, has probably contributed to the decline in the Democrats' ability to depend on the support of Catholic voters. (The ethno-religious distinctions between the major parties that go back to the early nineteenth century were in any case becoming somewhat anomalous in the party regime organized by New Deal issues.) The appeal of the new liberal agenda to many non-poor Americans has helped to create an 'inversion' of the New Deal class-party relationship, with the higher socio-economic groups becoming more liberal than the lower ones (Ladd and Hadley 1975: 242–6; Ladd 1976–7). Since 1980 and the beginning of 'Reaganomics' (tax cuts and domestic spending cuts), there has been a noticeable rise in the statistical relationship between party voting and income, with the percentage of lower-income voters voting Republican rising much more slowly than that of middle-income and upper-income voters; however, this holds true only for income: longer formal education and higher occupational status – both associated with public-sector employment – are still statistically linked to Democratic voting (Petrocik and Steeper 1987: 42–3).

CONCLUSION

If there is a new party system emerging today, it is significant that it does not yet have a name. It is commonly called simply the 'post-New Deal' party system. A clearer definition of major party differences and of the party system as a whole would be possible if a major party realignment, along the lines of the 1850s or 1930s, were to occur. In Chapter Four we shall explore that possibility. But first we turn to have a closer look at the technical development of parties in the nineteenth and early twentieth centuries, a development that was occurring alongside the history of party policies and coalitions that we have surveyed in this chapter.

3   Party development*

As we have seen, the system of competition between two major parties for the control of American government began soon after the Constitution of 1787 had become the framework of government. Table 3.1, which summarizes some of the party history that we surveyed in the previous chapter, shows the results of this competition in terms of the partisan control of the three elected federal bodies in that government: the presidency and the two houses of Congress. Several significant features of that control are illustrated by this table, and it will be referred to in later chapters as well. In this chapter, we turn away from the policy and interest group aspects of parties, to focus more on the development of attitudes towards party and techniques of party organization during the formative period of the party system. Examination of this development will elaborate and clarify the dual nature of the party system that we have already seen in that system's combination of principles and interests.

THE FIRST PARTIES AND THE CONSTITUTION

In spite of the early emergence of the party system, the development and acceptance of that system proceeded somewhat unsteadily over the course of its first half century. As we have seen, this development was not anticipated by the framers of the Constitution. James Madison, the 'Father of the Constitution' himself, had some second thoughts about the way that he described and defended the Constitution after he had begun to invent modern party politics in the 1790s. Yet even supposing that a national party politics had been anticipated by the framers of the Constitution, it is difficult to imagine how they would have changed the Constitution in order to

* Some of the material in this chapter first appeared in Richard Maidment and John Zvesper (eds) (1989) *Reflections on the Constitution* (Manchester University Press). We thank Manchester University Press for their kind permission to reprint.

Table 3.1 Shifts in partisan control of the federal government

Party system and presidents	Years	Presidency	House	Senate
First party system				
Washington	1789–93		non-partisan	
	1793–5	F	R	F
Washington, J. Adams	1795–1801	F	F	F
Jefferson, Madison, Monroe	1801–25	R	R	R
J. Q. Adams	1825–7	NR	NR	NR
	1827–9	NR	D	D
Second party system				
Jackson, Van Buren	1829–41	D	D	D
W. H. Harrison, Tyler	1841–3	W	W	W
Tyler	1843–5	W	D	W
Polk	1845–7	D	D	D
	1847–9	D	W	D
Taylor, Fillmore	1849–53	W	D	D
Pierce	1853–5	D	D	D
	1855–7	D	R	D
Buchanan	1857–9	D	D	D
	1859–61	D	R	D
Third party system				
Lincoln, Johnson, Grant	1861–75	R	R	R
Grant, Hayes	1875–9	R	D	R
	1879–81	R	D	D
Garfield, Arthur	1881–3	R	R	R
	1883–5	R	D	R
Cleveland	1885–9	D	D	D
B. Harrison	1889–91	R	R	R
	1891–3	R	D	R
Cleveland	1893–5	D	D	D
	1895–7	D	R	R
Fourth party system				
McKinley, T. Roosevelt, Taft	1897–1911	R	R	R
	1911–13	R	D	R
Wilson	1913–19	D	D	D
	1919–21	D	R	R
Harding, Coolidge, Hoover	1921–31	R	R	R
	1931–3	R	D	R
Fifth party system				
F. D. Roosevelt, Truman	1933–47	D	D	D
	1947–9	D	R	R
	1949–53	D	D	D
Eisenhower	1953–5	R	R	R
	1955–61	R	D	D
Kennedy, Johnson	1961–9	D	D	D
Nixon, Ford	1969–77	R	D	D
Carter	1977–81	D	D	D
Reagan	1981–7	R	D	R
Reagan, Bush	1987–93	R	D	D

Notes:

F = Federalist
R = Republican
NR = National Republican   Federal elections occur in even-numbered
D = Democrat   years, preceding the year in which
W = Whig   presidential administrations and
                            Congresses begin.

accommodate political parties. They might have made such minor adjustments as the one that was actually made shortly after these parties appeared on the scene, by the Twelfth Amendment. (This Amendment separated presidential from vice-presidential voting in the Electoral College – a procedural change that acknowledged the role of partisanship in these elections.) However, it is a mistake to assume that the framers' dim views of parties would have made them all recoil in horror from the presence of a national party or parties, and try to counter party with constitutional devices. As we have seen in Chapter One, their condemnations of parties were condemnations not of political parties as they later developed (with the help of many of the framers themselves), but of 'factions', that is, entirely non-public-spirited interests and cliques. The prior existence of national political parties might actually have reassured the framers on some points; for example, many feared that the Electoral College – at least after the departure of George Washington, the obvious first candidate for the presidency – would regularly fail to produce a majority for any candidate, thus breaking down the separation of powers by making presidents owe their election to the House of Representatives. But the prior existence of such parties would probably not have altered very much the considerations that went into the deliberations that produced the institutional arrangements set up by the Constitution. So the mere fact that the Constitution was framed before political parties were developed does not explain the tension between constitutional government and party politics in America; if parties had already been developed, the Constitution would still have worked to some extent against the grain of party politics. Perhaps it is simply the case that constitutional government, with its attempt to treat all citizens evenhandedly, is necessarily somewhat at odds with party government, with its bias against some citizens in favour of others, the party faithful.

It may sound a bit naive to talk about a situation in which national parties did not exist. The framers of the Constitution were quite familiar with a kind of partisanship at the national level. The contest between patriots and loyalists in the struggle for independence from Britain was a national party contest. So was the contest between the framers themselves – the Federalists, as they somewhat misleadingly called themselves – and their Antifederalist opponents in the ratification battles of 1787 and 1788. The framers of the Constitution had experienced national party conflict, as well as numerous factional conflicts at the state and local level. When Madison explained and defended the incipient Republican party opposition to Alexander Hamilton's policies in 1792, he cited the nation's previous experience of 'general' party conflicts – patriots versus loyalists, and Federalists versus Antifederalists – as precedents (Madison 1900–1910, 6: 106–19). He and other framers had failed to foresee that the need to appeal to these precedents would arise so soon after the Constitution was adopted. But the precedents were at hand, and were more or less recognized as such in Madison's and even Hamilton's reflections in *The Federalist* (26, 28, 40 and 43). It was not necessary for Madison and other Federalists to abandon their support for the Constitution in order to lend their support to a general political party.

However, the tension between Constitution and party remained. It was necessary for Madison and others who moved from support of the Constitution to party action against Hamiltonianism to stop emphasizing the need to strengthen the central government and to start emphasizing the need to strengthen the influence of public opinion outside the government, public opinion marshaled by the Republican party. Of course, the Constitution provided many limitations on central government, but it was the product and the vehicle of a movement designed to increase the 'energy' of the central government, a movement which could be seen to culminate logically in Hamilton's economic programme. Opposition to that programme was based not only on hard economic interests but also on Madison and other Republicans' judgement that partisanship was needed to erect public opinion as a supervisor over 'the various authorities established by [the] constitutional system' (Madison 1900–1910 [1791], 6: 67–70).

Much of Madison's case for the large and economically heterogeneous republic (discussed in Chapter One) had hung on the fact that the greater difficulty of communication in a larger country would help keep the selfish designs of interest groups 'secret', unexpressed in public and therefore unco-ordinated with potential allies who together might form 'an unjust and interested majority' (*The Federalist* 10). It would be more difficult for potential 'interested combinations of the majority' (*The Federalist* 51) 'to discover their own strength and to act in unison with each other', because of the intrinsic difficulty of publicly revealing and privately co-ordinating a party based on 'a consciousness of unjust or dishonorable purposes' (*The Federalist* 10). Now, however, Madison was able to promote the combination of the Republican party without completely reversing his earlier views, because this party was to be primarily a 'party of principle', based on consciousness of just and honourable purposes, which are both easier to express in public and more conducive to the mutual trust and internal unity of a party. What was required now that a challenge to the principles of republican government had appeared was an emphasis less on the heterogeneity of the selfish interests across the country than on the homogeneity of a united public opinion to reestablish these principles, through 'a general intercourse of sentiments', assisted by the use and perfection of such means of public communication as 'good roads, domestic commerce, a free press, and particularly a circulation of newspapers through the entire body of the people, and Representatives going from, and returning among every part of them' (Madison 1900–1910 [1791], 6: 70). One of the first steps taken by Republican party organizers was the establishment of the *National Gazette*, which publicized the party's views.

The first modern partisans were not quick to reach for the weapon of mass partisanship. At first they hoped that congressional reapportionment following the census of 1790 would produce a congressional majority against Hamilton's policies. When this technical tactic failed, they tried to challenge the constitutionality of those policies in the courts, and privately to persuade President Washington to abandon Hamilton. None of these tactics worked, and in the end the leaders of the Republican party had to inspire a popular electoral revolution – the 'revolution of 1800' – by which the Republicans captured control of the presidency as well as Congress. This strategy of focusing popular attention on the presidential election has been repeated by successful American parties ever since. This has altered the balance between the legislative and executive branches, which the framers of the Constitution had expected (or feared) would tilt clearly in the direction of Congress, because of its closer ties to the people. A president who can claim to be a tribune of the people can enjoy great policy-making power. This power can be even greater if the president's electoral fortunes can be linked credibly to those of Congressmen, but it has been significant even in those periods (such as the current one) when presidents have had very short coattails (McKay 1989).

However, the Republican leaders themselves did not seek to set a precedent that would be repeated regularly or routinely. Having beaten the unrepublican party (except in the judiciary, where Federalists clung on), there seemed to them to be no reason to maintain a permanent party system in the republic. Their attitudes towards parties remained rather traditional (no public respectability need be given to parties), moving occasionally towards the early modern attitude that public respectability might be accorded to one party only (see pp. 4–6). Party politics was, they thought, an emergency device, to be used only when there was a real danger of successful unrepublican policies and policymakers. Although Madison and Thomas Jefferson came to speak of the naturalness of an opposition between republicans (optimists, who love popular government) and antirepublicans (pessimists, who fear it), they did not think it was necessary for this natural antagonism to be institutionalized in republican government. While defeated Federalists might share the hopeful prediction of John Adams – the defeated incumbent in the presidential election of 1800 – that American government was becoming 'not a national but a party government' (Adams 1823), with regular transfers of power from one party to the other, Republican leaders had other ideas, and over the years they and events did largely succeed in reducing national party competition by eliminating the Federalist party from that competition. The tension between this 'first party system' and the Constitution was in this way perhaps somewhat reduced: a party system that was expected to wither away – and during the presidency of James Monroe, the third Republican president, did in fact do so to an extent that now seems incomprehensible – was an unlikely permanent rival to the constitutional ways of policy making.

A second reason that this tension was less than it might have been was that the Republican policies were in a sense quite negative. The Republicans were trying not so much to get the central government to act in certain ways as to get it to stop acting in certain ways. Hamilton's programme was the one that required central government action; the Republicans required less energetic central government. (Patronage rewards for their party workers were therefore thinner on the ground than they would have liked.) Perhaps it would be more accurate to say that Hamiltonianism required – and Republicans attacked – central *administrative* action. Hamilton was less a politician than an administrator. Federalists had a large administrative agenda but (even with George Washington on their side) insufficient political support; Republicans had political support but much less on their administrative agenda. At some later times in American political history, and at almost all times in American political science, the expectation has been the other way around: that parties would be the source of active and ambitious policy, and that governmental inertia, based on the constitutional separation of powers, federalism and socio-economic pluralism, would be the resisting object of partisan attentions. But American parties 'were first organized at a time when popular rule meant the limitation of government power' (Piereson 1982: 48). The Jeffersonian Republicans saw themselves as the true conservators of the Constitution. The decentralizing and restraining purposes of America's first real party – the Jeffersonian Republicans – have never entirely disappeared from major American parties, and this feature has made them appear very un-partylike to many foreign observers as well as to many Americans dissatisfied with their peculiarly unambitious parties.

However, there remain two important ways in which even the first American party – the Jeffersonian Republicans – did establish a tension between party and Constitution. The first way has already been noted: the role of extra-governmental public opinion as a power in the land. The first partisans, very like later (and current) ones, enhanced this role by their partisan use of the media and ideological political action committees (the Democratic-Republican Societies of the 1790s, which were modeled on the committees of correspondence of the Revolution). In earlier thinking about this role, such as in *The Federalist*, popular protests against governments had been conceived as occasional, *ad hoc* movements, appealing to natural right and working through informal, extra-constitutional channels – a democratic response inspired by tyrannical government or by imprudent use of executive prerogative, a response and an inspiration fully provided for in Lockean political philosophy. The institution of party politics reduced the occasional quality (at least in appearance) and made the channels more formal, but maintained the anti-or extra-constitutional bearing of this role. Party statesmen who can lead and direct the force of partisan public opinion can thereby overcome some of the limitations on statesmanship imposed by the necessity of acting in a party. Party can thus serve as an instrument of popular or statesmanlike discretion, versus rigid constitutionalism. The philosophic appeal to natural standards, versus adherence to established constitutional procedures, can thus play a part in American politics, and appeal not only to the Revolutionary precedent of 1776 but also to the Jeffersonian partisan precedent. The defects of the rule of law and constitutionalism – their over-generality and relative insensitivity to different and changing circumstances – can be addressed and to some extent corrected by partisan politics. Amendments and reinterpretations of important provisions of the Constitution have resulted from the pressures of party action, especially after those watershed realigning elections of the 1790s, 1850s and 1930s.

This brings us to the second way in which the Jeffersonian Republicans established a durable tension between party and Constitution. A qualification must be added to our observation of the relatively unambitious policy agenda of the Republicans. That agenda was not blank, and even if it had been, various decisions – perhaps the most important was the purchase of Louisiana – thrust themselves upon it. Relative to Hamiltonian Federalism, the Republicans may have had a negative approach to central government, but they had policies, some of them quite positive, and they did not hesitate to use the machinery of their party to gain support for these policies in Congress and in the country. The development of party politics by the Republicans facilitated popular majority mandates, bursting through the constitutional restraints of separated powers and federalism. This potential for majoritarian party government was more fully developed by Jacksonian, progressive and New Deal presidents, but they owed something to the Jeffersonian precedent. One of the reasons for the insistence upon strict construction of the Constitution's grants of power to the central government by Madison and other thoughtful Republicans after the emergence of parties was precisely their recognition of the danger that Republican partisanship could lead too easily to the assumption that the majority party was always right – that *vox populi vox dei*. Popular partisanship can address the defects of constitutionalism, but popularized constitutionalism can also address the defects of popular partisanship.

Have these tensions between the Constitution and party government in the USA been healthy or destructive? It seems to many observers that this tension was in some important ways healthier in the nineteenth century, especially in the mature party system built after the first parties died down, than it has been in the twentieth century, which has seen a series of attempts to reform the party system to make it more progressive and less partisan. For this reason, it is helpful to examine in some detail the 'mature party system' that was assembled in the nineteenth century, not in order to revive it, but simply in order to understand it and its successor more clearly.

THE MATURE PARTY SYSTEM

As we saw in the previous chapter, the second set of major parties in American national politics were the Jacksonian Democrats and the Whigs, whose conflicts lasted from the 1830s to the 1850s. This period of American party history is generally and not altogether inaccurately characterized as the period during which the party system reached 'maturity'. In part this maturity consisted in structural democratization and organizational sophistication: the replacement of state legislatures by popular elections in the choice of presidential electors, the expansion of the electorate, the expansion of the number of elective offices, the increasing frequency of electing Congressmen by districts (rather than at large), the introduction of the presidential and lower-level nominating conventions (replacing nomination by 'caucuses' – meetings of party members or leaders), and the proliferation and perfection of local party organizations. It is a little misleading and rather patronizing to look back from the vantage point of this mature 'second party system', with its close resemblances to the current party system, and see the 'first party system' as a case of immaturity and 'arrested development' (Goodman 1967: 85). The first partisans developed such organization as they thought they needed (it was actually quite extensive and sophisticated: Cunningham 1957); they did not intend for that organization to endure, so they should not be chastised too much for setting up a system that 'failed to survive' (*pace* Goodman 1967: 85, and McCormick 1967: 95). Nevertheless, the 'second party system' did exhibit much more of that characteristically American exuberant if rather chaotic participation and organization seemingly for the sake of participation and organization rather than for the sake of some programmatic set of policies.

However, one must be wary of letting the party organizational and structural innovation in this period lead one to conclude that here we truly have the first real American party system, with patronage and party loyalty proving themselves to be sufficient forces to hold the system together and to keep it functioning with only a marginal, insincere and halfhearted recourse to the kind of programmatic or ideological appeals that had been so rife in the first party system. It is true that the kind of party being developed in this period was based in part on the New York ('Albany Regency') model of party, which stressed organizational solidarity above policy and ideology, and that often involved 'that lack of consistency and clarity on ideas and issues that is so often the despair of critics of the American party system' (Hofstadter 1969: 26) (and the point admired by some of its conservative defenders). But organizational virtuosity was not enough.

In the first place, it was not enough to make it durable. If one is considering systems that 'failed to survive', one must consider the fate of this second party system. For it, too, 'failed to survive'. In the 1850s and 1860s it was replaced by the third American party system. If it was organizationally so 'mature', and it even lacked the handicap of 'immature' attitudes towards the necessity of party politics, why did it so soon collapse?

But in the second place, organizational virtuosity was not as a matter of fact enough to define and to energize the second party system. It also had a strong ideological element. The Jacksonian Democrats could not have endured as long as they did, nor have become the nationally dominant party in this period, if they had been characterized solely by politicians like Martin Van Buren, the 'Sly Fox' and 'Magician' of the Albany Regency, unaccompanied by politicians like 'Old Hero', Andrew Jackson. Van Buren's slippery style is captured in the story told against him by his rivals: asked if the sun rises in the east, he replies that he thought this was the 'common impression', but as he always slept until after sunrise, he could not speak from his own knowledge. Yet even to Van Buren himself, 'the character of career politician was... a doubtful and precarious identity...', and he sincerely admired and even envied the heroic Jackson (Meyers 1957: 144–5, 147). While there was significant organizational and structural innovation in the second party system, there was also (as we have seen in the previous chapter) some significant continuity between these parties and the first parties in terms of issues and ideologies. It is not at all clear that the Jacksonians would have been able to become the dominant party of the second party system – or even that party politics at the national level would have been revivable in this period – if 'the Jacksonian persuasion' had not revived ideological issues.

'Party is organized opinion.' Benjamin Disraeli's compact definition of political parties points to their two-sided nature: they need and are organization, but they also need and are opinion. Major American parties have conformed to this pattern. Successful parties of interest and patronage have also been parties of principle and issue, most clearly in their origins and establishment into hegemony, but also in their subsequent lives. American political parties have not been uniquely unideological parties, although their critics and their defenders have often criticized and defended them for being so.

The history of the first two American party systems illustrates the dual nature of American party politics. It is misleading to see the politicians of the first party system groping in the dark, blindly fumbling their way towards the tolerant, professional mature second party system. The first party organizations were more or less sufficient to their needs, which were considered temporary but urgent; the idea of long-term party competition was not accepted, but the idea of party as an emergency device was well established. So the organizational aspect was visible even here. Likewise, it is inaccurate to see only this aspect in the second party system; the organizational professionalism and civility of the politicians and voters of the second party system were clear, but so were their ideological crusades and intolerance of opposition. Both sides of the party system have always been present in the history of that system, although the balance between them has varied over time and space. In the first party system, the programmatic, crusading, principled aspect was more pronounced; in the second – and in the urban machines of later periods (on which see Chapter Six) – the pragmatic, accommodationist, patronage-oriented aspect was to the fore. But both aspects have always co-existed, and both need to be recognized for a thorough understanding of the American party system.

If this dual nature of American political parties had not been passed on from the first parties to the second ones, it would have been not easier but more difficult for this generation of politicians to develop, as they did develop, a justification for partisanship that accepted and encouraged the permanent place of parties alongside the Constitution. In politicians' and citizens' changed opinions about the desirability of a permanent party system, and about the way in which such a system can be compatible with the Constitution, there is real novelty in the second party system, and some reason to rename it the *first* party *system* – the first coincidence of the practice of party with its systematic justification.

Martin Van Buren left us the best statement of that justification, and of the more (not to say perfectly) complete integration of parties with the Constitution and with democratic constitutionalism that was possible in the generation that succeeded the framers. Van Buren is the true founder of the American party system. The subtlety and depth of his views on that system deserve the close attention of students of American politics (Ceaser 1979: Chapter 3; Weatherman 1982 and 1984).

When Van Buren was elected to the Senate in 1821, he left for Washington, DC, consciously intending to repeat at the national level what he had done in New York: to revive the party conflict, to end the blurring of party lines, and to overcome 'the Utopian notion of... the amalgamation of all parties' (*Albany Argus*, 29 July 1822, cited by Cole 1984: 104). This was not an easy or straightforward project. He backed the wrong horse in 1824, when he hoped to revive the old alliance between New York and Virginia by supporting William Crawford for the presidency. Crawford was the 'regular' candidate, nominated by the Republican congressional caucus. In the confused state of party loyalties following the demise of the Federalist party, Crawford was opposed not only by a National Republican candidate from New England – John Quincy Adams – but also by two western candidates: Henry Clay and Andrew Jackson. Van Buren soon became willing to see the Democratic party basing itself farther west, and resting on – or rather, supplying the basis of – the candidacy of Andrew Jackson. Jackson won the presidency in 1828, after the election of 1824 had been 'stolen' from him, who had won a plurality of Electoral College votes, by the 'corrupt bargain' between John Quincy Adams, who was elected in the House of Representatives in the end, and Henry Clay. (Clay had come fourth in the Electoral College vote, and therefore had been eliminated from the contest when it was moved into the House of Representatives. He threw his weight to Adams, and Adams appointed him secretary of state.) The alliance between Jackson and New York was crucial to Jackson's victories in 1828 and again in 1832. From the beginning, Van Buren insisted that Jackson's candidacy should depend on and perpetuate not his personal appeal as a candidate, but 'old party feelings'. Jackson's 'personal popularity' was an asset, but also a danger; it would be a grave error to let Jackson get himself elected because of 'his military services without reference to party'. For the sake of the future of the country as well as of the party (including, of course, Van Buren's own future, as Jackson's successor in 1836), Jackson's election had to be and to be perceived as 'the result of a combined and concerted effort of a political party, holding in the main to certain tenets and opposed to certain prevailing principles....' (Van Buren 1827).

Why was Van Buren so confident that a system of political parties, openly avowed, would be a valuable addition to the American political system? Forty years before, when the Constitution was composed, and even thirty-five years before, when the first parties under the Constitution were forming, political parties (as distinguished from 'factions', which meant interest groups or personal followings) had been treated as secret weapons, to be deployed only in emergencies, not in everyday politics. How had circumstances changed, to make public principled parties more desirable? Following Edmund Burke's reasoning that political parties need to be made more respectable when great statesmanship becomes rare or extinct (Mansfield 1965), one could argue that the departure of the great statesmen of the Revolutionary and constitutional eras did make a system of parties more desirable in America.

The visit of Lafayette and the laying of the cornerstone of the Bunker Hill monument in 1825 reminded Americans that half a century had passed since the Revolution. The passing of the founding fathers caught the attention of the nation. The remarkable coincidence of the deaths of Jefferson and Adams on the Fourth of July 1826, brought home the fact that most of the old heroes were gone.

(Cole 1984: 102)

Party principles and regularity can provide a democratic substitute for the discretion and discrimination of heroic statesmanship. Moreover, 'years of work in party-building and... the exacting discipline of party loyalty' (Hofstadter 1969: 241) can be the democratic politician's answer to the rather oligarchic assumption of some of the older-style anti-party politicians that they were born to rule, as well as to the demagogic danger of an ambitious and popular leader like Jackson, unconstrained by party ties. Richard Hofstadter describes the Albany Regency politicians in these terms: 'They were... modern political professionals who loved the bonhomie of political gatherings, a coterie of more-or-less equals who relied for success not on the authority of a brilliant charismatic leader but on their solidarity, patience, and discipline' (Hofstadter 1969: 242). As we shall see in Chapter Six, this reliance on the social, 'solidary' incentives of party activists has continued to be of central importance in American parties, especially in the most common type of party organization, the cadre-caucus type.

In addition to the need to compensate for the limits and dangers of democratic politics – limits and dangers not always modestly acknowledged by democratic politicians, citizens and intellectuals, but confronted by Van Buren – it is reasonable to speculate that the passage of time itself made party politics more tolerable under the less-than-brand-new Constitution: 'Only after our institutions of government were well-established could politicians look to differences of opinion as something that might be organized to serve as a positive political force in American politics' (Weatherman 1982: 22).

But perhaps the crucial difference between Van Buren and the anti-partisan generation of American politicians that preceded him was not a difference in circumstances, but Van Buren's disagreement with their judgement that American citizens could all be expected to be of one party, the Republican party. Van Buren thought it was too optimistic to expect all Americans to become and to remain loyal to truly republican ways of thinking; there would always be unrepublican partisans, who (because of their wealth and connections) could organize covertly more easily than republicans, so it was best to have them openly identifiable, by open party organization. Van Buren argued that the 'Utopian' expectations of anti-partisanship led to a corruption of the good, Republican party, as well as to an unsafe obscuring, rather than an obliteration (which was impossible), of the bad, anti-republican party. The experience of the country under Monroe and

John Quincy Adams supported Van Buren's less utopian view: Federalist policies and partisans had not disappeared from the politial arena, they had simply infiltrated the ranks of the Republicans themselves. John Quincy Adams – the son of the last Federalist president – presented himself as a Republican, but proposed (quite unsuccessfully) transparently Federalist policies. Van Buren thought the American people would support the right policies if only the choice were made clear to them, rather than obscured by this blurring of party lines.

In fact, Van Buren argued – again, with a fair degree of support from American experience – that trying (with President Monroe) to amalgamate the old parties and to suppress principled partisanship merely made partisanship break out in forms that were not only messier, less manageable and less comprehensible (a disadvantage particularly important in democratic politics), but also – and more seriously – lower, meaner and pettier. Van Buren had experienced this problem in New York politics; in 1824, it manifested itself in the presidential election. Personal rivalries produced unedifying campaigns that began years before the election itself. Van Buren began his *Inquiry into the Origin and Course of Political Parties in the United States* (written largely during his retirement in the 1850s, and published posthumously in 1867) by contrasting the successful administrations of Jefferson and Madison – who had, 'throughout, recognized and adhered to the political party that elected them' – with the political atmosphere presided over by the party amalgamator, Monroe, which became 'inflamed to an unprecedented extent' by a regression to unprincipled rivalries:

> In the place of the two great parties arrayed against each other in a fair and open contest for the establishment of principles in the administration of Government which they respectively believed most conducive to the public interest, the country was overrun with personal factions. These having few higher motives for the selection of their candidates or stronger incentives to action than individual preferences or antipathies, moved the bitter waters of political agitation to their lowest depths.
>
> (Van Buren 1967: 3–4)

It is important to appreciate the extent to which Van Buren regarded his novel and detailed defence of a party system as a defence also of political moderation and constitutionalism. He made his defence of political partisanship with the understanding that 'the inviolate sanctity of a written Constitution [is] the life of a republican government' (Van Buren 1967: 213). As already noted, systematic partisanship depersonalizes politics to some extent. This moderates personal political ambitions, and makes the necessary concessions of the compromises and coalitions of a moderate politics less personally painful. Van Buren's solution to the problem of strong personal ambitions in the pursuit of the presidency – ambitions tempted (as in 1824) to resort to extreme and inflammatory appeals, was his system of parties, which 'would restrain presidential aspirants, inducing them to take moderate positions' (Ceaser 1980: 102). Van Burenite partisanship is not partisanship that is constantly challenging the moderating influences of the Constitution.

However, it is also important to appreciate the occasionally less moderate, more decisive, more fully partisan function of the party system founded by Van Buren. This function is implicit in Van Buren's descriptions of the seriousness of the points at issue between the major parties, even if he does not explicitly draw attention to this function, and even though he does concentrate on the parties' differences on 'specific programs and policies instead of general theories' (Weatherman 1982: 13) (the former being closer to party interests and farther from convulsive regime politics). This function is also apparent, if only as an 'amendment to his earlier views' (Ceaser 1980: 103; 1979: 142–3), in Van Buren's becoming the presidential nominee of a third party in 1848 – the highly principled Free Soil Party (with Charles Francis Adams, the grandson of the last Federalist president, as his running mate!) – which challenged the stable, moderating competition between Democrats and Whigs.

James Ceaser provides a reasonable synthesis of these two views of the functions of partisanship, both contained within Van Buren's system – the moderating, 'inside', 'institutional' view, and the 'insurgency', 'outsider', more highly partisan view:

> Normally, the electoral system should work to prevent major pressure for change from translating itself too quickly into party policy. This bias is built into the system in the belief than an open system removes restraints on presidential aspirants and encourages them to appeal to dangerous and immoderate currents of opinion. Yet the moderation of the existing parties itself needs a check; occasional demands for change and renewal must be accommodated. These objectives can be accomplished by permitting a new party to be created or an old one to be reconstituted. Under this method, change takes place when a party sets forth a new program in response to some particular substantive problem and then attempts to win the political power to enact it.
>
> (Ceaser 1980: 103)

In this synthesis, most of the time American parties are rather status-quo-oriented, and quite compatible with and protective of constitutional government; but occasionally they respond to a powerful issue outside of the current party mainstream, and pursue policies that require radical changes, extending possibly to the constitutional fabric itself. The tension between American constitutional government and American political partisanship remains within the mature party system founded by Van Buren. Perhaps that tension is reduced by this system's institutional bias against radical change. Those proposing such change have to persevere against this bias, and can only hope to thrive from time to time, not in every election. Nevertheless, the openness of the system to such proposals – whether from 'third parties' (which are thus 'integral elements of the so-called two-party system': Ceaser 1979: 326, quoting V. O. Key) or from major party insurgents – constitutes an advantage of the mature party system, although or rather because it reintroduces, at least potentially, the tension between the party system and the calmer politics anticipated by the Constitution.

Thus, the answer to the question posed above – if the second party system was so perfect and mature, why did it 'fail to survive'? – is that this 'failure' was actually a success: the decision to stop compromising on the issue of freedom and slavery was a just decision, made through the party system itself, by the replacement of one of the major parties – the Whigs – with a 'third party' – the Republicans – and by the realignment of the electorate to support the dominance of the Republicans. Of course, Van Buren himself did not see it that way when these events occurred, towards the end of his life (he died in 1862). In spite of his previous support for the Free Soil cause, he supported Stephen Douglas in 1860. He had always been deeply concerned with sectional rivalries; these represented one the kinds of conflict that his party system had been intended to suppress. Nevertheless, it was clearly Van Buren's party system that made and reinforced the realigning decision of 1860, and it is not against the spirit of Van Buren's work to contend that the second party system was mature because it gave way to the third. True, Van Buren had consciously chosen not to call up a new party alignment so much as to recall and to reinstate the old one, and he did this with one eye on the necessity of having such issues as were embodied in this alignment as sustainers of party morale. And true, there was always something suspiciously artificial about the issues of the second party system; the 'Jacksonian persuasion' (like the Jeffersonian persuasion to which it was the heir) was a nostalgic protest against an inevitable socio-economic reality – call it the dynamics of capitalism – as much as it was an affirmation of 'substantial goods' (Meyers 1957: 274). Nevertheless, the invocation of such a moralizing persuasion as an essential element in the mature second party system made more possible the more genuinely moral decision of 1860.

THE DECLINE AND REFORM OF THE MATURE PARTY SYSTEM

Van Buren succeeded perhaps better than he knew, in establishing not only a relatively open party system (open to challengers such as the Free Soil and

Republican parties, as well as to darker ones such as the nativist Know Nothings), but also relatively closed parties (biased in favour of party discipline and regularity, and against incorporation of new issues). After the Civil War the party system brought forth a line of presidents whose lack of charisma and indebtedness to party were all that Van Buren could have asked for and more. The closed parties, especially the dominant Republican party, helped keep presidents relatively weak, and Congress relatively strong. The strong moderating effects of party were complemented and boosted by social and economic developments. Industrialization ensured that parties were by no means at odds with strong economic interests; in fact, the party system and the economy ran rather more in tandem than Van Buren, with his suspicion of the money power, would have liked. After all, the Republican party was the heir of the Whigs' pro-business policies. Abraham Lincoln's fear that after the Civil War the businessmen would enjoy too much political power proved to be well founded. The celebration of the robber baron businessman in turn made corrupt party machines seem acceptably American. Urbanization and immigration ensured that there was a large market in which the party machines could trade their favours – to the poor as well as to the rich – for votes and organizational help; the party drilling became even less likely to turn into a radical force than it was in Van Buren's day. In short, the moderate or constitutionalist tendency of the party system became extremely narrow and absolute.

Not surprisingly, the reaction against that tendency, when it came, was a rather extreme reaction, offering to reform the party system in the opposite direction, and even attacking the Constitution in order to make that reformation seem desirable and possible. The all-too-realistic profile assumed by parties during the last thirty years of the nineteenth century inspired a particularly strong anti-party ethos in America, in contrast to other liberal democracies. 'Nowhere else in the western democratic world did parties look so evil, at least to middle-class citizens, as they did in the United States' (Epstein 1986: 159). This was partly because the ideal of participation – difficult even for a party organization of the European mass membership kind to live up to – was higher in America than elsewhere, but it was also partly because the realities of party organization were often actually considerably lower than elsewhere. Over the past century, a series of laws, legal decisions and internal party practices have embodied the high-minded, reformist reaction against the lowly realities of party politics. Such reforms as the reduction in the resources for party patronage (by judicial decisions as well as by civil service reforms), tight legal regulation of internal party affairs, the use of non-partisan elections, nomination by primary elections, and a variety of campaign finance rules, have formed a changing but constantly relevant and significant context for the conduct of party politics in the twentieth century. (We shall be examining many of these reforms individually in later chapters.)

In twentieth-century America, the understanding of the party system has thus alternated between two rather extreme viewpoints. On the one hand, there has been a hard-headed 'conservative' view (accepted, sometimes reluctantly, by many liberals with a realistic political education), defending an exclusively constitutionalist, consensus, patronage, professional, congressional, status-quo orientation. (An excellent example of this type of apology for the low-minded party system is Banfield 1961; the classic of this type is probably Herring 1940.) On the other hand, there has been a high-minded 'liberal' view, tending toward an exclusively anti-constitutionalist, alternatives, issue, amateur, presidential, change orientation. Rarely has there appeared, much less dominated, in either theory or practice, a balance between these two sets of tendencies comparable to that achieved by the mature party system founded by Van Buren.

The founding father of the reformed party system, the moving spirit to set against Van Buren, was Woodrow Wilson (Eidelberg 1974: Chapter 9; Clor 1976; Ceaser 1979: Chapter 4; Kesler 1984). Wilson, a progressive intellectual and politician, outlined at the beginning of the party reform era the essential purposes and shape of this reformation. Most prominent in Wilson's view of the party system – and in the characteristic liberal view ever since – is the necessity of using this system to add to the constitutional system as a whole a constantly active 'leadership' with energy and 'vision'. In this view, the need for such leadership is (at least in the contemporary world, as distinct from the sleepier world of eighteenth- and early nineteenth-century America) not occasional, as the mature party system assumes, but continuous. The mature party system provided opportunity for major policy change and party realignment, but the assumption was that such opportunities would not be used very often; in the reformed system the assumption is that major policy change will frequently be needed. Therefore party power, especially at the state and local levels, must be made to yield to candidate and leader power.

At first Wilson had proposed the abolition of the separation of powers, to produce a more parliamentary system of government in America, to achieve the levels of governmental unity, leadership, activity and change that he thought were necessary. But he later accepted the difficulty of such a proposal, and urged instead the transformation of the presidency into a constant source of such leadership. The stasis of *Congressional Government* (the title of Wilson's famous critique of American government, published in 1885) – which he recognized was caused by the fragmentation of Congress into 'committee government' – could be overcome by presidential government, with a more national party, designed not (like Van Buren's) to limit the powers of presidential candidates and presidents but to 'be an instrument at the leader's command helping to further the principles and programs for which he had won approval in his direct appeal to the people' (Ceaser 1979: 174). Not the 'worn-out' traditional principles and programmes of his party, but newer, more up-to-date principles and programmes, were to comprise the popular leader's mandate. Party leaders need to be in direct contact with a public opinion from which all traces of constitutionalism have been removed, because they must owe their power not to the Constitution but to the people. For their proper function is not constitutionally definable. It is moral leadership which requires them to interpret the sometimes vague longings of the public into a coherent public policy. It is to have a 'vision' that is a privileged glimpse at the next stage of the historical process, and to be able to move the public in that direction, by building on the public's progressive opinion and helping it to suppress its non-progressive opinion. This process needs to be repeated again and again, in fairly rapid succession; therefore it was insufficient for Wilson simply to replace the worn-out principles of the existing parties with new ones, in the relatively difficult and rare manner allowed by the mature party system. It was necessary rather to change the party system itself, to make it much more productive of continual change, to keep the country in step with historical progress.

One of the major problems with reforming the party system in this way is that it makes the whole notion of party loyalty and discipline more than a little suspect. The supremacy of political leadership and political leaders over party entails a denigration of the respectability and usefulness of party. Parties are required to be sources of constant change, and with no particular end in view, for historical progress is seen to be endless. Besides, progressivism denies the reality of fixed natural standards by which (as we have seen) parties can justify a certain amount of departure from strict constitutionalism. The strong party government sought by progressive reformers is thus distinct from most actual western party governments, in that these have generally taken as their model party a socialist movement, with a quite well-defined end (a socialist society) justifying party activity. Lacking that final justification, progressive American parties have lacked a firm justification for their existence. Every party is 'worn-out' as soon as it makes its particular contribution to political progress. The usefulness of political parties can be no more durable than that of individual political leaders – perhaps less so, since parties are if anything more constrained by their own histories. In this perspective, it seems doubtful that any party system, formed however differently from the mature party system, could produce parties that are anything but instantly obsolete; a party system must always be by nature not mature but senile.

Thus, there is a distinctly non-partisan or anti-partisan cast to Wilson's and the general reform view of parties. (There are other reasons for the decline of party in recent decades, but a hundred years of reform and of reform-minded political education is prominent among them. Even the rise of the use of the non-partisan media as part of the new candidate-centred campaign techniques, one of the most often-noticed of the other causes of party decline, was itself prompted by the progressive anti-party legislation of the early twentieth century.) In the reformist view, elected offices, especially the presidency, as the representative of the whole nation, but other elected offices as well, are seen as above partisanship. Voters themselves are expected to avoid or to be easily weaned away from 'irrational', habitual partisan attachments, which may be essential to parties but are clearly obstacles to the rapid change demanded by progressive politics. This position recalls the originally anti-party attitudes of the framers of the Constitution, but it incorporates a much more sanguine, plebiscitary view of elections and of elective offices. The party reformers' emphasis on the need for government leadership and activity is comparable to the framers' emphasis on the need for energetic government, but they do not supplement this emphasis with a comparable insistence on maintaining some distance between elected officials and the electorate, and on maintaining the separation of powers as a means of controlling as well as of enabling officeholders. Thus, the system proposed by the party reform view is much more hostile to the Constitution than is the mature party system. Since Wilson, it has been more common among political scientists and practising politicians to condemn the Constitution as a worn-out 'Newtonian' political system, too fixed in its eighteenth-century orbits, which needs to be replaced in effect if not in fact by a more progressive, more easily evolving, 'living', 'Darwinian' political system. (Merriam 1968: 305–27) The greater hostility to party in the reformed party system makes it more, not less hostile to constitutional government.

CONCLUSION

For the past century, then, a 'conservative' version of the mature view of the party system, emphasizing the parties' production of consensus and playing down their production of alternatives, has coexisted uneasily with the 'liberal', reform view, emphasizing alternatives and relegating consensus-building to the darker and unacceptable side of party politics. The first view has been quite compatible with the Constitution – although inclined to overlook those elements of the Constitution itself that anticipate the need for periodic renewal, such as the provision for amendments and the stipulation that presidents undertake to 'preserve, protect and defend the Constitution' (not merely, as other officials, 'to support this Constitution'). The second view has been compelled to go on living with the Constitution, but has been bent on altering it to make the political process less fragmented, by altering the party system.

Accordingly, the democratization and organizational sophistication of the party system developed by the middle of the nineteenth century have been overlaid by reforms starting in the late nineteenth century and advanced especially in the progressive era of the early twentieth century and in the 1970s. These reforms have tended to favour more open parties and more candidate-centred politics. They have not particularly favoured stronger parties or stronger partisanship. In the next chapter, we shall see that these party reforms and the attitudes underlying them have in fact posed considerable difficulties in the operation of both the party system and the Constitution.

4 Party realignment

The first 'scientific' accounts of voting in the United States were done (as were those in Britain) during a period when there was relatively little deep ideological disagreement between the two major parties and therefore not much evidence either of such dramatic events as critical, realigning elections, or of the levels of voters' and leaders' interest and ideological polarization that accompany such events. In 1960, *the* study of *The American Voter* (Campbell *et al.* 1960) was based mainly on the elections of 1952–58. Not surprisingly, that study did not report the kind of electoral awareness, excitement and division that was to come to the fore in the 1960s and 1970s. But by the 1970s, political scientists had to begin talking about *The Changing American Voter* (Nie *et al.* 1976); the political times had changed, and although turnout in elections fell steadily, electoral apathy and ignorance seemed to reign less widely in the Johnson and Nixon years (1963–75) than in the Eisenhower years (1953–61). It is always dangerous to take a snapshot of a political system at a certain point in time and assume that it accurately captures the character of the system. This proved to be particularly the case with the paradigm of the American voter and party system constructed by many readers of the first 'scientific' studies of the American electorate, which were done at a time when the critical realigning potential of this electorate was not much in evidence. The authors of those studies themselves were rightly cautious about inferring too much from their 'observations... of a relatively brief interval' in American party history (Campbell *et al.* 1960: 43; see also 531–8).

Today not only academic political scientists and historians but also American politicians themselves frequently reflect or at least speculate upon the presence of or the prospects for major realigning elections in the current political scene. The concept of critical (or major realigning) elections and the recognition of the cyclical character of American party history, the tempo of which has been determined by such elections, has trickled into the world of journalism and practical politics. In this chapter we review the way that political scientists and historians have come to understand party competition during past periods of critical realignment, both to understand more precisely how the American party system has functioned, and to consider the possibilities of such realignments in the present and future. In spite of all the wishes of some American voters and politicians to the contrary, such possibilities seem slighter today than they might have been in similar circumstances in the past. Political scientists are beginning to doubt the usefulness of the concept of critical realignment for understanding contemporary American politics (Ladd 1989b). Yet even if the pattern of past realignments cannot or will not repeat itself today, knowing the reasons why this may be true can illuminate our understanding of contemporary American politics. Therefore we also begin to examine in this chapter the effects of certain barriers to critical realignment that have grown up in the twentieth century. Moreover, we shall see that some of the partisan dynamics best explained by the concept of critical realignment are still occurring, so it would seem premature to expunge this concept from explanations of the current party system.

THE AMERICAN ONE-PARTY SYSTEM

Although the American party system is and has always been largely a two-party system, there is an important sense in which this system is actually a one-party system. This can be seen in Table 3.1 (p. 39), which summarizes the results of elections to federal offices for the entire history of the American party system. Since the electoral 'revolution of 1800', the dominance of federal office holding by one of the two major parties has been striking. In the twenty-eight years from 1801 to 1829, the Republicans (or National Republicans) controlled the presidency, House and Senate together for twenty-six years. In the following thirty-two years (1829–61), the Democrats held all three bodies for eighteen years, their opponents only for two years. In the seventy-two years from the election of Lincoln to the election of Franklin Roosevelt, the Republicans controlled all three for forty years, their opponents for only ten. Finally, in the sixty years from 1933 to 1993, the Democrats will have held all three for thirty years, their opponents for only two years. In other words, the dominant parties in each of these periods (the Republicans from 1801 to 1829, the Democrats from 1829 to 1861, the Republicans from 1861 to 1933, and the Democrats since 1933 – although their failure to dominate the presidency since 1968 is a notable fact which we shall consider in a later section of this chapter) have elected the president and majorities in the House and Senate for a total of 114 years; their opponents have done this only fourteen years. (The continuity in the names of the parties is of course a little misleading, as we have seen in Chapter Two: the Republican party from 1860 was a new party, not the same as the

Jeffersonian Republicans, and the New Deal Democratic party from the 1930s became a new coalition, organized on different principles from the Democratic party of previous periods.)

More importantly, the dominant party in each period of party history has managed the policy-making agenda, and the subordinate major party in each period has had to learn to conform to the policy preferences established by the dominant party. Important choices have been made by conflicts within the dominant party, especially in their presidential nomination battles. The subordinate parties have had to offer an echo, not a choice, in order to survive as well as they can. In presidential contests, they have been well advised to nominate military heroes with rather obscure party loyalties rather than party regulars or ideologues too readily identified with energetic opposition to the dominant party. (This was the successful formula of the Whigs in 1840 and the Republicans in 1952; in 1964, with the nomination of Goldwater, the Republicans neglected this strategy and were soundly defeated. By 1980, the dominant Democratic party was no longer dominant in presidential elections, so the advice no longer applied.)

Samuel Lubell described this feature of the American party conflict in a revealing metaphor:

> Our political solar system... has been characterized not by two equally competing suns, but by a sun and a moon. It is within the majority party that the issues of any particular period are fought out; while the minority party shines in reflected radiance of the heat thus generated.
>
> (Lubell 1965: 191–2)

One finds in the writings of American politicians from the first party conflicts onwards a recognition of this fact, and of the justice of this fact. For example, Thomas Jefferson referred to the electoral 'Revolution of 1800', as a decisive establishment of true republican principles. If only one party is true to American republicanism, then it deserves to enjoy a hegemony over the other party. In a deep and important sense, the American political system has not experienced *The Rise of Legitimate Opposition* (the somewhat misleading subtitle of Richard Hofstadter's study of the American attitude towards party politics in the first half-century of the republic [Hofstadter 1969].) In their origins, each of the dominant major parties – the Republicans under Jefferson, the Democrats under Jackson, the new Republicans under Lincoln and the new Democrats under Franklin Roosevelt – has claimed superior legitimacy over its rival, and therefore a right to a dominant position in the political system.

Lubell argued that the transition from one period to another occurred when the majority party coalition, always subject to the centrifugal pull of its various elements, flew apart. 'The more heated the frictions within the majority sun... the more luminous are the chances of victory for the minority moon'; and when the majority sun party is 'shattered to its core... both parties are reshuffled and a wholly new political solar system is created' (Lubell 1965: 194–5). While this focus on the problems faced by the majority party in maintaining its coalition of diverse elements does help to explain what has happened in those elections in which the subordinate party has been *temporarily* victorious (for example, the presidential victories of the Whigs in 1848 and of the Democrats in 1884, 1892, 1912 and 1916), it is less helpful in understanding those few elections (or series of elections) in which the dominant party coalition has been established in the first place (1792–1800, 1828–32, 1860, and 1932–36). In the case of these elections, more attention has to be focused on the appeal of the emergent new dominant party than on the troubles of the old one, in order to understand what has happened. Understanding these rare but era-forming elections is the primary aim of the theory of critical elections.

CRITICAL AND UNCRITICAL ELECTIONS

The American political scientist V. O. Key was the first to propose 'A Theory of Critical Elections' (Key 1955). Key differed from many of his more 'scientific' colleagues in the political science profession by his conviction that the American electorate was more rational and responsible than some of the voting studies paradigms gave them credit for being (Key 1966). The theory of critical elections thus has implications for democratic theory. 'Realistic' critics of the 'classical' view of democracy follow in the footsteps of Machiavelli, who argued that democracy is an impossible regime because most people are too apolitical to be active citizens. The 'realistic' portrait of American voters offered by the new voting studies of the 1950s encouraged this scepticism about the possibility of democracy, even democracy by means of elections; if voting is largely an 'irrational' act based on unthinking, habitual identification of voters with one party or another, electoral direction and control of government can hardly be described as an attractively democratic process. Yet if in some elections, at least some voters act in a way that addresses and resolves a political crisis, then democracy looks more actual. Critical election theory offers 'to redefine democracy as a process which is more continual than continuous; more periodic than constant; more sudden, dramatic, abrupt, shattering, and monumental than smooth and incremental' (Trilling and Campbell 1980: 4). In fact, one could go farther: the democratic cast given to American politics by critical elections could be seen not only in the critical periods themselves, in which habits of party identification are established, but also in the stable periods that follow the crises, since even in these periods the democratic decision made in the critical period is maintained by means of elections, albeit voters are then acting more habitually.

Key argued that voters' own recognition that some elections are much more important than others made their inconsistent levels of interest and excitement, and their usual dependence on habitual party identification, seem quite reasonable. Key's theoretical account of the deservedly exciting 'critical' elections pointed to five characteristic features of these elections:

1 the durable transfer of dominance from one party to another,
2 durable changes in the loyalties of the groups that comprise each party's usual coalition,
3 a marked increase in the intensity of interparty and intraparty conflict (often associated with the mobilization of new groups of voters and an increase in turnout),
4 the emergence of a new set of issues as the basis of conflict, and
5 the loosening of inherited party loyalties in the face of these new issues.

Key also recognized a process of 'secular' party realignments (Key 1959), because he saw that realignments of the electorate sometimes occurred in slower motion than they did in critical realignments, as long-term drifts rather than as sudden waves. Critical elections are associated with critical realignments; secular realignments occur more gradually and more frequently.

The comprehensiveness of Key's theory probably helped make it the starting point for so many later studies. Yet even Key's theory probably paid too little attention to two things: first the role of political leaders in making or failing to make elections critical – a point explored by later theorists, and one which seems particularly germane when contemplating the absence of critical elections in the 1980s; and second, the very distinctive, evangelical quality of the political appeals made by leaders such as Jefferson, Jackson, Lincoln and Roosevelt during their critical election periods. All of these party leaders called for salvation of the republic, by a renewed dedication to the principles of the Declaration of Independence, which they claimed were being forgotten or distorted by their partisan opponents. The similarity of the rhetoric voiced by the winners of all of the critical elections makes more reasonable the continuity in the names of these parties: they are all called Democrats or Republicans – or in the case of Jackson's party, both – because only democratic republicans win these decisive contests in American politics (Jaffa 1965). The American party system is thus in an even more profound sense a one-party system. As we have seen in Chapter Two, what is at issue in these elections is the meaning of loyalty to democratic republican principles. This meaning can be deeply controversial, even though the controversies of American politics are not extended to encompass non-democratic or non-republican options.

Key's typology of elections – the division into critical and uncritical elections – has been elaborated by later writers. Angus Campbell's 'Classification of Presidential Elections' (Campbell *et al*. 1960: 531–8) divided the category of uncritical elections into 'maintaining' and 'deviating' elections. Maintaining elections – a category that includes the large majority of American elections – are those 'in which the pattern of partisan attachments prevailing in the preceding period persists and is the primary influence on forces governing the vote'; whereas in deviating elections, although 'the basic division of partisan loyalties is not seriously disturbed,' the majority party is nevertheless defeated, because personalities or events change voters' attitudes sufficiently to produce 'a temporary reversal' in the fortunes of this party that nevertheless continues to hold 'a clear advantage in the long-term preferences of the electorate'. Having been reminded of a further possibility by the results of the 1960 presidential election, Campbell and his colleagues added to their scheme of classification a third type of uncritical election: 'reinstating' elections, those in which 'the party enjoying a majority of party identifiers returns to power' (Converse *et al*. 1961). Gerald Pomper has argued in favour of a further category of uncritical elections, to reflect a distinction between critical elections proper and merely 'converting' elections, which resemble critical elections in the intensity and quality of the conflict and in the durability of their effects, but result (as in 1896, called a critical election by some) not in the displacement of the currently dominant party, but merely in the reassertion or strengthening of its dominant position (Pomper 1967). The presidential election of 1964, in which the Republicans offered in their nominee Barry Goldwater a 'choice' rather than an 'echo' (overwhelmingly rejected by the voters), and the presidential election of 1972, in which the 'deviating' result of 1968 was increased to landslide proportions by the voters' rejection of the Democrats' candidate George McGovern (felt by many voters to be out of the mainstream of the Democratic party), provided examples of a third type of election. This is a 'reinforcing' election, which can be basically either maintaining (as in 1964) or deviating (as in 1972), but which punishes whichever party offers a choice perceived to be too far out of step with the underlying consensus established in the last critical realignment.

THE ESSENCE OF CRITICAL REALIGNMENTS

What is necessary, and what is sufficient, to constitute a critical election or realignment? Everyone agrees that these phenomena are marked by durable changes in the electoral universe. But what must durably change?

We are inclined to accept James Sundquist's argument in favour of E. E. Schattschneider's emphasis on the effects of critical realigning elections on 'the agenda of American politics' (Sundquist 1983: 13, citing Schatt-schneider 1960: 88). Key's criteria for critical realignments concentrated too much, according to Sundquist, on changes in the composition of the parties and too little on the terms of political conflict. Sundquist proposed to reserve the term 'realignment' to those elections or periods when there has occurred 'a change in the structure of the party conflict and hence the establishment of a new line of partisan cleavage on a different axis within the electorate'. He argued that such 'conflict displacement' (for example, the replacement of conflict on the slavery issue by conflict on the issue of government intervention in the economy), rather than shifts either in relative party strength or in changes in the parties' group coalitions – both of which could be expected to be associated with such displacement – is best regarded as '*the* characteristic that identifies a party realignment' (Sundquist 1983: 13).

Treating conflict displacement as the essence of critical realignment makes the line between critical realignment and secular realignment less necessary to draw. Sundquist pointed out that '[m]uch of what appears as secular realignment is simply a later stage, or a later series of stages, of a preceding critical realignment – the aftershocks, so to speak, as the fault lines created by the initial political earthquake settle into place,' as happened during several decades following the New Deal realignment (Sundquist 1973: 8). Thus the perfectly reasonable tendency of commentators to talk of 'realigning periods' or 'eras' rather than a single 'realigning election'. Even critical realignments have their 'secular' phases, if by that is meant simply that they have some important long-term manifestations, such as northern liberals finally getting around to identifying and registering with the Democratic party, and southern conservatives with the Republican party, thirty years after the New Deal elections that defined the Democrats as the home of these northerners' kind of liberalism and these southerners' kind of conservatism (Sundquist 1983: Chapters 11–12). Therefore it can be confusing to focus our attention on the pace of the realignment process.

Sundquist also argued that the magnitude and geographic scope of the change were inessential features. As to magnitude, '[h]ow significant is significant enough?' and as to geographic scope, why insist – against everything we know about the decentralized and geographically uneven way that the American party system functions – that the change take place nationwide? Even durability as a criterion of realignment needs to be qualified by the recognition that there are some realignments that might have been durable if events had not intervened to shorten their lives – such as when the Great Depression obliterated or at least drastically modified the realignment of 1928 (Sundquist 1983: 6–10). So Sundquist concludes that it is better to follow Schattschneider's lead and to define a critical realignment – or rather, any party realignment strictly speaking (as opposed to a mere 'shift in the party balance within an established and continuing alignment') – 'in terms of the nature of the phenomenon rather than the electoral consequences that the phenomenon produces, in terms of the underlying process rather than its surface manifestations' – in other words, by the movement of 'the line of cleavage between the parties' to 'cut across the electorate in a new direction', so that the party system has 'shifted on its axis' (Sundquist 1983: 13–14). The essence of critical realignment is the establishment of such cross-cutting issues as the most important ones, supplanting the older issues dividing politicians and the electorate.

Even if one does not follow Sundquist's advice in every particular, his argument that realignments should be defined with reference to changes in the major issues that the party system deals with is persuasive. It is this kind of change that has made it plausible for historians and political scientists to talk of an essentially new party system coming into being with every critical election period, and to look at American political party history as a series of four or five such 'party systems' (Chambers and Burnham 1967, Burnham 1970, Kleppner *et al.* 1981). Critical elections are the American substitute for revolutions: they are 'constituent acts' that redefine 'the broad boundaries of the politically possible' (Burnham 1970: 10), and thereby usher in a new party system.

CRITICAL REALIGNMENT: SOCIAL OR POLITICAL?

Like students of other political phenomena, students of party realignments are divided on the question of the extent to which political phenomena should be explained in terms of socio-economic causes. Are critical elections and realignments, which everyone admits have great effects on the course of partisan conflict and public policy, fundamentally political events, involving a fair degree of conscious choice by individual voters and politicians? Or are they results of less rational changes in the arrangements of the parties' group coalitions, with the interests of some groups shifting them into one party and those of other groups shifting them into the other party, resulting in a net change in the balance between the parties? That is how the classic post-war studies of American voting behaviour preferred to see durable electoral changes occurring, because individual voters' judgement of the issues of the day seemed less likely to influence their long-term party loyalty than did the socially reinforced attitudes of their group's opinion: 'Attitudes rooted in social groups are likely to be more stable than are attitudes that are denied the status of group norms,' and changes in groups' party loyalties 'tend to be associated with issues that persist through time,' such as the issues linked to economic class (Campbell *et al.* 1960: 536). Moreover, although V. O. Key tended to be less cynical about the rationality and responsibility of voters than some of his colleagues in the political science profession, his own statement of the critical election process had emphasized the extent to which these important events in American party politics are associated with durable changes in the habitual loyalties of the groups that make up the parties' coalitions.

One can present the history of American party politics with an emphasis on this underlying coalitional dynamics and still recognize the different historical 'party systems' that have emerged during that history. But in order to do that, one has to trace these different systems to underlying socio-economic changes, rather than to autonomous political choices made by the electorate or some considerable portion of the electorate. In this account of the history of American party politics in terms of 'social change and political response' (Ladd 1970), each successive party system appears not as the result of political issues decided by critical elections but as the natural political expression of the current state of socio-economic development. Parties in the 'rural republic' give way gradually to parties in the 'industrializing nation' of the late nineteenth century; these in turn give way to the parties of the 'industrial state' of the twentieth century, and finally perhaps to the 'post-industrial state' of today. In this account, the emphasis shifts from political changes (such as those produced by elections) to social changes. What appears to be a critical election turns out to be merely an election that happens to occur during a social crisis: 'the election is but one current in the sweeping tide of sociopolitical change. Critical realignments take place primarily as *effects of* other major changes occurring in the society' (Ladd and Hadley 1975: 25, original emphasis).

This subordination of politics to sociology may seem natural and necessary in a society like the United States 'which has achieved a high measure of consensus around its constitutional arrangements'; with no fundamental political conflict:

> the source of lasting change in the structure of conflict must be transformations of the social system:... the appearance of broad new sets of political interests, drastically altered expectations within the citizenry, marked increases in the numerical strength of established interest groups, and the like.
>
> (Ladd and Hadley 1975: 90)

But the American experience of critical elections throws doubt on the hypothesis that such a consensus has been achieved. What is at issue in the critical elections if not precisely the shape of that consensus itself, or in other words the meaning of democratic republicanism? The 'consensus' view of American political history is today widely (and rightly) questioned. Those who are more impressed with the depth of political conflict in the United

States in certain periods, and with the importance of certain decisive elections, emphasize with Sundquist (here explicitly disagreeing with Ladd) the fact that social changes 'do not in themselves produce realignments. They must first give rise to genuine *political* issues.' Sundquist points out that 'a profound change in the structure of society, particularly one that occurred gradually, might never produce a political issue of realigning force; on the other hand, a major political issue might arise in the absence of fundamental structural change' (Sundquist 1983: 299). The realignments that elevated the parties of Jefferson, Jackson, Lincoln and Franklin Roosevelt all involved quick political actions, rather than merely political reactions to slow socio-economic developments. Only the combination of interest-group politics with ideological politics describes and explains critical elections. As we saw in our survey of party history in Chapter Two, interest-group politics does not disappear in critical elections, but it is accompanied by principled conflict.

In fact, principled conflicts are not absent in other periods of American party history, and it is interesting to ask why the rise of principled conflicts has not always led to critical elections. How have critical elections been avoided in many cases, in spite of the existence of cross-cutting issues of realigning potential? Addressing this question should help relieve the uneasiness felt by some that critical elections and realignment studies must neglect long periods of American party history to concentrate only on actual critical elections, which have been very few in number. It should also bring more into the centre of the picture the importance of political leaders' actions and failures to act, instead of leaving the behaviour of the electorate to dominate the scene on its own. Doubtless there have been occasions in American political history – perhaps particularly in cases of ethnic or religious quarrels – when potentially realigning issues deserved to be ignored or suppressed, in spite of their actual or potential appeal to the electorate. Political leaders deserve to be judged on (among other things) how well they have perceived such occasions and acted accordingly, as well as on how skilfully or how badly they have exploited realigning issues that deserved to be effective. When the times cry out for inaction, cooling the electorate's passions can be as praiseworthy as warming them up can be at other times. Statesmanship does not always have to deal in the stuff of tragedy. Uncritical elections can in this way be as interesting and as demanding as critical ones.

As we shall see in Chapter Nine, the exploitation of realigning issues by political leaders has occurred not only in critical elections themselves, but also in government policies afterwards, which in at least some cases have helped make the preceding elections durably critical. Electoral victories have simply provided the opportunity for 'decisive and innovative policy actions', and it is these actions that have been necessary 'to convert temporary electoral strength into lasting partisan support and loyalty' (Clubb *et al.* 1980: 32). Like vintage wines, critical elections can be proclaimed only in retrospect, when the durability of the changes they bring has been seen; but perhaps they depend even more than good wines on the way they are handled after the harvest. After the votes are counted, it remains to be seen what the victors will make of their spoils. 'Vigorous policy action... can be seen as reinforcing and, indeed, rewarding voting behaviour and as necessary for the final element of [a] realignment, the formation of a new and lasting distribution of partisan loyalties....' (Clubb *et al.* 1980: 260). This perspective can help to resolve conflicting interpretations of the significance of the mobilization of new voters versus the conversion of existing ones, in a given realignment. (Such conflicting interpretations have been especially evident in the literature on the New Deal realignment, some studies emphasizing the role of mobilization [Anderson 1979], others that of conversion [Erikson and Tedin 1981, Sundquist 1983: 229–39], still others the contributions of both forces [Campbell 1985].) Even newly mobilized voters need to be 'converted' in the sense that they need to become party loyalists rather than merely instrumental voters for the party for the time being.

These last two points – the absence of critical elections and realignments in certain times of principled political conflicts, and the importance of political leaders' actions both during and after potentially critical elections – have figured prominently in studies of the party conflict of the last twenty years, and in considerations of the prospects for realignment today.

INSTITUTIONAL BARRIERS TO CRITICAL REALIGNMENT

From Table 3.1 (p. 39), it can be seen that the legislative branch of the federal government – the House of Representatives and Senate – has been controlled by the Democratic party since 1955, with the exception of the first six years of Reagan's presidency, when the Democrats lost control of the Senate. During the same period, the Republican party has controlled the White House for all but twelve years. Divided party control of the federal government seems to have become the normal situation. The Republicans' apparent 'lock' on the presidential Electoral College is more than matched by the Democrats' 'lock' on congressional elections. During this period, all but the twelve years of Democratic presidents have been years of divided government; in other words, there has been divided government about two-thirds of the time. During the previous 162 years of American party politics, one can calculate from Table 3.1 that there was divided government for only about one-fifth of the time.

The Republican presidential victories of Eisenhower in 1952 and 1956 could (and still can) be seen mainly as deviating elections. In these elections, a military hero *not* known as 'Mr Republican' (that was Robert Taft, who was rejected for the nomination) helped the subordinate Republican party temporarily to defeat the presidential ambitions of the dominant Democrats (and, even more temporarily, their congressional ambitions). But the victories of Richard Nixon in 1968 and 1972 were accompanied by greater speculation about the possibilities of lasting shifts of the electorate towards identification with the Republican party. Some observers discerned an *Emerging Republican Majority* (Phillips 1970). The Watergate scandals checked any such emergence, at least for a few years, but the victories of Ronald Reagan in 1980 and 1984 (and Republican majorities in the Senate from 1981 to 1987 – however slight and diminishing) led to further speculation about a major realignment of the party system. Academics immediately voiced much scepticism about the existence of such a realignment, pointing out that the Democrats maintained firm control of the House (as well as of the majority of state legislative branches); more than forty per cent of the House Democratic incumbents who faced Republican challengers in both 1978 and 1980 actually improved on their 1978 vote (Jacobson 1983: Chapter 6). Furthermore, the exit polls in 1980 and other indicators of public opinion showed little evidence that voters thought they were giving the Republicans a conservative mandate (e. g. Ladd 1981, Schneider 1981). More evident than any realignment trend was a continuing trend towards party *de*alignment and decline. Burnham (1970: Chapter 5) and others had pointed to the evidence of a long-term decomposition of the party system, stretching back to the end of the nineteenth century, and such dealigning trends as low levels of partisanship, high levels of incumbents' success when seeking re-election, split-ticket voting, low turnout, the erosion of traditional ties between certain ethnic and interest groups and the major parties, the volatility of opinion and voting decisions, and the use of party-bypassing devices such as referenda and initiatives, all seemed to persist in spite of the 'Reagan Revolution'. (Party dealignment is discussed in more detail below, in Chapters Eight and Ten.)

Of course, dealignment is nothing new in American party politics. Evidence of dealignment has been spotted in previous historical party systems. It is a natural feature of the cycle of party history, both because of the difficulties of maintaining enthusiastic party loyalty long after the critical election battles have been fought and won, and because of the confusion of party loyalties in pre-realignment periods. Previous dealigning periods – the 1840s, the 1880s – also included high levels of divided government (Table 3.1; Beck 1979: 149). Could not the current period of dealignment and divided government simply be setting the stage for a contemporary critical realignment? The moderate and conservative wings of the Democratic party (for example, the Democratic Leadership Council, a group of southern and western Democratic officeholders formed after Walter Mondale's defeat in the 1984 presidential election) do seem to have been trying to move the Democrats into a moon-like 'me too' position, at least on economic issues. When even a leading liberal Democrat like Senator Edward Kennedy concedes that conservative fiscal concerns may sometimes come before liberal social welfare concerns, there appears to have been a shift of the centre ground of politics towards the right, with the prospect of the Republican party becoming the agenda-setting sun of the electoral solar system. Several Democratic electoral victories in the 1980s owed something to the Democratic candidates' ability to adopt 'me too' positions. For example, when Virginia elected a Democratic governor, lieutenant-governor and attorney general in 1985, Frank Fahrenkopf, the chairman of the Republican national committee, attributed this Republican defeat to the fact that 'We allowed the Democrats to out-Republican us.' Thus the current party system can be explained partly in terms of realignment theory, even though no complete critical realignment has taken place.

This raises two further and final questions about party realignment in the contemporary period: are political leaders currently exploiting the opportunities for realignment as well as they might? And are there any difficulties in the way of realignment that make such exploitation harder today than for political leaders in the past?

Ronald Reagan was a more enthusiastic Republican party booster than some other recent Republican presidents have been, but even many conservative supporters of Reagan have come to doubt that he served their cause and the Republican party as well as he might have done. His 1984 campaign, in particular, in spite of (or because of) its leading to a presidential landslide, seemed singularly lacking in any major and timely attempts either to define a set of polarizing issues and gather a presidential mandate or to spread the Republican electoral victory farther down the ballot. Reagan was well adapted to the cool politics of television, but little interested in carrying on hot and divisive political battles of the kind that have been essential to critical realignments in the past. Critical realignments require political leaders who are not afraid of being hated as well as loved. Reagan's personal popularity rarely dipped very low, but the percentage of the electorate with a Republican partisan identification at the end of Reagan's two administrations was not remarkably higher than it was at the beginning (and was still well below the percentage with a Democratic identification). For his electoral victories, he relied more on 'Reagan Democrats' than on massive conversions of voters or mobilizations of new voters as loyal Republicans. In 1984, he defended the satisfactory character of the status quo – which happened to include Democratic domination of elected offices other than the presidency and Senate. In his 1984 stump speech, Reagan reminded voters that he himself had been a Democrat most of his life, and denied that he was asking them to abandon the Democratic party and convert to Republicanism. Thus, it was not surprising to see the *New York Times–CBS News* exit poll in November 1988 finding that half of the Democrats who had voted for Reagan in 1984 supported the Democratic nominee, Michael Dukakis, and that first-time voters split fairly evenly between the presidential candidates, with George Bush receiving 51 per cent of their votes, to Dukakis's 47 per cent (in contrast to 1984, when Reagan received 61 per cent, to Walter Mondale's 38 per cent). In elections to the House of Representatives, first-time voters, who had split evenly between the two parties in 1986, gave a lead of about ten percentage points to Democratic candidates in 1988 and 1990.

This is not to deny the fact that Bush may well owe his election to his discovery of the power of the cross-cutting social or cultural issues that appeal to many of those Democrats who have recently voted for Republican presidential candidates. The Bush campaign transformed a seventeen-per-centage-point lead for Dukakis in the polls in the summer to an eight-point lead for Bush in the election in November, mainly on the strength of what was called 'negative' campaigning. Bush's attacks on Dukakis's record on the punishment of crime (the prison furlough issue) and on dedication to American political principles (the pledge of allegiance issue) may have been distasteful to many observers, both in America and abroad. But the success of these attacks clearly proves that the conventional wisdom of the 1960s and 1970s of television campaign professionals who taught that such 'negative' tactics were too risky now needs to be revised at the presidential level, just as it has already been revised at other levels of American politics. Dukakis and his advisers seriously underestimated the effects of these attacks. Failing to see that many American voters would take these issues seriously, Dukakis unwisely chose to ignore them at first, and when he did respond, he failed to respond to the charge made, which was not that he was (as he now admitted) a New Deal, Roosevelt–Truman–John Kennedy–Johnson liberal, but that he was – on the social issues – a 1960s, McGovern–Carter–Ted Kennedy–Jesse Jackson liberal (Wattenberg 1988: 20; Schneider 1989: 48, 56–7). The Bush 'negative' campaign helped to double between July and October the percent-age of the electorate with negative ratings of Dukakis, largely because it succeeded in identifying Dukakis clearly as a liberal on social and foreign policy issues (however much he was a fiscal conservative), in the minds of key groups in the electorate, including many socially conservative Demo-crats and independents. The *Times–CBS* exit poll showed liberals favouring Dukakis at a higher rate (81 per cent) than they had favoured Mondale in 1984 (70 per cent), in fact at the same high rate by which conservatives favoured Bush (and by which they had favoured Reagan in 1984). But only

18 per cent of the electorate called themselves liberals, while 33 per cent called themselves conservatives.

However, it seems unlikely that President Bush will prove any more inclined or able than President Reagan was to transform socially conservative support into a partisan realignment. Although he may owe his election to his stand on certain social issues, he clearly felt more uncomfortable than Reagan did in fighting on that ground. He may have helped to demonstrate that television can after all be used for heated partisanship, but he seemed more interested in being known for a 'kinder, gentler' politics than for a divisive partisanship. He was not the social conservatives' candidate in the nomination contest (Jack Kemp and Pat Robertson occupied that position), and in spite of his campaign tactics he is still distrusted by many of them. Even his economic conservatism is more flexible than Reagan's was. There was a brief lull in conservative complaints about Bush's avoidance of ideological battles during his first months in office, but following the defeats of Republican gubernatorial candidates in New Jersey and Virginia in November 1989, these complaints began to resurface. Bush will be anxious to maintain the support of social conservatives, and will therefore do things that they will applaud (especially things like conservative judicial appointments, which divert the partisan battle between social liberals and conservatives into the courts). But Bush emphasizes the need for bipartisanship, which does not rally the electorate to the Republicans. He will probably not be trying to reshape the American electoral universe by forcing a public, partisan choice between social liberalism and social conservatism – if only because he has already failed to use this tactic to persuade the electorate to vote for Republicans in general, who did much worse in 1988 than in 1980 or 1984. The Republican party continues to grow in the traditionally Democratic southern states, but elsewhere the Democrats have stopped losing support to Republicans. So not only did the Democrats in 1988 and 1990 increase their majorities in the Senate and House of Representatives, they also put a stop to the drift of state legislative seats to the Republican party. The Republicans, while remaining the minority party in most state legislatures, had nevertheless enjoyed a net gain of more than 300 of these seats in 1980 and 1984, but they lost a net total of twenty-nine of them in 1988 (although gaining twenty-seven in the south). After the 1990 elections the democrats controlled nearly three quarters of the state legislative chambers.

In addition to television and the other modern techniques of contemporary American political campaigns, many of which do interfere with any attempt to strengthen candidates' and voters' partisanship, there are other institutional difficulties in the way of realignment today that did not exist in the past. The chief example of these barriers must be the level of incumbency protection that has become established by Congressmen, making any serious bid by the Republicans for control of the House of Representatives seem out of the question. (In 1988, out of all of the Democratic incumbents running for re-election in the House and Senate, only two representatives and one senator were defeated. Incumbents' average margins of victory were slightly reduced in 1990, but about 96 per cent won.) It can be seen from Table 3.1 that in the past (1827, 1855, 1859 and 1931) the partisan control of the House of Representatives has reacted more quickly than that of the presidency to critical realignments of the electorate's partisan loyalties. Today the House is much less likely to act as such a sensitive barometer.

Associated with this high level of congressional incumbency protection, and further inhibiting realignment by further dividing congressional from presidential elections, are the different methods of campaign finance now obtaining in congressional as opposed to presidential races. Following the reforms of the 1970s, presidential races are now largely publicly financed, with much more money going to individual candidates than to their parties. Congressional races are still mainly privately financed, and the reformed system of legal limits on individual contributions to congressional races – but not on the totals spent – generally helps incumbents and discourages challengers, and ties the winners more firmly to the network of private business contributors than to other winners with the same party label, be they Congressmen or president. Winning presidential elections and winning congressional elections have always been distinct activities, but they have not always been as divorced from each other as they have become in the last two decades.

It may also simply be the case that no single realigning issue or set of issues of sufficient potency has been available in the last two decades, in spite of the apparently greater importance in party politics since the 1960s of issues and ideologies in general, and of social issues in particular. With no such traumatic event as a civil war or a massive economic depression, realignment on the scale of 1860 or 1932 may be nearly impossible. The least that must be said here is that the scenario of the last two decades more clearly resembles that of the Civil War realignment, when the critical moment came only after several years of partisan confusion, than of the New Deal realignment, which occurred more abruptly and sent out shock waves for several years thereafter. For the moment, American public opinion has not been forced by events or by political leaders to choose between social conservatism and social liberalism. Some voters may be tired of the middle, but more are afraid of the extremes. The *Times–CBS* exit poll in 1988 found moderates (45 per cent of the voters) still far outnumbering liberals (18 per cent) and conservatives (33 per cent). Split ticket voting, producing conservative Republican presidents and liberal Democratic Congresses, accurately reflects the indecisiveness of public opinion, which when polled indicates support for conservative sentiments in general, but for liberal policies in specific areas. The president, as the one national representative, and as the official most constitutionally responsible for foreign policy, has come to represent the general support for conservatism, while Congress, with its stronger influence on the day-to-day administration of particular domestic programmes, represents the continued public support for these programmes. Divided government reflects indecisive public opinion.

Perhaps relatively rapid swings of electoral support between the two major parties, with (if anything) very short-term one-party domination – such as occurred in the 1840s, 1880s and 1910s – is the most plausible prognosis for partisan alignment and realignment in the current party system. A more genuinely two-party system is seen emerging in the United States by those observers who anticipate this scenario (Cavanagh and Sundquist 1985: 62–7). Alternatively, one could argue that, given the greater institutional barriers to realignment in the late twentieth century, the transformation of the terms of political debate since 1980 has already been sufficiently great to constitute a durable new direction in partisan debate and public policy (Chubb and Peterson 1985: 30). But this argument that the Reagan realignment has been impressive precisely because of its ability partially to overcome these greater barriers seems to us to place the emphasis the wrong way around: the growth of the barriers has been far more impressive than the effectiveness of the 'Reagan revolution' in overcoming them. More likely than either a more genuinely two-party system or a more consistently conservative one is the continued division of the branches of the national government between liberal Democrats and conservative Republicans.

PARTY REFORMISM AS A BARRIER TO PARTISAN REALIGNMENT

The greater difficulty of critical partisan realignment in twentieth-century American politics must be considered not only as it relates to the institutional and historical factors discussed above, but also in the light of the anti-partisan, reform-minded attitude towards party that emerged in late nineteenth- and early twentieth-century America. As noted in Chapter Three, this high-minded attitude to the American party system, first elaborated by Woodrow Wilson, developed as a reaction against the lowly realities of that system, and both of these extremes undermined the synthesis of Constitutional moderation and partisan change established at least in the thought if not also by the deeds of Martin Van Buren.

The party reforming reaction, most effective in the progressive period just before the First World War and in the post–1968 Chicago Democratic convention and post-Watergate reforms of the 1970s, has produced a host of legal and institutional changes affecting the practice of party both at the state and local levels and at the national level: 'professionalization' of the civil service (including city managers), non-partisan municipal elections, referenda, initiatives, recall devices, voter registration, government-printed ballots, heavy regulation of internal party activities (forbidding such terrible conspiracies as communication between county committees and the state committees: an extreme example, but a real one), widespread use of the direct primary election (with primaries coming to dominate nominations at the presidential level as well since 1972) and (the most recent large innovation) public financing of some campaigns in several states and in presidential primary and general elections. The experience in various places and in various elections differs, but the general tendency of these reforms clearly has been to promote voters' independence from partisanship, and to discourage existing party organizations, thus encouraging candidates' own organizations and campaign efforts, rather than dependence on parties. (These developments are discussed in greater detail in Chapter Seven.) Furthermore, in so far as party organizations have also been helped by these reforms, it has been the duopoly of Democrats and Republicans that has been propped up, thus closing the party system even while opening up the major parties. Primaries and other party-opening reforms allow new groups to compete within the existing major parties, rather than encouraging them to work through new or existing third parties; legal regulations burden minor parties more than major ones; and public financing helps major parties far more than minor ones. The party reform movements have promoted candidate-centred politics, as a replacement for a party system that they have made in some ways even more stale and status-quo-directed than it was before they started complaining about this failing. The subordination of party to candidate was one of the effects most clearly intended by the progressive reforms, and one which most clearly sets the reformed party system apart from the mature party system described in Chapter Three. The emphasis of the 1960s and 1970s reform movement was more on wider participation than on better leadership, but both this and the progressive reform movement were primarily concerned to open up the parties to publicity, and to purify them from the corrupting influence of professional politicians uninterested in either the establishment of the administrative state or the politics of high principle.

The reform movements have succeeded in transforming the party system and the larger political system to some extent, although the anti-party thrust of party reform has tended to undermine its unifying leadership thrust. Plebiscitary leadership has been encouraged, but, as might have been expected, the unifying and enduring qualities of this leadership have not been so apparent. It is now commonly expected of both conservative and liberal politicians, especially executives, that they will lead in a Wilsonian manner, relying less on Constitutional powers or party ties than on popular leadership, based on their whole constituency and on public (not party) opinion. The 'modern presidency' and the modern administrative state are Wilsonian in spirit, although they have not succeeded in reducing the 'extraordinary isolation' of the presidency noticed by Wilson. Furthermore, it is now widely accepted that the best voters are independents, not party regulars. Not even potential party regulars: the dealigning American electorate are more decidedly dealigned than other dealigning electorates; their attitudes to their major parties are less hostile than they are neutral, viewing them as irrelevancies in the political system (Wattenberg 1982).

Even the New Deal in the 1930s, which is often seen as an episode that revived American partisan politics for a time, can be seen more penetratingly as an attempt by Franklin Roosevelt's leadership to replace partisan politics with presidential administration, pursuing not Jefferson's or Van Buren's lead, but Hamilton's. The New Deal, like its successor the Great Society in the 1960s, and not unlike the Reagan assault on the Great Society in the 1980s, was less a partisan programme than an exercise in extending 'nonpartisan administration'; it was intended to be 'a party to end all parties' (Milkis 1985, 1987). Roosevelt tried – inconsistently and unsuccessfully – to reinforce partisanship by making the Democratic party a more purely liberal party. But apart from the fact that ideological purity and partisan loyalty are two different things (so success with this project might not have revived so much as stifled partisanship), Roosevelt easily consoled himself when this project failed, because he saw (as he said in 1940 – in his Jackson Day Speech!) that

> the future lies with those wise political leaders who realize the great public is interested more in government than in politics, that the independent vote in this country has been steadily on the increase, at least for the past generation, that vast numbers of people consider themselves normally adherents of one party and still feel perfectly free to vote for one or more candidates of another party, come election day, and on the other hand, sometimes uphold party principles even when precinct captains decide 'to take a walk'.

> (Milkis 1985: 498)

The overt and covert hostility of the reform view to partisanship itself, and therefore to any party system, however formed or reformed, has helped to create the current situation, in which weak partisanship both in the electorate and in elected officials makes durable partisan and governing coalitions difficult if not impossible for politicians to construct, and therefore makes political leadership itself more difficult. Wilson himself already found that his re-election to the presidency in 1916 on a personal rather than a party basis stored up problems for his second term of office, during which he was greatly handicapped by the absence of the backing of an organized party. In the modern American political system, political leadership is (as expected by the reformers) in greater demand but (contrary to their expectations) shorter supply. Partisan majorities, when they appear, are extremely short-lived. Policy successes, when they appear, are equally ephemeral. The danger of mistaking personal convictions for popular mandates (again following Wilson's precedent) is ever present. This situation can be attributed in significant part to the failure of twentieth-century political science and politicians to achieve such a constructive level and kind of tension between the party system and Constitutional government as were achieved by the politicians of the early nineteenth century. This failure constitutes one of the main barriers to durable critical realignment of the party system in the twentieth century.

CONCLUSION

In spite of the contemporary barriers to major party realignment, such realignment remains a possibility for American politicians to pursue or to avoid, and is therefore still a leading characteristic of the American party system. The statistically more normal, 'uncritical' functioning of American parties depends for some of its vitality on the heat generated by these rare but crucial moments in the history of the party system. If that heat were truly no longer possible to sense or at least to imagine, there might be real danger of a collapse of the party system. And in fact, at least in presidential politics, the ideological stuff of critical realignment has not yet completely dissipated.

As we have seen in this chapter and in Chapter Two, the experience of major realignments has had the effect not only of rejuvenating the party system from time to time, but also of shaping it into a two-party system, by promoting a division of the electorate into two parts, on the basis of a powerful central issue. In the next chapter, we examine further the causes and effects of this duopolistic character of the American party system.

5 A two-party system

Each of the five historical party systems described in Chapter Two consisted of two major parties. In this chapter we seek to describe, account for and assess the impact of the two-party system. In addition, we will discuss the performances of those other parties (collectively referred to as 'third parties') which have, briefly, made the deepest inroads into two-party domination.

We begin by demonstrating the strength and durability of the two-party system in America. Second, we seek to explain why it thrives in a diverse society. In this section we devote particular attention to a feature unique to America in western party systems, the absence of an electorally relevant socialist or social democratic party. In the states one-party dominance is a common alternative to two-party competition. In the third section we seek to account for the absence of a competitive party system in some states. We then consider the performance of third parties in presidential elections where, in the twentieth century, their strength has been greatest. Finally, we identify the consequences of the two-party system for American politics.

THE MAJOR PARTY DUOPOLY

Democrats and Republicans currently exercise a virtual duopoly over elective office in the United States. Independents, many of them in local office which is legally required to be filled by non-partisan elections in many areas, constitute most of the exceptions to duopolistic control. In 1989 the president, every senator, member of the House of Representatives, state governor and all but four of the 7,406 members of the state legislatures which allow partisan elections were either Democrats or Republicans. All four exceptions in the state legislatures were independents rather than members of other parties.

Election contests are usually confined to the two major parties. In recent times few offices below the presidency have attracted candidates from third parties. In 1986, of 435 districts used for elections to the House of Representatives, only 27 per cent were contested by third parties or independents. The exceptions to the norm of two-horse races were concentrated in the two largest states, New York and California where a majority of seats were contested by third parties. The Libertarians, the most active of the third parties, ran candidates in less than one seat in ten. In Vermont, Ben Sanders, a socialist running as an independent, won to breach the two-party duopoly of representation in Congress for the first time in a decade. It is over forty years since a third party won a state governorship (though Maine did elect an independent in 1974). Third-party representation is now weaker than ever before in American government (Schlesinger 1984).

A duopoly has characterized most of American electoral history. Each of the historical party systems consisted of only two major parties. They dominated the presidency, Congress, governorships and state legislatures. The principal exception to duopolistic control was the almost instant transition of the Republicans from third-party competitor in 1856 to dominant party in 1860. Thereafter the two-party pattern was quickly re-established.

The characteristics of a two-party system have been defined by Giovanni Sartori (1976). His definitions are concerned with the prospects for single-party government (while recognizing that in the non-parliamentary system of the United States there are two seats of government, Congress and the presidency). Adapted for the American context Sartori's four conditions of a two-party system are:

1 Two parties are in a position to compete for an absolute majority of seats in Congress.
2 One of the parties wins a sufficient majority.
3 One of the two parties controls the presidency.
4 Alternation or rotation in power between the two parties remains a credible expectation.

The first three conditions have been fulfilled repeatedly. The last condition is more doubtful. There have been lengthy periods when one party had uninterrupted control of one or both seats of government. Each of the historical systems has been characterized by an imbalance in the electoral strength of the two major parties. One party was in the ascendant in each era, usually obtaining majorities in Congress and winning the presidency. The other party was, with occasional exceptions, in the minority or it controlled only one branch of government. Control by the majority was most stable in the years immediately following the realignment. The majority party controlled both the presidency and Congress for more than a decade after each realignment. In the later phases of each era the majority's support was more fragile and the minority party disrupted its monopoly of power.

Sartori's fourth condition focuses upon the expectation of alternation rather than its occurrence. Expectations are difficult to decipher in the past. But there is little evidence in any era of party elites regarding the relationship between majority and minority as unalterable. In particular, the minority party do not seem to have accepted their fate.

If party government, for which there are only two realistic contenders, were to be a condition of a two-party system then simultaneous control of both presidency and Congress would be an appropriate test for the United States. The enactment of a programme requires collaboration between president and Congress. Where both institutions are controlled by the same party the prospects for the enactment of a programme are likely to be enhanced. In the past this demanding condition was regularly satisfied. From 1828 to 1968 the same party controlled the presidency while simultaneously possessing a clear majority in Congress for eighty-eight years of the 140-year period, 63 per cent of the time (Burnham *et al.* 1978). In recent years synchronized control has been the exception. In the period 1945–90 only nineteen of the forty-six years have provided simultaneous party control of the presidency and Congress. Democrats have controlled the House of Representatives continuously since 1955 but they have won only three of the nine presidential elections in that time.

The states exhibit diversity in the degree of competitiveness between the two parties. Three gradations of competitiveness are identifiable. First, there are competitive states where election results are often close and control of the governorship and legislature switches between the parties. Divided control is common with neither party simultaneously holding the governorship and both houses of the legislature. Secondly, there are the instances of uneven competition. One party is commonly but not permanently in control of the legislature. Majorities in the legislature switch between the parties but only on rare occasions. Elections for governor are more competitive and may frequently be won by the party which is usually the legislative minority. A third category of states are virtual monopolies. In the legislature, majority–minority status does not change over long periods. Gubernatorial elections are competitive with the legislative minority securing some victories. (See Table 5.1 for a classification of the states also showing which party is dominant in the legislative branch.)

Only eleven states are closely balanced between the two parties. In the remainder the parties are unequal in the legislative branch though more competitive in control of the governorship. The advantage enjoyed by one party in state contests is not necessarily reproduced in federal elections where the balance is often tipped towards the minority by appealing candidates, stances on national issues and the advantages of incumbency. Of the twenty-nine states in which Democrats have an edge (virtual monopoly or uneven

Table 5.1 Party competition in state elections, 1965–86

Virtual monopoly	Uneven competition	Two-party competition
Democratic	*Democratic*	Alaska
Alabama	California	Delaware
Arkansas	Connecticut	Illinois
Florida	Michigan	Iowa
Georgia	Minnesota	Maine
Hawaii	Nevada	Montana
Kentucky	Oregon	New Jersey
Louisiana	Washington	New York
Maryland		Ohio
Massachusetts		Pennsylvania
Mississippi	*Republican*	Wisconsin
Missouri	Arizona	
New Hampshire	Colorado	
New Mexico	Indiana	
North Carolina	Kansas	
Oklahoma	North Dakota	
Rhode Island	South Dakota	
South Carolina	Utah	
Tennessee	Vermont	
Texas	Wyoming	
Virginia		
West Virginia		
Republican		
Idaho		

Note: Nebraska excluded because legislature non-partisan
Source: Adapted from Malcolm E. Jewell and Samuel C. Patterson, *The Legislative Process in the United States*, 4th edn (New York: Random House, 1986).

competition) all but one were carried by the Republicans in the 1984 presidential election.

Unified control of both branches by one party is now rarer than it used to be. In 1989, of the forty-nine states which permit partisan elections of both branches (Nebraska has a non-partisan legislature), only eighteen were controlled by one party. This tendency towards divided party control has grown in recent years from the modest competitive trend in state elections (Table 5.2). Today even the most solid one-party states do evidence competitive races for governor. In these contests the issues and the candidates gain more salience than in elections for lesser offices, depressing the impact of party loyalties on the vote. Beginning from the mid–1960s even the formerly solidly Democratic south began to yield Republican governors. By 1986 only Georgia and Mississippi continued to hold out against a Republican for governor. However, in state legislative elections traditional loyalties are more resilient. In only two southern states, Florida and Tennessee, do

Table 5.2 Growth of divided control in the states, 1950–90

Year	Divided control (% all states)
1950	23.9
1960	37.5
1970	41.7
1980	51.0
1990	61.0

Republicans constitute a third of the members of both houses of the legislature.

CAUSES OF TWO PARTYISM

The USA is a heterogeneous society. Its population is diverse in religions, races, ethnic backgrounds, occupations and geographical location. Despite this diversity the two-party pattern has prevailed. For all the 'raw material' provided for a multi-party system, America has consistently been a duopoly.

Two sets of factors account for the two-party system amidst social diversity:

1 Institutional provisions;
2 Socio-cultural influences.

Institutional provisions

Various aspects of laws and constitutions, federal and state, promote a two-party rather than a multi-party system. First, the single member, first-past-the-post (plurality) election system penalizes parties unable to obtain the relative majorities necessary to win seats. In contrast, proportional representation systems, by lowering the threshold of first-choice preferences necessary to secure election, facilitate the proliferation of parties. Proportional representation has been used in some local elections with predictable consequences. In New York city's ten-year experiment with PR, beginning in 1938, even two Communists were elected to the city council.

The principal exception to the plurality rule for election is the requirement in presidential contests of an absolute majority in the Electoral College. To achieve this objective popular vote pluralities have to be won in a sufficient number of states to convert into half plus one of the presidential electors. This requires a geographical spread of support which concentrated strength would not achieve. Only a broad coalition can carry the Electoral College.

The capture of the presidency was one of the original stimulants to the formation of national parties in America, and the presidential election continues to shape the party system. Those parties capable of contending for the single most powerful office in the US political system enjoy a public credibility that their less advantaged competitors lack.

By having a single executive office, the presidency, multi-party coalition governments are precluded. Executive power cannot be shared between parties in the United States as it can be in cabinet systems. There is thus no prospect of sharing power for a party with a small minority of the vote. In cabinet systems this possibility exists and the West German Free Democrats have repeatedly demonstrated the scope for winning office for a small party which holds the balance of power. In the individual states executive power is divided between several elected officials, of which the governor is the most prominent. But the elections for each office are usually discrete contests. Each office is indivisible between parties. Moreover, each office has constitutionally defined responsibilities, there is little sense of collective leadership in which power could be distributed between parties.

Modern election laws have been enacted by legislatures dominated by the two major parties. In at least two respects the laws are designed to protect the duopoly. The two major parties qualify more easily to appear on the ballot and to obtain financial assistance towards funding their campaigns than their third party competitors. To qualify to appear on the ballot in many states requires either a specified percentage of the vote to have been obtained in a previous election or the submission of a petition signed by a stipulated number of voters. The major parties usually qualify via the first provision. Third parties and independent candidates have to meet the petition requirements. This can entail obtaining vast numbers of signatures. For the 1980 presidential election it has been estimated that 1.2 million signatures were needed to satisfy the petition requirements of the fifty states. Clearing this hurdle cost John Anderson's independent campaign $3 million either in obtaining signatures or mounting court challenges to the state laws that required them (Rosenstone *et al*. 1984). Some states require petitions to be lodged with election authorities months before the contest, a severe handicap to candidacies which only develop in election year as Anderson's did. States vary in their requirements. The very diversity adds to the burden on third parties seeking to mount national campaigns.

Recent campaign finance legislation has accentuated the inequalities in resources available to third parties compared to their major opponents. Under the 1974 Federal Election Campaign Act contributions by individuals and groups (organized into political action committees) were restricted to $1,000 and $5,000 respectively for each candidate. Large contributions were prohibited (though independent campaigns separate from, but on a candidate's behalf, can still be mounted without a financial limit). Generating large numbers of contributions under $5,000 is often attainable for major parties and incumbent office-holders. But third parties and their non-incumbent candidates often struggle to raise sufficient finance to mount a credible campaign.

Public funding of presidential campaigns was also provided for in the 1974 Act. But the law discriminated between parties in its generosity. The major parties received contributions in advance to offset the cost of staging national conventions and running campaigns. Other parties and independents qualified only if they obtained 5 per cent of the popular vote in the previous election or if they went on to cross that threshold in the current one. The effect of the latter regulation was to deny funds to third parties until after the election. Similar advantages are conferred on the major parties by some state public financing provisions.

The permeability of the major parties further handicaps their third party opponents. Legal regulation of internal party affairs is more extensive in the United States than in any other western democracy. A recurrent objective of legal regulation has been to promote public participation in party affairs. The direct primary for choosing candidates is a token of this tendency. Since its inception at the end of the nineteenth century parties have lost influence over the nomination and the rules by which they are decided.

Public laws more than party rules define the criteria for participation in a primary, either as voter or candidates for the nomination (see Chapter Seven). In neither case are the conditions usually onerous. Where the thresholds to participation in the major parties are so low the stimuli to the formation of other parties are weak. Historical evidence shows that competition from third parties receded after the inception of primaries (Galderisi and Ginsberg 1986). Proponents of new issues and group interests can seek to mobilize within the existing parties to mould them to their priorities rather than create new organizations. Alternatively, existing third parties can invade major party primaries as a more plausible route to power than competing against them. This latter strategy was recently adopted by the National Democratic Policy Committee (formerly the US Labor party) led by the maverick Lyndon La Rouche, who believes that Queen Elizabeth operates an international drug-trafficking conspiracy. In the 1980s La Rouche supporters succeeded in winning several Democratic nominations including that for the lieutenant governorship of Illinois.

Election petition requirements and the accessibility of primaries may reinforce one another to channel activity into the major parties. Where petition requirements for the election are more demanding than the qualifications to run in a major party primary, the latter may be preferred by emerging political forces. Inclusion within a major party offers an easier route to the electorate and to office than a third party strategy.

Socio-cultural influences

Despite its social heterogeneity the US escaped the politicization of several socio-cultural cleavages which in many European countries gave rise to separate parties (Lipset and Rokkan 1967). Divisive conflicts such as those over church–state relations, owner versus employee, democracy versus some authoritarian alternative, peripheral cultures resisting that of the core, did not fragment the American population as they did in much of Europe. Since independence there has been little opposition to a secular, capitalist, democratic nation-state.

Founded after the Reformation and Counter-Reformation as a refuge from persecution, America escaped the political schisms resulting from religious conflict. The prohibition of an established church entrenched in the First Amendment of the Constitution precluded the institutionalized national religion around which many European church–state conflicts pivoted. Without integral links to the state, no church was in a position to translate its doctrines into national public policy. Religious values and clerics have regularly been involved in political debates, as in the nineteenth-century campaign against slavery and the contemporary opposition to abortion. But disputes over an institutionally privileged church have been absent.

Mass democracy developed in America earlier and with less conflict than in most of Europe. The elitist features of the original federal and state constitutions progressively eroded in the early nineteenth century as the franchise was extended beyond property holders and elective offices multiplied. Resistance to the democratizing trend was fragile at least so long as the beneficiaries were confined to white males. The US lacked a monarchy and an aristocracy. No monarchical absolutist state had to be defeated to entrench democratic practices. Nor was there an aristocracy seeking to preserve its privileges by excluding other classes from power.

Despite the severity of the Depression in the United States in the 1930s fascism failed to develop a mass appeal. Demagogues such as Huey Long and Father Charles Coughlin did gain popular support in that period but they have not usually been regarded as fascists. Antagonism to democracy, a defining characteristic of European fascism, was not articulated by Long, and by Coughlin only after his popularity had begun to decline. Mass organizations never developed around either figure.

Many of the social and historical antecedents of fascism were absent in America. Modernization had taken place under the auspices of the bourgeoisie rather than the aristocracy, the latter lacking from the American scene. In the 1930s democracy was neither recently established nor unstable. There was no militant working class nor sizeable communist party to scare the bourgeoisie into the defence offered by fascism. There had been no national humiliation in the First World War, and dissatisfaction with the Versailles settlement had been expiated by the Senate's rejection of it.

The southern secession of 1861 constitutes the egregious exception to the rule that separatist movements have been weak in America. For most of the white population original incorporation into the United States was voluntary. The populations of newly settled territories applied to join the Union. Immigrants voted with their feet to live in America. For non-whites incorporation entailed violence. Indian territory was forcibly annexed and most blacks were enslaved but both groups were long denied the political rights to challenge incorporation that they lacked the force to resist. Federalism provided a governmental outlet for a differentiated population to find expression. A decentralized political system enabled geographically concentrated cultures to be articulated through the laws of the various states. Diverse practices thus co-existed within the nation-state.

The Civil War provides the explosive exception to decentralized harmony. States' rights were shown to preclude secession from the Union. Though slavery was ended many novel devices for subjugating the black population were introduced after the withdrawal of Union troops in 1877. Southern re-incorporation was thus eased by the latitude extended to the state governments to define policy on racial matters. Thus after 1877 federalism facilitated a distinctive approach to race relations in the south within the confines of the nation-state.

Racial separatism has been a persistent strain among black political and religious movements without ever becoming the majority sentiment. On the contrary, most blacks have wanted integration with whites rather than racial segregation. The plausibility of black separatism has been undermined by the absence of a territorial core that could form the homeland of a new nation-state. Identification with Africa has never been widespread and has found expression in culture rather than in mainstream politics.

The absence of religious, anti-democratic and separatist parties distinguishes the United States from the party systems of most other western democracies. Most possess at least one of these types of party though there are a handful of other states, such as Australia and New Zealand, where none of them exist. Where the United States is exceptional is in the absence of a politically significant socialist or social democratic party. In most western nations such parties have held power in the central government. In the handful of cases where this has not been achieved, as in Canada, a party of the democratic left accounts for around a fifth of the national vote. But in the US there is no such threat to the major parties from the left. There is no sizeable vote for a party of the left nor has such a party ever held power in Washington. Not since 1948 has a candidate of a left-wing party obtained even 1 per cent of the vote in a presidential election. In 1990 a candidate from the left won a seat in Congress against major party opposition for the first time in over forty years. Because the absence of a large party of the left is a uniquely American phenomenon we pursue at length the reasons for it.

Explanations for the failure of the left in the world's largest capitalist democracy are legion (Laslett and Lipset 1974). All such theories seek to identify what is unique to the US or to its working class which in turn explains its exceptionalism in lacking a socialist or social democratic party. Though there are many theories the causes they attribute to the US's exceptionalism can be distilled into three broad explanations:

1 Class consciousness is absent in the US.
2 Class consciousness is present in the US working class but it is not politicized.
3 Historical events and strategic errors disrupted the potential of the Social-ist party, historically the most promising movement on the American left.

The absence of class consciousness

Sociological, economic and political factors have been adduced to account for the impediments to US working-class consciousness. Below we summarize the major arguments.

Sociological factors

US value system

There is a consensus on liberal values in the United States. Individualism, freedom, property rights, equality of opportunity and the limited state enjoy virtual unanimous endorsement. These values conflict with the ends of socialism such as common ownership and equality of result. The US value system is subscribed to by the working class, rendering it unsympathetic to socialism (Samson 1935, Lipset 1967).

Intellectuals have embraced the value system rendering them unreceptive to socialist ideas. They have largely rejected a materialist interpretation of history, given primacy to status rather than class, to individualism in pref-erence to collectivism. Professional social science exemplifies the distance between American thought and socialism. Emerging in the late nineteenth century, coincident with the acceleration of the industrializing process, professional social science stressed technical problem-solving within the confines of a capitalist system which was taken for granted. Critical social science is and always has been a rarity in the United States (Watson 1981). Lacking a secure foothold among intellectuals deprived American socialism of both leadership and influence through socializing agencies such as universities and the press.

Absence of feudalism

Capitalism did not displace a feudal system in the US. Feudalism is a stratified pre-capitalist order. Its stratification engenders class consciousness particularly among the bourgeoisie who emerge within it and are the proponents of its transformation. A stimulus to bourgeois class consciousness and action was lacking in America, which had a lasting impact on the nature of class domination. Without a self-conscious ruling class, a stimulus to working-class consciousness has also been absent (Hartz 1955).

Social mobility

Upward social mobility, at least during industrialization, was more prolific in the US than in other capitalist states. Escape from the working class through upward mobility beckoned. The fluidity of the social structure militated against class identity and loyalty (Thernstrom 1970).

Religious and ethnic diversity

Mass immigration produced a heterogenous American working class. Religious and ethnic identities cut across class boundaries. These identities fragmented the working class, precluding the formation of a common consciousness (Handlin 1951, Aronowitz 1973).

Economic factors

Working-class affluence

American workers enjoyed higher living standards than their European counterparts in the industrial era. Able to afford adequate food, housing and clothes, American workers were not discontented with the status quo. In a famous formulation, a European author captured the impediments to radicalism deriving from wealth, 'All Socialist Utopias come to nothing on roast beef and apple pie' (Sombart 1976: 106).

Availability of land

Free land offered an escape from industrialism for the working class. Land acted as a safety valve for the discontented of the city. The prospect of geographical mobility discouraged a perception of the working-class condition as permanent, weakening identification with it (Commons 1966).

Political factors

The principal political explanation for the failure of working-class consciousness to develop is the timing of manhood suffrage. The enfranchisement of white men was complete in most states by the 1830s. Manhood suffrage originated before the development of a proletariat. A stimulus to working-class consciousness and organization – the injustice of disenfranchisement – was denied to American workers (Perlman 1970).

Failure of class consciousness to become politicized

For all the attention devoted to explaining its absence, there is considerable evidence of working-class consciousness in America. Surveys have found many Americans prepared to identify themselves as working class, express a preference for associating with members of their own class and attribute social inequalities to structural rather than personal causes (Jackman and Jackman 1981). The militancy of the trade unions could be interpreted as class-conscious behaviour. Industrial disputes are frequent and sometimes violent. Days lost in strikes per worker have frequently been higher in America than in several European countries including Britain (Armstrong *et al*. 1984: 378).

There is an apparent paradox between the presence of working-class consciousness and the absence of a party to represent it. The thesis that there existed impediments to that consciousness becoming politicized provides a resolution of the paradox (Katznelson 1982). The impediments are constituted by the mixing of machine-style parties, mass immigration, ethnic segregation in housing and a decentralized system of government.

Party machines were already in existence before the onset of industrialism. When industry developed, the demand for additional labour was met by the influx of large numbers of immigrants. Ethnic groups among the immigrants tended to cluster together in homogeneous communities in the big cities. Party and governmental decentralization facilitated a political sensitivity to ethnic groups in the large urban areas. Parties accommodated the new voters by a mix of ethnic appeals and material benefits.

In the workplace, geographically separate from the communities where people lived, the different ethnic groups intermingled. Subjected to the same conditions they developed a common consciousness facilitating unity in industrial action. But this class unity was confined to the workplace. No such intermixing and combination took place in the residential communities. A decentralized political system allowed considerable autonomy in managing the community and the party machines avoided appeals in class terms.

Historical events and strategic errors

The foregoing theories explain why American socialism was weak or non-existent. But early in the twentieth century there were many signs of the vigour of American socialism. The Socialist party did make inroads into the duopoly of the two parties. In 1911 the Socialists won elections for mayor in over seventy towns and cities. By 1912 there were over a thousand Socialist elected officials. That year the party's candidate for president, Eugene Debs, polled 6 per cent of the national vote. The party's membership exceeded 100,000.

In 1912 the American Socialist party's electoral strength was on a par with its counterparts in several other western nations in the years prior to the First World War (see Table 5.3). Though laggard compared to Australia and Scandinavia, the American Socialist party was of similar strength to the British, Belgian and New Zealand parties. Where the experience of the American Socialist party diverged from that of its western counterparts was in its development after the First World War. The election of 1912 proved to be the US party's peak. In other countries several socialist parties made sufficient electoral gains in the 1920s to win power. The exceptionalism of the American Socialist party resides in its post-war failure to build on apparently promising foundations. A rapid decline rather than a failure to emerge characterized socialism in America (Weinstein 1967).

Two features of the Socialist party of America distinguished it from its counterparts in other western countries at the time of the First World War. First, the US party's greatest electoral strength was not the urban proletariat. Small farmers, workers in the lumber and mining industries were the party's principal supporters. These groups were primarily constituted by native-born Americans whereas the urban proletariat consisted of many foreign-born recent immigrants. States containing few immigrant voters such as Oklahoma, Nevada and Colorado registered the largest shares of the vote for Eugene Debs in the 1912 presidential election.

Second, unlike other parties in the Second International, the Socialist party of America opposed its own country's involvement in the First World War. This stance alienated many native-born Americans from an allegedly unpatriotic party. An exodus of native-born party members followed. The

Table 5.3 Electoral support for socialist parties in Western nations before the First World War

Nation	Party	Year	% Vote
Australia	Labour	1913	48.5
Germany	Social Democrats	1912	34.8
Sweden	Social Democrats	1914	30.1
Denmark	Social Democrats	1913	29.6
Norway	Labour	1912	26.3
Switzerland	Social Democrats	1911	20.0
Netherlands	Social Democratic Workers	1913	18.5
Italy	Socialist	1913	17.6
France	Socialist	1914	16.8
Belgium	Workers	1912	9.3
New Zealand	Labour	1911	8.8
United Kingdom	Labour	1910 (December)	6.4
United States	Socialist	1912	6.0
Canada	Labour	1911	0.1

Source: Thomas T. Mackie and Richard Rose (1982) *The International Almanac of Electoral History*, 2nd edn (London: Macmillan)

party was also subjected to punitive legal treatment for its stance. Debs, for example, was sentenced to a twenty-year prison term for sedition in advocating opposition to the war.

Both the membership and electoral support for the party was transformed by its anti-war stance. The foreign-born (organized in language federations) became over half of the total membership. Electoral support underwent a similar shift. The immigrant centres of the northeastern states became the party's strongholds. Immigrant influence within the party also grew. In consequence, the party's strategy came to be prompted by those least familiar with American conditions. In the early 1920s the party shifted beyond the confines of American radicalism where it had formerly resided. Sensitivity to the peculiarities of the American socio-economic context declined as did party membership and electoral support.

The split in the international socialist movement following the Bolshevik Revolution also proved severely damaging to the Socialist party of America. Breakaway communist parties were formed by revolutionary socialists. In the year following the split in 1919 Socialist membership fell by 60 per cent.

Despite the loss of revolutionaries the Socialist party continued on a radical course. The Soviet Union was viewed with approval and the party applied to join the Third (Moscow-led) Socialist International in 1920. In the mid–1920s radicalism was de-emphasized but by this time party membership had fallen to under 10,000. Farmer-labour parties, and the Democrats (by the late 1920s) pre-empted the Socialists' appeal to the discontented.

ONE PARTYISM IN THE STATES

American national politics has nearly always consisted of two-party competition. But as Table 5.1 revealed, the degree of competitiveness within the various states is uneven. Few states are closely balanced between the two parties, particularly in legislative contests. In the past, competition was even rarer. Now the most visible contests – for the presidency, governor and Congress – are not monopolies for the dominant party of the area that they once were. As the southern states demonstrate, the historical minority party can win in their former barren areas, and in the most salient offices they can even have the advantage, as Republicans now do in presidential elections in the south.

Three explanations have been offered for the absence of two-party competition. The first emphasizes the continuing effect of a legacy of the past. The second stresses the social characteristics of the state's population. The third offers an organizational explanation of one-partyism. The experience of the Civil War in solidifying the south around the Democratic party is the most egregious example of the effect of history on partisan competition in the states. More than a century after the Civil War the large Democratic majorities in southern state legislatures testify to the survival of that experience as a factor in the loyalties of southerners. A second variant of the historical legacy thesis is the state-level effect of national partisan realignments. Each realignment gradually resulted in shifts in the voting allegiances of many state electorates. Many states reproduced the national trend, shifting towards the new dominant party. A few states were propelled in the opposite direction. For example, states such as Rhode Island, Maryland and Missouri, still predominantly Democratic in state elections, first moved decisively in that direction as a result of the New Deal realignment. Conversely, Nebraska shifted towards the Republicans in the 1930s.

Population characteristic explanations identify social homogeneity as conducive to one-partyism (Key 1956, 1964). Social diversity, in contrast, is conducive to two-party competition. Different social classes, occupations, races, religious and ethnic groups and residential settings promote distinctive partisan loyalties. For example, blacks today tend overwhelmingly to be Democrats, while whites are more likely to be Republicans.

States characterized by diversity have the raw material for two parties. Where a state population is homogeneous, and demographic characteristics reinforce one another in favour of a single party, the social basis for two-party competition may be absent. For example, states with predominantly white Protestant populations lacking large industries and big cities, such as North Dakota and Vermont, tended to be one-party strongholds.

Organizational explanations link the capability of party structures to electoral viability (Cotter *et al.* 1984). Where party organizations are non-existent or inactive they fail to recruit candidates, raise funds and mount sophisticated campaigns. Organizational weakness is likely where the party's core constituency is in short supply, preventing it from mounting effective electoral challenges. All other things being equal, the electoral prospects of such parties are meagre. They may fail to field candidates in many contests or they are of poor quality. Campaigns are paltry and amateurish. While the Civil War legacy provided southern Democratic parties with a vast reserve of electoral support, the inertia of the Republican party organizations in the region ensured that their dominance lasted into the second half of the twentieth century. The growth of Republican state party capacity in the 1960s, itself a legacy of the activism inspired by Goldwater's 1964 presidential candidacy, enhanced the challenge that was mounted to the Democrats in elections thereafter.

THIRD PARTIES IN PRESIDENTIAL ELECTIONS

Electoral challenges to the two major parties are rare for offices below the presidency. Two of the most active third parties in the 1986 elections were the Conservatives and the Liberals, in New York State. Each has a symbiotic relationship to one of the major parties. The Conservatives shift between running independent candidates to endorsing Republican nominees. The Liberals adopt the same pair of tactics, in their case allying with Democratic nominees.

Third-party candidates do contest presidential elections. In 1988 the two major party nominees faced competition, in at least some states, from candidates of thirteen other parties, including the Libertarian, Populist, New Alliance, Consumer, Socialist Workers, Workers World, American and Workers League parties. Combined, these parties accounted for approximately 0.8 per cent of the total vote.

Only one third party, the Republicans in 1860, has ever won the presidency and that date marks their transition to major party status. Though no third party has won, subsequently several have had an influence on the margin of victory by drawing votes disproportionately from one of the major parties though not to the extent of altering the outcome. On occasions during the election campaign the support for a third-party nominee promised to be of such size as to deny any candidate an Electoral College majority. However this threat has never materialized on election day. But third parties have periodically broken the duopoly of the vote in presidential contests (see Table 5.4).

In the nineteenth century the strongest inroads into the duopoly were made by candidates of a perennial third party which obtained an untypically large

Table 5.4 Largest third-party share of the vote in presidential elections, 1828–88

Year	Candidate	Party	% Vote
1832	William Wirt	Anti-Masonic	7.8
1848	Martin Van Buren	Free Soil	10.1
1856	Millard Fillmore	American	21.5
1860	Abraham Lincoln	Republican	39.1
	John Breckinridge	Democratic (southern breakaway)	18.1
	John Bell	Constitutional Union	12.6
1892	James B. Weaver	People's (Populist)	8.5
1912	Theodore Roosevelt	Progressive	27.4
	Eugene Debs	Socialist	6.0
1924	Robert La Follette	Progressive	16.6
1968	George Wallace	American Independent	13.5
1980	John Anderson	Independent (no party)	6.6

Source: Thomas T. Mackie and Richard Rose (1982) *The International Almanac of Electoral History*, 2nd edn (London: Macmillan)

vote on one occasion. Such parties participated in several presidential contests also running candidates for lower level offices. In the twentieth century the highest third-party totals have been obtained by impromptu candidate organizations (with the exception of the 1912 Socialist vote). These have been parties in name only. They were rudimentary as organizations, contested few other offices and often disintegrated after one election. (The Progressive parties of 1912 and 1924 were separate entities.)

The changed character of twentieth-century third 'parties' is probably attributable to alterations in law and in the nature of election campaigns. Legal changes mandating primaries helps to channel activity into the major parties. Second, more personalized forms of campaign organization are now the norm, evident also among the major parties. Individual candidates construct their own organizations. Capital-intensive forms of campaigning such as television advertising and direct mail render a party workforce dispensable in modern elections (see Chapter Seven).

Many of the most successful third-party candidates have been deserters from the major parties. Van Buren, Fillmore and Theodore Roosevelt had all served as president under the aegis of one of the major parties. Breckinridge had served as vice president. Others had been elected to Congress or state office on major party tickets. In several instances (Breckinridge, Theodore Roosevelt, Anderson) third-party campaigns were adopted after efforts to capture a major party nomination failed.

Third-party strength has been explained as a consequence of major party failure (Mazmanian 1974, Rosenstone *et al.* 1984). Where issues salient to a bloc of votes have been neglected by the major parties the gap has been filled by a third party. In the late nineteenth century the Greenback and Populist parties espoused the concerns of farmers on issues such as debt repayment which the major parties ignored.

Where major parties fail to adopt policy stances that appeal to all voters, third parties have profited by espousing a distinctive position. In 1968 George Wallace adopted hawkish positions on Vietnam, law and order and civil rights. He captured voters on these issues unattracted by the centrist positions of the major party candidates.

Major party failure in office has prompted third-party voting. This has not been registered on the general economic performance of major party administrations with any consistency. Third-party strength was absent in 1932, for example. But declines in farm prices were a cue to third-party strength in rural areas in the nineteenth century.

Attractive candidates win votes for third parties. The most successful third-party nominees have been established national figures. As mentioned above, several had held major elected offices. Several had contested for a major party nomination before adopting a third-party strategy. Unappealing major party nominees have profited third-party candidates, a factor in John Anderson's vote in 1980.

National crises, 1932 excepted, have favoured third parties electorally. In such periods public opinion is unusually fractured. Issues have assumed untypical salience. Divisions within the major parties have been deeper and more intense. Under such conditions the capacity of the major parties to accommodate the electorate has been severely strained, and the intensity of political conflict has overcome the disincentives to embracing a third party.

The latter phases of the historical party systems have been conducive to third-party strength. Elections immediately following realignment have produced minute third-party votes. The largest third-party votes have occurred at least five elections after realignment. As the time since the realignment lengthens so the loyalties forged in that period weaken. New generations of voters enter the electorate lacking the strength of party loyalty of their elders.

Large third-party votes have on occasion heralded new realignments. Their strength has indicated that the major parties' capacity for accommodating the electorate has eroded. This has eventually resulted in a new party system. Either the existing major parties have recaptured the entire electorate with new appeals or a new party has emerged. The realignment of the 1890s exemplifies the first possibility. The Democrats embraced Populist concerns undermining the third party's distinctive appeal. New voters were won to the Democratic standard but other groups formerly supportive of the party were repelled by its style and programme. The 1850s realignment demonstrates the second scenario at work. Anti-slavery sentiment, previously expressed by the Liberty and Free Soil parties but also existing in the major parties, was amalgamated into an electoral majority by the Republicans.

THE EFFECTS OF A TWO-PARTY SYSTEM

Where two parties exert an electoral duopoly over a heterogeneous society it is inevitable that they will exhibit great internal diversity. They are catch-all parties or their duopoly would end. This necessitates the manufacture of inclusive appeals, particularly in presidential contests where the diversity of the electorate is most pronounced. Broad themes, attractive personalities and the promise of material benefits have been staples of election campaigns.

Issues are not ignored but competitive pressures restrain their use. Sharp issue differences between the parties rarely become apparent in campaigns. Rather than taking contradictory positions, candidates adopt different but non-conflictual stances, tending to talk past each other rather than oppose the competition (Kelley 1960, Page 1978, Monroe 1983). Issues that risk fracturing the parties' potential coalitions tend to be neglected or fudged. For example, the Democratic party from the 1930s onwards frequently eschewed commitments on civil rights that would have divided its white southern conservative and northern liberal–black blocs from one another. In office Franklin Roosevelt refused to propose measures explicitly favouring blacks for fear of alienating the large and influential southern Democratic group in Congress.

The ascendancy of one of the parties evident in each of the electoral systems and in many states still today deters distinctiveness on issues. Where one party dominates but the other is a plausible contender for power, there are incentives for the minority party to imitate the majority to attract votes. During the various national party systems the gap separating the parties on issues tended to narrow over time. The minority party gradually accommodated itself to the hegemony on issues established by the majority. For example, Democrats early in the twentieth century desisted from the demand for free silver and Republicans in the late 1930s accepted the New Deal. Other examples of this electoralism have occurred where new preferences are deemed to appear among a majority of voters without partisan realignment. In the wake of the Republican victories of 1980 and Reagan's subsequent popularity the Democrats developed concerns for budget deficit reduction and increased defence spending. Both commitments were included in the 1984 party platform.

In the states, policy differences between the parties have been most visible at the poles of competitiveness, monopoly and two-party competition. In the latter the parties have diverged on issues central to the New Deal such as welfare-state provision and trade union rights (Fenton 1966). This has been attributed to the distinctive class bases of the parties' support. In states such as Michigan and Minnesota, Democrats tended to be dependent on working-class support, Republicans on the middle class. Each party reflected the preferences of their different supporters. They were both plausible contenders for power without making deep inroads into the traditional support of their opponents which would have required compromises on policy.

Some uncompetitive states outside the south have exhibited an ideological polarization between the parties. Where one party is so dominant that no feasible strategy is available to the minority to become the majority, the incentives towards convergence on issues are weak. In addition, such electoral hopelessness is likely to deter all but the most dedicated from becoming involved in the minority party. Lacking voters and activists, such an uncompetitive party has few defences against ideologues who want to clarify the differences between the parties. This tendency towards purism rather than pragmatism has emerged in recent years among the minority Republican party in states such as Massachusetts and Rhode Island (White 1983).

Diversity within the parties frequently translates into internal conflict and disunity. So factionalized have been the parties that one author maintained that America had not a two-but a four-party system, the Republican and Democrats each split between their presidential and congressional wings (Burns 1963). Party unity voting in Congress is modest compared to that in many parliamentary systems as are the efforts to impose discipline.

Durable factions have been evident in the national, and many state parties. At national level the divisions have tended to follow geographical (sectional) lines. The north–south split persists in the Democratic party but with declining vigour now that racial conservatives are fewer in the party. For the first half of the twentieth century eastern–midwestern conflicts in the Republican party tended to be coterminous with internationalist–isolationist divisions. Different regional economic interests now divide both parties between those from the sunbelt centres of new development against the declining traditional industries of the rustbelt.

Durable factions in state parties have taken several forms. In some parties the cleavage is ideological, as in the liberal–conservative split among Virginia Democrats. Elsewhere the factions follow territorial divisions (north versus south in both California parties, Chicago versus downstate Illinois Democrats) religion (as in the Connecticut party divisions between Protestants and Catholics), pragmatism versus purism in the Massachusetts Republicans, political dynasties such as the pivotal role the Long family and associates once played in dividing the loyalties of Louisiana Democrats.

Monopoly parties usually exhibit great internal diversity. In such areas all political forces tend to be channelled into one party without any offsetting impetus towards unity to withstand electoral competition. Primaries, particularly those for the governorship, have provided the principal venue for factional competition. Rarely have such factions been ideologically defined.

In consequence, primaries lack ideological alternatives and the status quo is unchallenged.

CONCLUSION

In this chapter we have demonstrated the duopolistic control of elective office exerted by the two major parties. Most of the states fall short of effective two-party competition so that far from there being signs of multi-partyism the limit of competitiveness is but two parties. We suggest that the channelling of political forces into, effectively, two alternatives contributes to the distinctive character of the American parties. Their internal diversity and disunity, their lack of discipline and, traditionally, the absence of policy cleavages between the parties are all promoted by the institutional and socio-political forces that funnel political activity into two parties. What remains to be established in subsequent chapters is if parties are anything more than labels. Are they empty shells or do they play a role in conducting campaigns, eliciting voter loyalties and governing?

6 Party organization

In this chapter we look at how the parties are organized outside of govern-ment. Grassroots party organizations are one of the hallmarks of mass democracy. A mass electorate invites activity by parties to educate, persuade and mobilize voters for elections. Grassroots party organization emerged as the franchise was extended. The USA was the first mass democracy, and in consequence it was also the first to develop party organizations. From the early years of the Republic party-style organizations were in evidence linking elected officials to voters.

In this chapter we are concerned with the performance of the modern party organization. We identify and account for the principal characteristics of American party organizations. Here we are particularly interested in distin-guishing American party organizations from their counterparts in other western democracies. Second, we describe the formal structures that com-pose the organization. Third, we look at the variety of informal types of party organization which exist in practice. In so doing we describe the activity of parties at local, state and national level.

CHARACTERISTICS OF AMERICAN PARTY ORGANIZATION

It will become evident in the course of this chapter that not all party organizations in America are the same. They differ, for example, over the numbers involved in their activities, what motivates people to become active within them, the distribution of power within the organization and so on. But some generalizations can be produced to allow comparison with parties in other democracies. To make such generalizations we focus on features commonly though not universally found in the party organization in the United States and elsewhere respectively.

In general, American party organizations exhibit four major characteristics:

1 They lack mass membership.

2 Power within the party is decentralized.
3 Legal regulation is extensive.
4 They do not select candidates for public office.

A formal membership entailing the payment of subscriptions has been adduced as a defining characteristic of modern mass parties (Duverger 1959). But formal party membership is rare in America. Those who are active within the parties often lack formal status. There are party officials such as chairmen and committee members for each territorial division of the party organization but below these 'chiefs' there are no official 'Indians'. In many places the numbers active in the party are small. The organization consists of a handful of party officials (not all of them active) and a few helpers. Absence of formal membership deprives the organization of discipline and funds. Party officials have no formal means for controlling entry into party activity. Nor do they possess the means for controlling the conduct of activists available where formal membership can be withdrawn. Without membership dues the organization lacks a regular income which would facilitate an expansion of its activities.

In those rare instances where formal membership has been adopted recruitment remains a minute fraction of the parties' voters. California provides an example of membership clubs existing alongside the legally required party structure. But membership of the umbrella organization of these clubs on the Democratic side, the California Democratic Council, numbered under 27,000 in 1960 compared against a vote for the party's presidential candidate of 3 million (Wilson 1962). This represents a meagre ratio of party members to voters even when the membership of the clubs was larger than it is now. This proportion of members to voters is much smaller than in most European democracies where ratios of 1:10 are common (von Beyme 1985).

Each unit of the party organization possesses near autonomy. They are subject to little control or assistance from other levels. Each is responsible for recruiting its own activists, raising funds and conducting election campaigns. Figure 6.1 depicts the various rings of the party organization as it exists in many of the states. We have deliberately avoided picturing the party as a series of vertical tiers. Such a characterization implies a hierarchy, a chain of command that is inappropriate as a description of the relationship between the various rings of the American parties though it would be more pertinent elsewhere. Devices for securing hierarchical controls in American parties are few. Many state and local party structures are creations of state law rather than party rules. In consequence, disbandment or its threat cannot be utilized to discipline recalcitrant organizations. Nor, in the absence of formal membership, can troublesome individuals or groupings be expelled.

Figure 6.1 Rings of the party structure

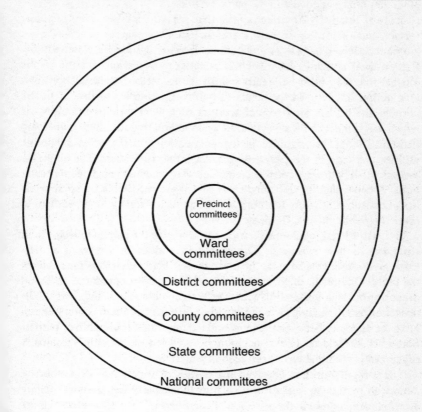

In many states parties are subject to detailed legal regulation. Massachusetts, an extreme example, has statutes relating to parties and elections which run to over 500 pages (Huckshorn 1976). State and local party structures are often required to exist by state law. (In 1989 the Supreme Court, in *Eu* v. *San Francisco County Democratic Central Committee*, freed parties from legally imposed internal structures. At the time of writing it is too early to assess the impact of this new-found freedom for parties to define their organizational form.) The methods for choosing party officials and convention delegates are usually legally defined. Laws also cover the processes for selecting candidates for public office, the sums that can be raised and spent in campaigns, the eligibility for participation in primary elections and many other activities conducted in the party's name.

It is a distinctively American approach to see parties as providers of public services but liable to abuse them, therefore requiring legal constraints. Parties are not conceived as private associations free to regulate their own affairs. Rather, their activities have such substantial ramifications for the public interest that they must be legally compelled to perform them responsibly. One author has likened the status of parties in America to that of public utilities, the private providers of services such as electricity and transport which are subject to legal regulation as an alternative to public ownership (Epstein 1986). The origins of the legal regulation of both parties and public utilities coincide in the progressive era. At that time there was abundant evidence that both were corrupt. Remedies were sought through legal restrictions. A belief that the deficiencies of parties are rectifiable by appropriate laws persists, continuing to inform contemporary efforts to compel them to serve the public interest (Ranney 1975).

Extensive legal regulation restricts the scope for the parties to shape their structures to their own needs. Organizations, with defined responsibilities, exist at various levels because the law requires them rather than the needs of the party. One result of these legal fetters is the development of informal organization and leadership which effectively constitute the party. The bosses of party machines which flourished into the twentieth century exemplify the disparity between the legal and the unofficial leadership of parties. Some bosses held no formal position yet they led the most hierarchically organized parties that have been seen in America.

Legal regulation has deprived the parties of functions. Most notably, American parties do not perform such textbook party functions as staging election campaigns and the selection of candidates. Many local elections are required by law to be non-partisan. In practice there is considerable variation in what constitutes a non-partisan election from the mere absence of party labels from the ballot paper to the absence of party activity at any stage of the electoral process (Adrian 1959). But non-partisan elections in some form are used in two-thirds of the cities with a population over five thousand, including Los Angeles, Boston, San Francisco and Detroit. Nebraska's legislature is also non-partisan.

Where non-partisan elections are more than a mere formality, parties are deprived of functions in local elections. Activist recruitment is hindered because one of the attractions of party work is absent for many elections. Voters are also discouraged from developing party allegiances, which are a precondition of activism. Potential candidates lack the incentives to be active within the parties as a preliminary to running for office. The direct primary, like non-partisanship an innovation of the progressive era, deprived the party organizations of a role in candidate selection. The convention, populated by the party activists, was displaced by primary elections open to voters. Initially party organizations able to mobilize large numbers of voters continued to exert effective control over nominations despite the adoption of primaries. But such cases are now exceptional. In many areas party organizations do not intervene in primaries.

Primaries are an obstacle to party government. They sever the connection between party organization and public officials which can promote cohesion and discipline in government. Without a role in selection or the threat of de-selection the party organization cannot curb independent behaviour in office. A force for unity is also lacking through the absence of a national veto over local nominations. As control over nominations is devolved by law to local electorates the national organization is precluded from enforcing ideological conformity throughout the party.

Thus in several respects American party organization is distinctive. Institutional and cultural influences have given the American parties their peculiar organizational features. The Constitution, anti-partisan attitudes and the laws which incorporate them have produced an environment unconducive to centralized, self-regulating, mass-membership parties. Though marginal changes and occasional exceptions have emerged, the durability of these characteristics suggests that the environment is a strong constraint on what type of party organization is possible in the United States.

Federalism has been the deepest constitutional imprint on the parties. By creating a legally empowered layer of states which in turn devolve many powers to local authorities, decentralization and fragmentation of government was promoted. Similar effects were registered in the parties. Each state evolved a distinctive political system contained within a particular constitutional framework and culture. The profusion of elective offices in local and state government encouraged a parochial focus within the party organizations. Concerned with local electoral considerations and patronage, a national focus was obscured.

Laws fostered decentralized parties. Most of the legal regulation of parties derives from state statutes. Varied in their content and extent, the laws differentiate state political environments from one another. Some states allow partisan local elections, some states prohibit them. Some states allow primaries open to all voters wheras others restrict them to self-declared party identifiers (unless party rules specify otherwise). Parties have to organize to conform to fifty different sets of state laws. Decentralized legal regulation has militated against centralized control because of the diversity that it has promoted.

The absence of mass party activism is also partially attributable to the impact of law. Legal requirements have compelled party structures into existence, irrespective of whether there is a core of activists available to sustain an organization. Where the party is unable to define its structures the consequence can be the inertia and irrelevance of those that are required by law. Activism is also discouraged by the deprivation of functions. In candidate selection and campaigning there are organizations other than parties available to citizens wishing to influence these processes. Interest groups, political action committees and candidate organizations may be stronger influences in determining their outcomes than parties. Moreover, as some incentives to activism depend upon winning office – to implement policy or obtain material benefits – successful candidates are unlikely to be influenced by organizations tangential to their victories. Activists interested in policy or patronage are encouraged to use other organizational vehicles to realize their objectives.

Anti-partisan attitudes find tangible expression in the legal regulation of parties. The means to control parties include their removal from some activities, public participation or rigorous regulation. Examples are non-partisan elections, primary elections and legally defined party rules. Each alternative denies parties autonomy in conducting their activities. They have structures imposed upon them. They have structures deprived of functions. They have candidates and officials they did not choose and cannot control imposed upon them by primary electorates. They conduct their affairs under rules they did not choose and which may be insensitive to their needs.

Some sense of the pervasiveness of anti-partisan attitudes is evident in the role of partisan office holders in enacting legal regulation. Governors, state legislators, presidents, members of Congress – elected on party tickets – have written laws detrimental to party organization. In some instances there was public pressure for action. More frequently, there was little public arousal, allowing officials room for inaction or less severe solutions. On occasion legislation debilitating to party organizations in the long term was used to tip the balance of power to the advantage of a particular faction. For example, primaries were introduced in some Republican-dominated northern states to strengthen reform forces with public support against the conservatives entrenched in the party organization. Even where the destructive effects of legal regulation have been appreciated office-holders have often refrained from revising the offending laws. In part this perhaps reflects the public legitimacy of anti-partisan devices such as primaries. Additionally, elective office-holders have come to appreciate the benefits of independence from parties. For example, primaries free officials from accountability to party organizations. Such independence releases officials from any conflict of interest between responding to their parties or to their electorates.

Negative public attitudes towards parties are unconducive to mass activism within them. Objects of distrust, the parties are hampered in generating allegiance and activism. For potential activists non-partisan mechanisms including interest groups, initiatives and referenda offer more legitimate vehicles for participation.

In elections there has been a trend since the 1950s among the public to see the role of parties as irrelevant (Wattenberg 1986). Voters have found parties dispensable. They are not needed to define issues, discriminate between candidates or decide how to vote. Such neutral attitudes, though distinct from hostility, are again unconducive to inspiring activism in parties. This trend towards neutrality is a distinctly American phenomenon. Elsewhere voters have become more negative about at least one of the parties but they have not become neutral towards parties in general (Wattenberg 1982).

FORMAL PARTY STRUCTURES

As has already been observed, many state laws specify a structure for the parties. This produces a variety of structures resulting from differences in state laws. There are differences, for example, in the number and nomenclature of the territorial subdivisions for which a party structure is required to exist. Not all of the rings portrayed in Figure 6.1 are universal. California has no precinct organizations and Alaska has no county parties, for instance.

Above the precinct, party institutions for each ring consist of chairpersons, committees and conventions though the latter may be absent for some of the smaller units. Chairpersons and committees perform tasks throughout the year. Conventions are constituted for short periods usually only in election years. A variety of methods are used to select party chairs, committee members and convention delegates. For at least the inner rings of the party structure there is usually provision for public participation in the selection process. In the precinct (a territory covering blocks of streets and several hundred voters) committee members and convention delegates are normally chosen in primaries or in public meetings known as caucuses. However, these positions are frequently uncontested and only rarely excite the participation of more than a handful of voters where there is competition. In practice many vacancies have to be filled by appointment.

For the outer rings of the party structure, covering the larger units, officials are more likely to be appointed than elected. Chairs are appointed by conventions or committees; committees chosen by conventions. But in a minority of cases election prevails at these levels. A quarter of state committees have some of their members chosen in primaries (Jewell and Olson 1978). A majority of national convention delegates are chosen by primaries or a series of conventions originating from precinct caucuses. Given that some party representatives are chosen by voters who then select other officials, all positions within the organization are filled by processes which include public participation.

Hierarchical controls within the party between the various levels are slight, as already discussed. This phenomenon of virtual autonomy of each layer has been labelled a 'stratarchy' (Eldersveld 1964). Since the late 1960s there has been some undermining of the independence of each unit in the Democratic party where state organs have been subjected to national guidelines in selecting delegates to the presidential nominating conventions (Epstein 1982). But the attention this development has attracted is attributable more to its novelty than to its magnitude. In all other spheres of state party activity, independence persists.

Communications between the state and local parties occur regularly. But state–national party interactions are infrequent (Crotty 1985). In part contact comes about through party meetings in which representatives of smaller units sit on the committees of larger ones. Precinct and ward officials claim regular contacts with the nearest levels of the organization, the district and county parties. Contacts are less frequent with state party officials. Little is known about the content of these communications though one study found that electoral concerns predominated. Organizational matters, issues or party goals are less salient (Eldersveld 1964).

LOCAL PARTIES

In this section the term local refers to all units of the party below the state level. This range extends from precincts covering a neighbourhood to county parties whose catchment population can run into millions. Attempts to generalize about American local parties are hindered by the shortage of information. Several hundred thousand local party units exist, but few have been studied. A handful of probably untypical cases (Chicago, New York) recur in the literature. Generalization is also complicated by the apparent diversity of organizational types that occur among formally similar party structures (see next section). To attempt to overcome these difficulties in this section we rely on national surveys or where similar evidence from several locales indicates a widely shared characteristic.

Precinct officials are the hub of the party, the innermost of the concentric rings which make up the organization. The number of positions to be filled, one or sometimes two per precinct, presents problems of recruitment. A survey of county chairs reported 5 per cent of Democratic and 15 per cent of Republican precinct positions vacant (Cotter *et al*. 1984). Additional officials are in post but inactive.

Of the outer rings of the organization, it has been the county party which has often been the most dynamic within the states. Elections, resources and geography account for the vigour (relative to other levels) of county parties. Several public officials are elected to county level posts, creating the incentive to collaborative electoral efforts which parties provide. County boundaries are also used to define other electoral constituencies such as Congressional and state legislative districts. A supply of patronage resources has also been available from county government which has been used to stimulate party activism at that level. Outside major conurbations the county seat is also a focus of local human activity. It is the centre of the local economy, social life and public administration (Sorauf 1980, Jewell and Olson 1978).

VARIETIES OF PARTY ORGANIZATION

Formal structures can be misleading guides to how party organizations function in practice. In some localities there is no party even on paper and in others lists of officials disguise inertia in practice while in other places the party consists of large numbers of activists. Party organizations differ across time and space and between the two parties in the same time and space.

In this section we seek to identify the principal forms of party in practice. In distinguishing parties we use two variables. First, we distinguish between the motivations that stimulate activism in parties. Here we draw on the work that has identified the incentives to activism in all types of voluntary organization devised by Peter Clark and James Wilson (1961). They have identified three types of incentive: material benefits such as jobs and money; solidary (social) rewards which include prestige, friendships and contact with others; and purposive (normative) motivations in pursuit of ideological or policy goals or conceptions of good government. Secondly, we distinguish parties by the distribution of influence within the organization. This can range from influence concentrated in a single leader or a small group or its fragmentation between many activists.

Of the several permutations that can be formed from these variables, we concentrate on three types we think are particularly pertinent to the American case. *Machines* combine centralized leadership under a single boss with activism based on material rewards. *Amateur clubs* have a broad diffusion of influence among activists motivated by purposive incentives. *Cadre caucuses* have influence concentrated in a leadership core and activism stimulated by solidary rewards.

Some of the terms used here occur frequently in the literature though the meaning attached to them is not necessarily consistent with our definitions. These characterizations are ideal types rather than a depiction of actual cases. In practice the ideal types are approximations which rarely appear in pure form. But we believe such characterizations are of value in reducing the volume of party organizations to a manageable number of types to be easily described.

MACHINES

The machine has been regarded as a peculiarly American style of party organization (Duverger 1959, Lowi 1967). They have also been regarded as the norm (Bone 1949). Neither of these perspectives is accurate. Parties approximating to the machine type have been identified in southern Europe and in the Third World (Scott 1969, Lemarchand 1981). In America, machines have never been the norm. Most machines have been found in the urban areas of the eastern side of the country (Shefter 1983, Mayhew 1986). Machines in rural areas, suburbs and the western half of the country have been rare. Even in eastern cities machines were never universal. The city-wide machine prominent in academic literature and popular fiction was always the exception. They were not a permanent feature of any city and in locales such as Boston they never emerged. The city-wide machine was a transient phenomenon, appearing only in some locales. Ward-level machines were more prolific (Brown and Halaby 1987). Moreover, the machine style flourished in a particular phase of American history, roughly spanning the Civil War to the Second World War, which saw the development of an urban, industrial society.

The machine is a party based on interests rather than principles. Fuelled by material benefits, machines have been likened to business organizations, specializing in winning votes and elections (Banfield and Wilson 1963). To thrive the machine needed to control the organs of government. From there it obtained the resources to generate activism, electoral and financial support. The activists consisted of an army of patronage workers chosen under the spoils system by which victors in elections obtained the right to fill appointive positions in government with their supporters. A study of Chicago in 1928 found 60 per cent of Democratic ward committeemen to be public employees (Gosnell 1968). Patronage workers were required to perform party tasks to remain on the public payroll, a goal that could be eased by appointment to sinecures.

Voters gave the machine electoral support in exchange for material benefits. In the absence of welfare state provision the party dispensed services such as jobs and cash in time of need on condition of electoral loyalty. Recent immigrants, in the nineteenth century usually able to vote, provided a constituency to whose needs the machine ministered. Business corporations, dependent upon government for contracts or lax legal regulation, funded machines in exchange for preferential treatment.

A variety of theories have been adduced to account for the development of the machine. We differentiate them by the factors attributed the greatest emphasis as respectively social, cultural, economic, political and intergovernmental explanations. *Social* theories locate the sources of machine growth in the conditions prevailing in American cities during industrialization. Populations grew rapidly with the influx of rural migrants and foreign immigrants. But public administration failed to keep pace with population growth and the associated problems of social dislocation and deprivation. City governments were inefficient and services inadequate. Machines filled the gap left by the deficiencies of government. On a selective basis they dispensed material benefits to those in need. By providing recognition, liaison with officialdom and introductions into community organizations they integrated new populations into city life (Greenstein 1970).

The *cultural* theory attaches paramount importance to attitudes in explaining the machine's emergence. Mass immigration resulted in a transfer of power between ethnic groups in northern cities. Older stock Anglo-Saxon groups were displaced in power by immigrants from Ireland, and those from southern and eastern Europe. Different attitudes towards government separated the old stock from the immigrants. The former subscribed to a public-regarding view of government, entailing ideals such as public interest and participation. In contrast, the immigrant ethos was private-regarding, emphasizing personal needs and loyalties over universal principles. The machine was the organizational expression of the immigrant ethos (Banfield and Wilson 1963).

Elite rather than mass needs are central to the *economic* theory of machine development. The party machine, like New York's Democrats of Tammany Hall, was a reliable conduit for business influence in government. The machine disciplined elected office-holders, curbing their independence and corruption. Prior to the development of the machine, business had suffered from the 'rapacious individualism' of those in office. Uncontrolled greed was antipathetic to stable profits. The machines provided stability. They were a business-political coalition which assured a durable hold on profit and power respectively (Shefter 1976).

The *political* theory traces the development of the machine to the conjunction of industrialization with a wide franchise. Uniquely in the US, the conflicts arising from industrialization found an outlet in electoral politics, an occurrence precluded elsewhere by the restricted suffrage. The machine was a party organization that mobilized the working class which was a patchwork of ethnic groups. Organization at the ward level facilitated sensitivity to the demands of and a distribution of benefits to different ethnic groups. The machine's operational style allowed cohesive parties to be forged out of an ethnically diverse working class from the beginnings of the industrial era (Bridges 1984).

The *intergovernmental* theory emphasizes the supply side of machine growth. Demand alone was insufficient to trigger city-wide machines into existence. Rather they could only emerge when one organization was able to exert a monopoly over the supply of machine-style rewards in a particular area. When one machine organization established a monopoly of patronage it attained electoral dominance by depriving its rivals of the resources with which to mobilize votes. To exert monopoly control required allies at other levels of government which distributed patronage in the city. Thus machine leaders had to forge alliances with state and federal politicians to gain monopoly control. In their absence a city-wide machine failed to materialize for want of resources (Erie 1988).

Party machines diminished in number and electoral leverage after the Second World War. Like their rise, the causes of the decline of machines is a subject of debate. The conventional wisdom attributes their decline to economic, political and social changes which began to register in America after 1945. Post-war affluence, the expansion of welfare state provision originating from the New Deal, the extension of meritocratic selection criteria for public employment, the diminution in the numbers of first-generation immigrants, and a more educated electorate have, it is argued, depleted the manpower and clienteles of the machines (Sorauf 1980, Epstein 1986).

Critiques of and qualifications to the conventional wisdom have been advanced by several writers. Wolfinger noted that many of the conditions in which the machine thrived still prevail (1972, 1974). Changes have not been so profound as to eliminate urban poverty, patronage and the benefits of preferment. The enhanced bureaucratization of government has enhanced not reduced the need for agencies which mediate on the citizen's behalf with government, a traditional machine function. Other writers, in a narrower critique, have questioned the contribution of the New Deal to the machine's demise. They have observed that the resources of some machines were expanded in the 1930s. Government became more active, provided more employment and distributed more benefits. In consequence, rejuvenation rather than decline describes the impact of the New Deal for some machines (Stave 1970, Dorsett 1977).

The evidence of machine decline does appear overwhelming, though its causes and timing may be disputed. Studies of surviving machines suggest several deviations from those of the past. Internal party discipline falls below optimum efficiency. Patronage appointees are politically inactive and contributors unrewarded (Johnston 1979). Some machines did survive and adapt to the conditions of post-war America. In Chicago, the Democratic party organization, the last of the big city-wide machines, flourished until the 1970s, winning middle-class support. Such an untypical machine electorate was generated by competence in government, a sensitivity to the needs of business corporations, low taxation and, particularly attractive to white middle-class ethnics, a sluggishness in promoting racially integrated housing. But the machine's reputation for competence was undone by the failure of city services in the severe winter of 1979. In the long term, machine control was loosened by the changing racial balance in the city. Blacks, never a major component of the machine's power structure but material beneficiaries of its control, were growing as a proportion of the city electorate. Lack of influence, aggravated by the cutbacks in welfare provision of the Reagan era, alienated the black electorate sufficiently to overturn the machine's control of the mayoralty in 1983 (Kleppner 1985, Erie 1988).

AMATEUR CLUBS

The amateur club is a party based upon principle. The title amateur was first used in the early 1960s to characterize a new style of activist in American party politics. Unlike professionals, regarded as the norm for party activists, the amateurs, predominantly middle class, were concerned with principle and policy rather than electoral victory and the compromises this entailed. In addition, amateurs were also devoted to internal democracy within the party organizations they participated in, a concern not shared by professionals (Wilson 1962).

Some of the foremost examples of the amateur club type have been formed outside of the party structure. In two of three cities in Wilson's original study, Los Angeles and Chicago, amateur clubs were extra-legal organizations. In the former, amateur clubs were the only form of grassroots organization where state law provides for party structures only from counties upwards. In Chicago, the clubs were organized in opposition to the machine. In their third city, New York, the clubs had successfully taken over the official party structures in some areas. In other cities the official party structure resembles an amateur club. The Democratic parties in Denver and Houston have resembled this style in recent years (Ware 1984, Mayhew 1986).

By the late 1960s the amateur club style was declining. Both activism and electoral success were receding. This decline was attributable to social and political causes (Ware 1984). Of social significance was the changing status of women, who had been numerous in amateur clubs. Increased female participation in the workforce (rising from a quarter to a half of all women from 1940 to 1980) reduced their availability for political activity. Of political relevance was both the substance and structure of issue politics of the late 1960s. The Vietnam War, escalated by Democratic presidents, divided the party and alienated many issue-conscious activists. Non-partisan mechanisms such as interest groups, initiatives, referenda and direct action gained in attractiveness thereafter for those who remained politically active.

CADRE CAUCUSES

The cadre-caucus style party is the norm in American experience. 'Cadre' refers to the reliance on a relatively few key members of staff, as opposed to a mass membership; 'caucus' refers to the relative autonomy of each organizational unit, as opposed to a more hierarchical 'branch' organization. Like the machine, and unlike the amateur club, the cadre caucus concentrates influence in a few leaders in each unit, but the units are generally rather loosely related to each other. In contrast to both the machine and the amateur club, the cadre caucus offers mainly solidary incentives to activists (although material and purposive incentives can also be present); thus it is this type of party organization that is most congenial to the mature party system developed and defended by politicians like Martin Van Buren in the early nineteenth century (see Chapter Three). Cadre caucuses are characterized by small numbers, absence of formal membership, localism, an electoral orientation and the separation of the organization from the candidates for public office (Duverger 1959, Ware 1984). There is considerable organizational slack in cadre caucuses. They can be understaffed, inactive and laxly disciplined. A national study of county parties in the late 1970s found that 10 per cent of Democratic and a fifth of Republican organizations lacked a full complement of officials. At the precinct level the same survey found 15 per cent of precinct positions unfilled in the Republican party and 5 per cent in the Democratic. As both sets of figures were supplied by county leaders probably unwilling to concede the full extent of organizational deficiencies within their party, they may well underestimate the problem of staffing (Cotter *et al.* 1984). A Detroit study in 1980 found a third of precincts unstaffed by Democrats and an even larger proportion in the Republican party (Eldersveld 1982).

Not all of those who occupy official positions are active on the party's behalf. An Indiana study found 10 per cent of precinct officials to be totally inactive in party work (Bartholomew 1968). Even in election activity, the focus of the precinct official's duties, many tasks are left undone. Of three election-related activities – registering voters, canvassing, election day mobilization – each one was not undertaken by from one-third to two-thirds of precinct officials in various locales (Crotty 1986). Shortfalls in efficiency are, of necessity, tolerated. Discipline cannot be enforced when the organization lacks resources that can be easily given or revoked to improve performance (Sorauf 1980). Nor is there a reservoir of manpower available to replace the inefficient. Interest groups help to supplement the deficiencies of party organization in some locales. In urban areas the aid given to the Democrats by trade unions exemplifies the alliance of party and interest group. The relationship varies from the integration of trade unionists into party activities, as in Detroit, to a separate mobilization by unions on the party's behalf, as in Los Angeles (Greenstone 1966). However, union activism and influence is now waning, diminishing their capacity to supplement party activity (Ware 1984).

Periodic studies of the same local parties show no trend toward inactivity. Precinct studies in Detroit and the national county survey show parties now as active as they were in 1956 or 1964 (Gibson *et al*. 1985, 1989, Crotty 1986). However, such data are only a partial guide to organizational effectiveness. The progressive decline in election turnout between 1964 and 1980, and in registration from 1964 to 1976, are indicative either of lower party activity or lower effectiveness. Parties are also facing greater competition to perform campaign functions such as canvassing and mobilizing on election day from candidate organizations, political action committees and television. These 'textbook' party functions are no longer their monopoly. A survey of campaign managers in the 1978 Congressional elections found only 27 per cent who thought party organization would be important or very important in determining the outcome of the election (Wattenberg 1986).

STATE PARTIES

Most state parties are of the cadre caucus type. Most of the local organizations that constitute the state party are themselves cadre caucuses. Only occasionally have state parties developed an identity distinct from the local organizations from which they are composed. Rivalries between various local organizations, along with conflicts over ideology and leaders, account for the frequency of factional divisions in state parties.

There are some exceptions to the cadre caucus norm among state parties. From the 1930s the Democratic parties in Virginia and Louisiana assumed machine characteristics under the leadership of Harry Byrd and Huey Long respectively. Interestingly, both were primarily rural states demonstrating that machines are not peculiar to urban settings.

In Louisiana, the Long-controlled faction of the party profited from the expansion of government activity in the states in the 1930s. This enlarged the scope for patronage and preferment to be used to supply disciplined activists and finance for the machine to function. In a reversal of the customary flow of influence in American parties, the state party extended its control into local government to swell its resources (Williams 1969).

The professionalization of state government in recent decades has attenuated the potential for patronage. Many more positions are now filled by meritocratic criteria than they were before the Second World War. Those discretionary appointments which remain often require the performance of specialized tasks requiring qualified appointees. There are states where patronage and approximations to the machine survive. Indiana is probably the best modern example. An electorally competitive state, both parties exhibit machine features. In the early 1970s one third of state employees were patronage appointees (Huckshorn 1976). Both parties engage in 'macing' – enforced party contributions from public employees.

The amateur club style has characterized a minority of state parties concentrated in the upper Midwest. In Michigan from the late 1940s the Democratic party became a liberal–labour alliance. Citizen activism was encouraged in pursuit of liberal programmes. Around the same time a liberal, participatory state party emerged in Minnesota from the amalgamation of the formerly separate Democratic and Farmer–Labor parties (Fenton 1966). Both major parties in Minnesota continue to encourage activism and policy discussion (Marshall 1980).

A notable trend in state parties in the last twenty years is that they have developed as organizations. They have become more professionalized, bureaucratic and productive. State party chairmanships are now usually full-time appointments. Nearly all parties have a permanent headquarters and several full-time staff. The organizations engage in activities including opinion polling, fund raising and providing services to candidates such as research. These services or the funds to finance them are also passed on to local parties (Cotter *et al*. 1984).

But organizational development is not synonymous with increased influence. In some respects the impact of state parties has diminished. Where patronage is available, many state governors distribute it independently of their party organizations (Huckshorn 1976). In presidential nominations state parties have been effectively removed as actors where they once played the leading roles. National convention delegations consist of candidate supporters rather than party workers. In elections state parties, like those at local level, vie for influence with other structures such as candidate organizations. Conspicuously, one of the few quantitative measures of state party activity that has registered a decline since the 1960s is in the number of candidates they recruit to contest elections (Gibson *et al*. 1983).

NATIONAL PARTIES

In the standard organization chart the national level appears as the highest tier. But in parties in which power is decentralized the national organizations have been anything but command centres. In fact, in the past the national parties were the least powerful and least active of the party rings. National parties lacked independent authority, being dependent upon the constituent state parties for the implementation of decisions. Unlike the federal system of government, the parties lacked autonomy at national level, prompting one author to describe the party structure as 'more nearly confederative than federal in nature' (Key 1964: 334). A study of the national committees published in the early 1960s was aptly titled *Politics without Power* (Cotter and Hennessy 1964).

National committees originate in both major parties from before the Civil War. Consisting of representatives of state parties across the country they met infrequently and were unassertive in dealing with the various layers of the party structure. The presidential campaign was co-ordinated by the national party chairman but between elections there was little activity. It was not until 1918 that a national party organization employed permanent staff. Between elections the official duties of the national committees principally consisted of deciding the venue and allocations of delegates to the states for the next national convention. For the party controlling the White House the national chairman acted as chief personnel officer for the administration. Requests and recommendations for appointments were channelled through the national chairman to the White House, departments and agencies. On several occasions the party chairman simultaneously served in the administration as postmaster general, presiding over the government department with the largest patronage payroll.

More active and assertive national parties emerged after the Second World War. The background to this development included the centralization of government promoted by the New Deal, improvements in communications contributing to the nationalization of American society and the increased salience of the civil rights issue, provoking southern–national conflict in the Democratic party. National party growth intensified in the 1970s so that they acquired an unprecedented degree of dynamism. National parties today engage in more activities and have closer links to constituent state and local parties than ever before (Cotter and Bibby 1980, Longley 1980a 1980b, Epstein 1982, Reichley 1985).

In the 1950s the focus of national party assertion was the states' methods of selecting delegates to national conventions. Formerly the principle of states' rights had prevailed in delegate selection. But this now became qualified. Republican rules defined acceptable selection methods and the Democrats sought to ensure the loyalty to the national ticket of state parties represented at the convention.

Delegate selection remained the focus of national regulation in the Democratic party beyond the 1950s. After the turmoil of the 1968 Chicago convention and the subsequent election defeat a systematic overhaul of delegate selection procedures was begun. A succession of *ad hoc* commissions, the first beginning in 1969 under the successive chairmanships of George McGovern and Donald Fraser, revised the rules of delegate selection after each presidential election from 1968 to 1980. But for a handful of exceptions, commission recommendations were endorsed by the national committee and made binding on the states parties. Strikingly, the national party succeeded in gaining compliance from the states. Litigation confirmed the right of the national party to delimit the independence of the state units in selecting delegates even where national party rules contradicted state laws (Crotty 1976, Wekkin 1984a).

The establishment of a code of delegate selection rules was part of a broader trend towards institutionalization of the national Democratic party in the 1970s (Hitlin and Jackson 1979, Wekkin 1984b). In 1974 a party charter was adopted, effectively the first constitution of a major party in America. Institutions created by the charter included a national finance council and a judicial council to review state delegate selection plans. A more substantial innovation was the provision for an optional mid-term policy convention, producing a new national forum for the discussion of issues previously confined to the conventions of presidential election years.

Mid-term conferences were held in 1974, 1978 and 1982. The first two were dominated by activists concerned over issues who at the second conference registered discontent over the performance of the incumbent Carter administration. Though many issues were debated, without a mechanism for binding elected officials to conference decisions their influence on government policy was slight. In 1986 the national committee abolished the mid-term conference, prompted by the party chairman Paul Kirk, who argued that they were wasteful and divisive.

The national Republican party also became more institutionalized in the 1970s (Bibby 1980, Herrnson 1988). The Republican national committee acquired a permanent headquarters and between 1972–84 underwent a twenty-fold increase in staffing. By the latter year the committee employed 600 staff though numbers fell subsequently. More staff produced greater activity, particularly focused on overcoming the party's minority status in the electorate. The short-term objective was to increase Republican representation among governors and state legislators prior to the redrawing of constituency boundaries following the 1980 census. In so doing, a national party organization became involved to an unprecedented degree in subnational elections.

To assist state and local parties the national committee placed money, personnel and expertise at their disposal. Funds were concentrated in areas offering potential for party development or, as in the 1982 congressional elections, where Republican incumbents were vulnerable (Jacobson 1985–6). Staff from the national committee have been seconded to state parties or subsidies provided to pay additional salaries. Advice from national party personnel on opinion polling, data processing, voter registration and fundraising has been provided. National party officials have sought to recruit candidates to run for office, and to offer training in campaign techniques. Enhanced Republican national party activity has been financed by the development of a lucrative fund-raising operation. Using direct mail a list of two million contributors had been established by 1984. Though individual contributions are modest the total is massive, amounting to $106 million in 1983–4. Armed with such resources the traditional direction of the flow of money in American parties has been reversed. For the Republican party the national organization now subvents state and local units.

The national Democratic and Republican parties differ in emphases in the activities they undertake. The Democratic national committee does provide aid to state and local parties in elections and its Republican counterpart has been involved in regulating delegate selection. But national Democratic services are restricted by both shortage of funds and the party's dominance of most electoral positions below the presidential level. For example, in the early 1980s 70 per cent of state Republican parties obtained aid from the national committee compared to 7 per cent of their Democratic counterparts (Herrnson 1988). Conversely, recent Republican successes in winning the White House have muted pressures for reform of the way its presidential candidates are selected. Republican national guidelines on delegate selection are advisory not mandatory so preserving the states' rights principle.

These unprecedented national activities have prompted the view that they constitute the outlines of a new style of American party (Kayden and Mahe 1985). In this new style party, the national level is the dynamic layer of the organization. Old-style party functions such as candidate recruitment and organizing campaigns are now undertaken at the national level. But this interpretation exaggerates the role of national parties. The potential for the national party to influence candidate recruitment is circumscribed by the continuation of the direct primary. State and local electorates decide nominations and in only a minority of locales does any layer of party organization exert a decisive impact on the outcome.

While national party influence has grown in some spheres it has diminished in others. The national party organizations no longer conduct presidential campaigns. It has been deprived of this function or forced to share it with the nominee's personal organization. Patronage is now channelled through the White House rather than the national party chairman. The Carter White House paid so little attention to the party in making appointments that it was condemned in a resolution of the Democratic national committee within four months of taking office. Where once the national party initiated patronage proposals, now it responds to White House recommendations (Bass 1984).

Patronage illustrates the subordination of the national party organization to presidential interests. When the party controls the White House the initiative of its national organs declines. Not surprisingly, the innovations in national party activity described above occurred after presidential election defeats. Several recent presidents have sought to control the national organizations to neutralize their influence. As long as presidents perceive the party headquarters as a potential rival best converted into a White House public relations department then they – allied with state laws, primaries and traditions of localism – will prevent the development of strong national parties.

CONCLUSION

In this chapter we identified the machine, amateur club and cadre caucus as informal types of party structure. Though their internal power structures and stimuli to activism differ, they have all undergone the similar experience of organizational decline at some time since the Second World War. Though the timing and sources of decline vary, all types of local party were experiencing it by the 1980s.

At state and national level there is evidence of organizational growth. Staff have increased in number and specialization. The national parties have also obtained a vast increase in funds which has facilitated greater activism. At both levels funds and services have been passed along to other territorial units of the party structure. These changes demonstrate that the decentralized character of the American party system is not fixed. Change is possible within the existing constitutional framework. But the impediments of the direct primary and, for the president's party, White House resistance, continue to prevent the development of a centralized party system.

7 Party in elections

As mechanisms for fighting elections parties have been in existence in the US for nearly two centuries. The parties have regularly assembled and reassembled coalitions of interests and principles, and readjusted the balance between the two, in the quest for electoral ascendancy. Periodically, critical elections have given primacy to particular principles and interests, and have reshaped the substance of political conflict and the direction of government. However, as we noted in Chapter Three, the capacity of the contemporary parties to provide elections with the raw materials for a political transformation has been attenuated by a hundred years of reform and legal regulation. For all their reputed preoccupation with elections, the contemporary American parties are probably more circumscribed in their influence on elections than parties in any other western democracy. There is no party monopoly of the selection of candidates, or of the financing or organization of election campaigns. Parties have to compete against other organizations and individuals, or at least collaborate with them, to perform these functions.

Limitations on the parties' role in elections began a century ago when the secret, official (or Australian) ballot was introduced. Replacing the 'tickets' distributed by the various parties, these innovations concomitantly diminished their control over the electorate. Formerly voters acquired the party ticket of their choice and placed it in the ballot box. Parties thus had detailed information at their disposal about who had received tickets, and how they had voted. Moreover, this method facilitated voting 'straight' party tickets. The time and physical hindrances to split-ticket voting deterred its incidence. These partisan assets disappeared with the introduction of the Australian ballot, inaugurating a century in which party influence in elections progressively declined.

In this chapter we analyse the contemporary role of party in elections. We begin by examining their role in recruiting candidates to run for office. Secondly, we examine the party role in the selection (nomination) of candidates in state, and in presidential elections. We then assess the type of parties that result from nomination by primary. Subsequently we depict the party role in financing campaigns. Finally, we examine the involvement of the parties in conducting the campaign.

RECRUITMENT

The process of narrowing the alternatives presented to voters begins with the decision of candidates to run for office. This stage winnows out the vast majority of the population to leave a minute proportion who opt to become candidates. As discussed in Chapter Five, outside of legally non-partisan contests elective office is a virtual duopoly of the Republican and Democratic parties' candidates. To win many elections an almost essential precondition is to be a candidate of a major party. Thus realistic efforts at winning office are usually channelled through the parties. The two-party stranglehold is probably greater than ever before as independents and third-party candidates are at an all-time low in electoral success (Schlesinger 1984).

Most county and state party chairs solicit candidates to run for office. A survey of county chairs found a majority involved in recruiting candidates for county, state legislative and congressional elections. Only 17 per cent of the sample were not involved in recruiting candidates for county contests. Much less activity was reported for instigating candidacies for town- and city-level contests where non-partisan elections are common. State party chairs also seek to recruit candidates, mainly for state legislative and congressional contests (Cotter *et al*. 1984). Party officials at units smaller than the county are rarely involved in candidate recruitment (Bowman and Boynton 1966).

Until recently the state and local levels of the party dominated candidate recruitment. But since the late 1970s both national party organizations have instigated candidacies, particularly for congressional and state legislative elections. The Republican party has been the more active of the two in this sphere.

Since the 1978 elections the Republican National Committee (RNC) has run a local elections campaign division. It liaises with state party organizations to acquire data on legislative contests. Profiles of constituencies are developed, electorally promising seats identified and candidates recruited. For example, in 1978 RNC representative Mary Crisp travelled through New England and the midwest attempting to attract Republican women to run as candidates (Bibby 1979). Similar activities have been undertaken by the party's campaign committees in Congress (the electioneering units of the legislative parties).

But parties are not the only initiators of candidacies. Some candidates are self-starters who make their decisions unprompted. Others are encouraged to run by interest groups such as unions, business and women's organizations. A study of state legislators found that only a minority of candidates were recruited by parties when they first ran for office. However, a majority did consult with party officials although the initiative for the candidacy originated elsewhere (Tobin and Keynes 1975). Though self-starters are also common in elections to Congress, many candidates have previously been active in their party (Kazee and Thornberry 1990).

The extent of party organization involvement in recruiting candidates varies. The principal variables are the type of organization (as defined in Chapter Six) and the electoral strength of the party. Machine-style parties are the most assertive in recruiting candidates (Sorauf 1963, Snowiss 1966). Public office is a resource husbanded by the machine. It is a reward for faithful service which promises a solicitousness towards machine interests when in office. Hierarchical controls within the party organization and loyal electorates provide machines with substantial resources with which to nominate and elect preferred candidates. These resources can also be employed to repel unwanted aspirants for office.

Neither cadre-caucus nor amateur-style parties attempt the degree of control over recruitment practised by machines. Cadre caucuses usually lack the resources to encourage or repel with any effectiveness. Amateur-style parties do not appear to be involved in recruitment activity. Perhaps where there is a participatory ethos such activity is unnecessary or unacceptable. Electoral weakness necessitates party activity to recruit candidates. Where the chances of electoral success are negligible few candidates are volunteers. (The tradition of localism discounts the prospects for a candidate who fights hopeless causes being rewarded with a safe seat elsewhere.) In such areas party officials struggle to conscript candidates to 'show the flag'. Volunteers are more plentiful where electoral prospects are brighter. Where one party predominates it is likely to be inundated with aspiring candidates for the most attractive offices unless there is a machine-style organization to constrict the flow.

NOMINATIONS IN THE STATES

The process of candidate selection (nomination) is distinctive in the US for the lack of control exerted by party organizations. This has not always been so. After the rise of the mature party system nominations were made by conventions composed of delegates drawn from constituent party organizations. But from the introduction of official ballot papers candidates had to satisfy legal criteria to appear on them. This constrained the parties' discretion over the selection process as it came to be regulated by law.

The attenuation of party control was compounded shortly afterwards by the inception of the primary to replace the convention as the means for deciding nominations. The primary is an election-like contest in which voters choose among a party's candidates to determine who will represent it in the general election. Wisconsin enacted the first primary law in 1902, inspired by its reforming governor Robert La Follette. By 1908 two-thirds of the states had adopted the primary to determine some nominations.

Primaries were advocated as a device to undermine the influence of corrupt machine party organizations over elected officials. By removing selection from the machines it was hoped to enhance elected officials' responsiveness to voters. The primary was one of a cluster of innovations enacted in the so-called progressive era of the early twentieth century aimed at destroying machine influence. Reflecting a resurgence of the anti-partisan ethos, additional reforms such as non-partisan elections and voter-controlled decisions through referendums and initiatives were also widely adopted at this time. Though the primary was advocated as a device to destroy machine influence, its adoption followed a different logic. Most of the states that first adopted primary laws were one-party strongholds (Key 1956). Wisconsin, for example, was dominated by the Republican party. Here, as in several other northern states, the primary was a method of shifting the balance of power within the Republican party towards reformers with an appeal to voters against the conservatives who controlled the organizations. In the south, where machines were rare, the primary was probably intended to consolidate one-party dominance. Opening up the dominant party to internal competition diminished the incentives to mobilize behind the Republicans or Populists. Throughout the country the introduction of the primary reinforced one-party dominance. Though intra-party contests intensified, competition between the parties waned.

Today every state uses primaries to make some nominations. Despite their universality there is no uniformity in primary laws. Moreover in some states there is scope for differences between the nominating methods used by the two parties. Two dimensions can be employed to differentiate primaries. *Decision phase* distinguishes the place of the primary in determining the nomination. *Participation* defines who is eligible to vote in the primary.

Three types can be located on the decision phase dimension. *Plurality winner*, the most common, awards the nomination to the candidate with the most votes in the primary. *Run-off* primaries, used in most of the southern states, resemble the procedures for electing French presidents. To be nominated a candidate requires more than 50 per cent of the total vote. If the initial ballot fails to produce a majority winner then another contest is held between the top two finishers in the first primary. The third type, *convention*, refers to those states where the primary is only a part of the nominating process. In states such as Connecticut and New York, party conventions choose nominees who can then be challenged in primaries. To qualify for the 'challenge primary' candidates must have obtained a legally specified share of the convention vote (20 per cent Connecticut, 25 per cent in New York). In Iowa nomination is made by convention if no candidate in the primary obtained 35 per cent of the vote. In several states primaries are optional. States such as Alabama and Virginia permit nomination by either primary or convention. This can produce differences between the parties as to how they make nominations. In Virginia, for example, Republicans in the 1970s nominated by conventions and the Democrats by primaries.

Four types of *participation* can be distinguished. *Closed* primaries restrict participation to voters who declare an allegiance to the party holding the primary. In some states allegiance is recorded on the electoral register. In other states a statement of party allegiance is required at the polling place to obtain a ballot paper. No other type of primary tests for the voter's party affiliation. Closed primaries used to be mandated by state law. However, in 1986 in *Tashjian v Republican Party of Connecticut* the Supreme Court held closed primaries to be an unconstitutional restriction on the freedom of association protected by the First Amendment. State laws can still permit parties to hold closed primaries but they cannot be required by law. To date few states have altered their laws or administrative practices in the light of the *Tashjian* decision. In the handful of instances where changes have been made they have taken the form of allowing individual parties to opt for open primaries. Unless this option is taken up the primary remains closed. So far it is the minority party (the Republicans in each case) who have opted for open primaries while the majority Democrats retain the closed system (Epstein 1989).

In *open* primaries voters receive ballot papers for both parties but they may mark only one. In a *blanket* primary there is a single ballot paper containing candidates for both parties. For each office voters cast one vote but can switch between parties to choose nominees for different offices. In Louisiana's *non-partisan* primary all candidates, irrespective of party, compete in the same primary for which all voters are eligible. A candidate obtaining over half the vote is automatically elected. Only where there is no majority is there a general election and this may involve candidates of the same party (see Table 7.1). No primary is effectively closed in practice. Some are less open than others but none succeed in limiting participation to the identifiers of the party in whose name the primary is conducted. Declaration of party allegiance is dependent upon the self-designation of voters which can be altered to qualify for a primary vote (in some states a lengthy period of advance notice is required). Nor is there any means of invalidating a statement of party affiliation: 'The fact remains that even in Illinois, New York or any other closed primary state you are a Democrat if you say you

Table 7.1 Types of gubernatorial primary

	Open	Closed		Blanket	Non-partisan
Plurality					
	Hawaii	Arizona	New Hampshire	Alaska	
	Idaho	California	New Jersey	Washington	
	Michigan	Delaware	New Mexico		
	Minnesota	Illinois	Ohio		
	Montana	Indiana	Oregon		
	North Dakota	Kansas	Pennsylvania		
	Vermont	Kentucky	Rhode Island		
	Wisconsin	Maine	South Dakota		
		Maryland (D)	Tennessee		
		Massachusetts	Virginia		
		Missouri	West Virginia (D)		
		Nebraska	Wyoming		
		Nevada			
Run off		Alabama			Louisiana
		Arkansas			
		Florida			
		Georgia			
		Mississippi			
		North Carolina (D)			
		Oklahoma			
		South Carolina			
		Texas			
Convention	Utah	Connecticut (D)			
		New York			
		Colorado			
		Iowa			

Note: (D) shows the Democratic practice. Republicans now use open primaries in these states

are; no one can effectively say you are not; and you can become a Republican any time the spirit moves you simply by saying that you have become one' (Ranney 1975: 166).

In some states primaries co-exist with legal opportunities for party organizations to exert influence over nominations. In states such as Connecticut the party convention decides the nomination unless challenged in a primary. In several other states, including Rhode Island and North Dakota, party conventions endorse one of the candidates in the primary. Endorsement usually confers some legal privilege like first place on the ballot paper or automatic placement where other candidates have to obtain signatures on a petition to qualify. In a third set of states, including Minnesota and Illinois, the parties make informal endorsements. Though conferring no legal advantages informal endorsements can benefit candidates by unifying activists and money around a preferred candidate. But these various devices are employed in a minority of states. In around two-thirds of the states neither legal mechanisms nor informal endorsements are used by parties to influence nominations.

Where party influence is asserted it is frequently successful. Convention decisions are rarely challenged in states like Connecticut and Colorado. Where challenges are raised they usually fail. Only New York Democrats' convention selections are regularly overturned. Parties' endorsed candidates often face competition in the primary but they usually overcome it (Jewell and Olson 1978, McNitt 1980, Jewell 1984).

There are signs that endorsed candidates are more vulnerable in some locales than they once were. The defeat of a Democratic gubernatorial informal endorsement in Pennsylvania first occurred in 1966. Endorsed candidates have failed to carry several other nominations in the state in the past twenty years. In Minnesota in 1978 both parties failed to secure the nomination for their endorsed candidates for US senator. In Chicago, last of the big city machines, preferred candidates lost the Democratic mayoralty primaries in 1979 and 1983. These slippages of party influence, combined with the rarity of any attempts to exert it, indicate the considerable degree to which party organizations are now divorced from candidate selection in the states.

PRESIDENTIAL NOMINATIONS

The selection of presidential candidates remained immune from the influence of primaries longer than that for other major elective offices. From the 1830s presidential nominations were made by national conventions composed of delegates representing state parties. Early in the twentieth century presidential primaries were appended to the national convention system but did not replace it. Presidential primaries were adopted in some states to allow voters either to vote for a candidate for the nomination (preference primaries) or to elect national convention delegates (delegate primaries) or both. They did not replace the national convention as a mechanism for deciding the nomination.

In 1912 twelve states held some form of presidential primary. Their number burgeoned immediately afterwards, producing twenty primaries in 1916. Reaction set in thereafter. In the 1968 Democratic contest only seventeen primaries were held.

For most of the period 1912–68 only a minority of states held presidential primaries. They accounted for only a minority of delegates to national conventions and many candidates declined to enter them. Several nominations were won by candidates who entered no primaries: Republicans

Wendell Willkie (1940) and Thomas Dewey (1944), Democrats Adlai Stevenson (1952) and Hubert Humphrey (1968) are examples. Lack of candidate interest, low turnouts and high costs accounted for a disenchantment with presidential primaries leading to a decline in their numbers (Davis 1967).

Because presidential nominations could be won without entering primaries there were few incentives for candidates to use them. At least until after the Second World War no nominees owed their nominations to winning primaries. Most national convention delegates were selected by processes usually controlled by party organizations: state party conventions or committees choosing a large majority of delegates. State conventions consisted of delegates chosen in a series of caucuses (meetings) for progressively larger intra-state territorial units. Access to caucuses varied between states. Some were confined entirely to party officials. In others, the first stage of caucuses, usually at the precinct level, were open to voters though turnouts were meagre.

Many national convention delegations were hierarchically controlled. Party or public officials (usually governors) dominated delegations through patronage and personal appeal. The need for delegation unity to maximize state influence over the nomination also encouraged control by the leadership. Candidates or their representatives campaigned for the nomination by cultivating state party elites. By establishing a personal rapport and striking bargains over policy and patronage, candidates sought to establish coalitions of state party leaders. In the absence of a majority on the first ballot (Democrats required two-thirds majorities until 1936), balloting and bargaining continued. Either one of the leading contenders struck enough bargains with party leaders and failing candidates to obtain the required majority, or leaders compromised around a previously obscure 'dark horse' candidate inoffensive to all major factions.

Candidates entered primaries to persuade the leaders who controlled delegations. The primaries could deliver a 'demonstration effect': proof that a candidate could win votes (Epstein 1978). Concerned, though not necessarily exclusively or even primarily for their party to win elections, leaders were alert to evidence of candidates' vote-getting abilities. Candidates such as Harold Stassen in 1948 and Estes Kefauver in 1952 forced themselves into contention for the nomination by winning primaries.

Two types of candidates were compelled to use primaries to prove themselves to party leaders. Insurgents used them to capitalize on their popular support in contrast to their lack of appeal to party leaders. Challengers to incumbent presidents of their own party such as Theodore Roosevelt (1912), Robert La Follette (1924), Kefauver (1952) and Eugene McCarthy (1968) were insurgent candidates. Second, suspect vote-getters used primaries to allay doubts about their electability among otherwise sympathetic party leaders. Previously defeated presidential candidates Stevenson (1956) and Richard Nixon (1968) used primaries to offset fears that they were losers. Similarly, John Kennedy in 1960 sought to disprove the 'lesson' of the 1928 election that a Catholic could not win.

Primaries did grow in influence over the nomination from the 1940s. Some primary losers were winnowed out of contention while others gained consideration by their victories. The rise to world power status of the US and the further homogenization of American society enhanced the desirability of the parties fielding presidential candidates with national appeal which primary victories could demonstrate. Kennedy's victory in 1960 depended on primary victories and several other nominations were facilitated by convincing vote-getting performances such as Dewey in 1948. However, it is a testimony to the continued control exerted by party leaders that no insurgents could win the nomination. Kefauver was electable but unacceptable to party leaders and he was defeated. Kennedy, electable and acceptable, was nominated.

In 1968 the legitimacy of this party-dominated process was severely strained. Opponents of the Vietnam War sought to depose President Johnson by denying him the Democratic party nomination. A challenge was organized around Senator Eugene McCarthy. Another administration critic, Senator Robert Kennedy, also mounted a challenge but it was abbreviated by assassination. Though Johnson withdrew, his support within the party was inherited by his faithful vice president, Hubert Humphrey.

McCarthy supporters encountered insurmountable obstacles to translating anti-war sentiment into national convention delegates. There were few primaries and several preference polls were not binding on delegates. In non-primary states McCarthy supporters struggled to participate. Where participation was limited to party officials there was little support for McCarthy. In nominally open caucus states access was denied in practice, meetings were conducted in a biased manner, and McCarthy strength was under-represented in the allocation of delegates. In many areas the party organizations closed ranks behind Humphrey.

The nomination of Humphrey was the peak but also the culmination of party organization control over the nominating process. Disquiet over delegate selection procedures, allied with inertia and confusion, prompted the convention that nominated Humphrey to mandate state parties to promote the participation of Democratic voters in future contests. The body subsequently created to secure that mandate, the Commission on Party Structure and Delegate Selection (known after its successive chairmen as McGovern-Fraser), pursued its task with vigour. Guided by a staff dedicated to undermining party organization control, the commission devised a set of standards to which future state delegate selection procedures were to conform (Shafer 1983). Among the Commission's guidelines were the requirement for caucuses open to voters and an end to ex-officio delegates; limits to the number of delegates chosen by party committees; and the representation of women, young people (aged eighteen to thirty) and minorities on delegations in proportion to their numbers in the population, effectively a quota system.

The rules widened voter participation, loosening party organization control over nominations. These effects were accentuated by an unintended, undesired consequence of the commission's proposals: the spread of presidential primaries. The new rules contributed to the spread of primaries as they were adopted to replace prohibited delegate selection methods or to evade the complex rules now regulating the caucus process. Another motive, unconnected to reform, was to capture a share of the media attention that primaries had attracted by the 1960s. In 1972 twenty-three states held a Democratic primary, producing two-thirds of the delegate total, many of them bound by the results of preference polls. Mandated by state laws, the proliferation of primaries also enlarged voter participation in Republican nominations.

The new rules shifted the balance of power over the nomination. In the first post-reform contest in 1972, the favourite of the party hierarchy, Senator Edmund Muskie, performed disappointingly in early primaries and withdrew. The anti-war Senator George McGovern showed surprising strength in early contests and went on to win the nomination. He triumphed despite meagre support from party leaders. He also espoused policy positions which placed him to the left of most Democratic identifiers.

Subsequent commissions in the 1970s (known after their respective chairs as Mikulski and Winograd) rewrote the selection rules while preserving the participatory process inaugurated in 1972. Quotas were replaced by less rigid affirmative action programmes but other changes were consistent with McGovern-Fraser objectives. For example, the links between voter preferences and the allocation of delegates were tightened. Winner-take-all primaries were abolished, proportional representation in delegates adopted and candidates given a veto over the seating of national convention delegates elected in their name (to guarantee their faithfulness). Though no commission advocated it, presidential primaries continued to multiply. For the 1980 Democratic contest there were thirty-five states holding primaries accounting for three-quarters of the delegates.

In the 1980s the reaction against the voter-dominated nominating process began to take institutional form. The Hunt Commission which devised the rules for 1984, reintroduced *ex-officio* 'super-delegates' consisting of public and party officials without binding commitments to candidates. Presidential primaries also declined. There were twenty-nine in the 1984 Democratic contest, accounting for 53 per cent of all delegates, though the number rose again in 1988.

But the dynamics of post-reform contests persisted. Victories in primaries were decisive in winning the nomination. Nominees such as Mondale in 1984 and Bush in 1988 were supported by party leaders but they owed their nominations to winning in primaries. Without such primary successes, party leaders' support would have been insufficient to win the nomination.

Showing strength unpredicted by media commentators in early contests, such as the Iowa caucuses or the New Hampshire primary, elevated previously obscure candidates into contenders for the nomination. As Gary Hart demonstrated in 1984, early successes translated into 'momentum' to generate media attention, a surge in popularity, financial contributions and a campaign workforce which strengthened the candidate for later contests. Neither policy positions more extreme than those of party identifiers nor apparent unelectability disbarred candidates from becoming serious contenders provided they won primaries, as Jesse Jackson did in both 1984 and 1988.

The primaries act as a winnowing process. Weak performers fail to generate momentum and withdraw. One candidate capitalizes on the shrinking field to capture a majority of delegates in advance of the convention. Despite large fields at the outset, the conventions can be uncontested. The experiment with Democratic super-delegates (the Republicans have no equivalent) has yet to have a decisive influence on the outcome. In both 1984 and 1988 their votes at the convention only inflated delegate majorities that the nominee established in the primaries.

Since 1972 presidential nominations have become more like those for other offices. Primaries now decide nominations. There are differences in that the presidential contest consists of a series of primaries and a convention still has the formal responsibility for selecting the nominee. But now from the presidency downwards nominations are decided by voters not party organizations.

National conventions still perform several useful functions for the parties. They serve as a pre-election rally for party activists. They can heal divisions in the party by compromises over the platform and vice presidential nomination. Television coverage captures national attention for the party and the nominees, helping to build support for the election. But the presidential nomination is ratified rather than decided by the convention (Shafer 1988).

THE IMPACT OF THE PRIMARY

Primaries are not unique to the US but they are longer established and more widespread than in any other western democracy. They have been formative influences in shaping the modern American parties and the party system. Among the effects of primaries are the following five results.

Weak party organization

Excepting the last redoubts of nomination by convention, party organizations have lost the control of the selection of candidates for public office, one of the principal functions of parties. Lacking an important function to perform, the American party has fewer incentives to attract activists than its counterparts elsewhere. The party organization is also attenuated by its lack of influence over elected officials. Candidates are compelled to create personal organizations to contest primaries, a forerunner of independent campaigns in the general election.

Weak party discipline and cohesion

Primaries deprive the party organizations of the resources to bind elected officials to party programmes. Lacking control over selection and de-selection, local party officials have no means for disciplining elected representatives. Moreover, a selection method both decentralized and voter-dominated obstructs the formation of cohesive national parties. The national party organization lacks controls over local electorates to produce conformity among candidates. Attempts to centralize influence over primaries – as in President Roosevelt's attempted purge of hostile congressional Democrats in 1938 – have been conspicuous failures. Nor is the party able to defend itself against unwanted maverick candidates who succeed in capturing the party label. When the former Ku Klux Klan leader, David Duke, was nominated and elected as a Republican to the Louisiana state legislature in 1989 he was denounced by the national party chairman, Lee Atwater. Yet the party organization was powerless to deny Duke the Republican title. Still disowned by the party, Duke in 1990 was the leading Republican in Louisiana's non-partisan primary for a US Senate seat.

Internal disunity

Primaries virtually compel the parties to 'wash their dirty linen in public'. Candidates of the same party are forced to differentiate themselves from each other. They also have to develop personal followings to mount a campaign. Unifying the party for the general election can be hindered by the infighting for the nomination. The academic literature on the electoral consequences of 'divisive' primaries (defined by some numerical standard of closeness of the result) is inconclusive (see Miller *et al.* 1988 for references). Most studies suggest that divisive primaries are an electoral handicap but all of these works are flawed by the absence of any pre-primary measure of internal party disunity. The deficiencies of the literature notwithstanding, many practising politicians see divisive primaries as damaging.

Reduction in inter-party competition

Primaries provide for competition within parties but diminish the potential for contests between them (see Chapter Five). The substitution of the primary for the convention made electorally dominant parties more permeable. Potential candidates, activists and voters had heightened opportunities to penetrate the majority party to secure their objectives rather than working through the minority or third parties. By channelling resources into the majority party others are depleted, accentuating their electoral disadvantages. For example, the Republican party in southern states frequently struggles to find candidates to warrant primary contests.

In so doing, Republicans forego the opportunities for party building which flow from the interest generated by media coverage, and the identification of sympathetic voters via registration or declarations to obtain the primary ballot. New parties are discouraged by the permeability of those already established. Unsurprisingly, the inception of primaries coincided with both the spread of one-party areas, and the decline of third-party voting.

Control over nominations by unrepresentative minorities

Turnouts in primaries are small, often attracting a half to a quarter of the general election vote. The exception to this standard is the south where the Democratic primaries, usually the decisive phase of the electoral process, once produced higher turnouts than in the general election (Jewell and Olson 1978). This is now changing in contests for major offices, reflecting the growing strength of the Republican party but it remains the norm for lower profile elections. Primary voters are an unrepresentative sample of the electorate and party identifiers. They tend to be disproportionately middle class and politically aware. They are also stronger party identifiers on average, different from voters in their ideological, issue and candidate preferences. This can produce nominees unrepresentative of their party's voters but the evidence is inconsistent (Key 1956, Ranney 1968, 1972, De Nitto and Smithers 1972, Kritzer 1977, Lengle 1981). In part, the inconsistency may reflect the variations in primary electorates. It seems likely that in some cases there are unrepresentative electorates and nominees but the paucity of studies precludes an accurate estimate of their frequency.

Primaries have enormous potential to promote intra-party democracy but much of it remains to be realized. Turnouts are often low and on occasions unrepresentative. Many primaries are uncontested. For example, in 1978 less than half of major party congressional primaries produced contests. Incumbent advantages in name recognition, popularity and finance are often so great as to deter all opposition. Close results are few and the unseating of incumbents rare. In 1990 only one out of the 407 congressional incumbents seeking renomination was defeated. However, there have been occasional primary upsets of senior politicians in Congress from one-party areas where the general election posed no threat. Victims of primary defeats include William Fulbright, chairman of the Senate Foreign Relations Committee, and Ed Koch, three-term mayor of New York City.

FINANCING CAMPAIGNS

American elections are vastly expensive. Some $458 million was spent in the elections for Congress in 1988. The large size of constituencies, the legal entitlement to buy highly expensive television advertising and the sophisticated, costly techniques of modern campaigns account for their expense. Spending has increased in each recent successive election and the rate of increase usually far outpaces inflation.

Parties in the US account for only a minority of the total money raising and spending effort in elections. The principal recipients of contributions are the individual candidates. The major sources of funds are individual contributors and political action committees alias PACs, usually the fund-raising units of interest groups (see Table 7.2). For both presidential elections and nominations the federal government also provides funds. Without reliable historical information it is impossible to date when candidates rather than parties became the main recipients of funds. But fund-raising organizations for individual candidates were well developed by at least the 1950s (Heard 1960).

Table 7.2 Sources of contributions to major party candidates for Congress, 1987–8(%)

Source	Contest	
	Senate	House
Individuals	64.2	46.8
PACs	23.2	36.7
Parties	0.6	0.8
Candidates	3.4	1.7
Loans to candidates	4.1	8.3
Other (interest, transfers, other loans)	4.5	5.7

Source: Statistical Abstract of the United States, 1990 (Washington, D.C.: Bureau of the Census, 1990).

The decline of party as a source of campaign funds was accentuated by the transformation of federal election finance law in the 1970s. The Federal Election Campaign Act (FECA) of 1971 (and the subsequent amendments of 1974, 1976, 1978, 1979) was stimulated by growing concern over the cost of elections and corruption related to the funding of campaigns. Remedies were sought in the public disclosure and legal limitation of contributions and expenditures. The new legislation had two major negative effects on parties.

Limits on party contributions to candidates

The restrictions on contributions applied to the parties. For Senate contests the national party (i. e. national committee and senate campaign committee) could contribute a maximum of $27,500 to candidates. State parties could contribute an additional $10,000. In House contests the national party was limited to a $20,000 contribution. State (or local) parties were able to donate a further $10,000. These sums fall far short of the cost of the average competitive campaign.

Ceilings on contributions also apply to individual donors and political action committees. Following the Supreme Court's decision in *Buckley* v. *Valeo* in 1976 the one source of funding which is unlimited is that of the candidates themselves. Wealthy candidates can thus escape dependence on any outside sources of funds including parties.

Growth of non-party sources of funds

FECA created one new source of campaign funds, the federal government (only for presidential contests), while promoting an existing one, the political action committee. Both are non-party sources of funds. Their development accelerated the relative decline of party election financing.

Candidates for major party presidential nominations qualify for federal government matching funds if they first raise $5,000 in individual donations of under $250 in each of twenty states. Thereafter all subsequent individual donations under $250 are matched (doubled up) by the federal government if the candidate applies for them. Candidates who accept federal funds are subject to overall expenditure limits on their campaigns (approximately $27 million in 1988) and in individual states. Since they first became available only John Connally in 1980 qualified but did not apply for matching funds, thereby avoiding the spending limits.

For presidential elections the major party candidates can obtain federal funds prior to the campaign. In 1988 each candidate received approximately $47 million. Recipients are prohibited from accepting or spending funds from other sources. So far, all major party candidates have used federal funding.

Minor party candidates who obtain at least 5 per cent of the vote qualify for federal funding after the election. The amount they receive is based on a sliding scale depending on their share of the vote. John Anderson, the third-party candidate who won 7 per cent of the vote in 1980, was reimbursed 29 per cent of the $14.4 million he spent.

Retrospective funding of minor candidates discriminates in favour of major-party nominees. They can rely exclusively on federal finance obviating the need for a fund-raising effort. In contrast, minor candidates' campaigns are side-tracked into the quest for money. Moreover, major-party candidates have the funds in advance, enabling them to plan their budgets and pay for services.

But this discrimination in funding, it should be noted, is between *candidates*. It is candidates, not parties, that receive funds. For both the nomination and election stages FECA promotes the financial independence of candidates from parties. At the nomination stage, party contributions are ineligible for matching, which diminishes their attractiveness compared to individual donations. At the general election stage, party contributions are impermissible if federal funds are accepted.

Political action committees burgeoned following FECA because they could provide five times more assistance to candidates ($5,000) than individuals. Business corporations, which previously encouraged individual shareholders and employees to make donation, now had incentives to engage in collective fund raising efforts to maximize their political influence. Formerly the preserve of trade unions, business and ideological PACs proliferated after FECA. By the 1980s PACs were second to individuals as sources of funds in elections to Congress.

FECA had an immediate depressing effect on the party share of campaign donations. In 1972, the last federal election before the amendments relevant to parties came into effect and the first for which detailed data are available, candidates received 17 per cent of their funds from parties. In 1974 4 per cent came from this source (Sabato 1981, Jacobson 1984). Though the party contribution recovered in the later 1970s, it declined again in the 1980s. Individuals and PACs bore the brunt of rising campaign spending.

There are some respects in which FECA gives parties a preferred status in campaign finance. They can make larger donations than individuals or PACs. They can receive larger donations from individuals and PACs than candidates ($20,000 and $15,000 respectively per year). They can also undertake co-ordinated expenditures on behalf of candidates. For example, parties can finance opinion polls supplying candidates with the results. In 1984 co-ordinated expenditures of over $18 million were made in elections for Congress. State and local parties can spend unlimited amounts on specified activities including registration, and get-out-the-vote drives in presidential elections. Such 'soft money' expenditures were worth $80 million in 1988.

Parties pursued more vigorous fund-raising efforts after FECA. In competing for funds, the Republican party has been by far the more successful, building on a capability established in the 1960s. Modern fund-raising techniques involving computers and postal solicitations (direct mail) have been utilized. By 1980 the Republican National Committee claimed 1.2 million contributors. Income exceeded $77 million that year. Similar methods were used by the Republican congressional campaign committees, that is the National Republican Senatorial Committee and National Republican Congressional Committee. In 1980 the two committees had a combined income of more than $40 million.

The Democrats' fund raising has been less successful. Strapped by debts originating from the 1968 campaign, the Democratic National Committee (DNC) was cutting its budgets in the 1970s. Its financial weakness became a vicious circle. Lacking capital, it could not finance modern fund-raising methods. Lacking such techniques, it could not generate capital. Some progress was made at the end of the 1970s, relying on a small pool of large contributions (several thousand dollars). In 1980 the Democratic National Committee's income of $15.4 million was a fifth of its Republican counterpart. The congressional campaign committees lagged even further behind the opposition. Attempts to generate a large pool of donors on the Republican model were made in the 1980s. By 1984 the DNC had widened its pool of donors, claiming a total of 400,000 contributors.

The wealth of the national Republican party is used to support candidates running for office. They receive both financial contributions and services. In both the Republicans far outspend the Democrats. In 1982 in open seats in Congress (with no running incumbent), where the potential for gains is greatest, Republican House candidates received an average assistance worth $42,935. Their Senate equivalents received $693,075. The corresponding figures for Democrats were $5,324 and $170,032 respectively. Over three-quarters of co-ordinated expenditures that year were made by the Republican party. Analysis of the congressional results suggest that the targeting of resources where seats were in danger limited Republican losses (Jacobson 1985–6).

State parties have also benefited from the wealth of the national parties. Beginning in 1978 the RNC attempted to improve the electoral performance of the Republican party in the states. The immediate aim was to increase representation in state legislatures prior to their redrawing of constituency boundaries (reapportionment) after the 1980 Census. The long-term objective was to overcome the status of minority party dating from the New Deal realignment. Assistance also comes in the form of services such as the secondment of RNC staff to state parties. By the late 1980s both national parties were also raising substantial sums of 'soft money' – the legally unlimited contributions for state parties to finance activities such as voter registration and get-out-the-vote drives. In 1988 the national committees channelled some $10 million of soft money to state parties, the previously penurious DNC accounting for more than three-quarters of the total. This top–down mode of assistance reverses the former intra-party flow of aid. In the past state and local parties channelled resources, including money, to the impoverished national committees to conduct presidential campaigns.

National party structures also liaise with PACs. The former have information, the latter money. PACs are solicited to provide funds. They are are provided with information such as the policy stances of candidates sympathetic to their interests. Close contests are identified and contributions encouraged where additional funds might have a decisive impact on the outcome. PACs are also encouraged to provide funds to the parties. In 1981–2 a third of all multi-candidate PACs made donations to the parties. Though there is collaboration between PACs and parties their interests are not coterminous. For example, some PACs donate to candidates from both parties.

Information about the financial condition of sub-national party organizations is sparse. One survey of county parties found that only a quarter had regular annual budgets. Two-thirds did engage in fund-raising efforts for election campaigns, and made contributions to candidates. A survey of state parties found that their budgets averaged $340,000, the range extending from the richest at $2.5 million to the poorest with $14,000. Most state parties make contributions to candidates though few provide assistance with fund raising. In the late 1970s the average state party contributed a total of over $135,000 to candidates (Cotter *et al.* 1984). In state, as in congressional contests, parties account for a minority of candidates' funds. A survey of a sample of states found the proportion of contributions made to candidates by parties varied between 31 per cent for Wisconsin statewide contests to 1 per cent for state legislative elections in Missouri. Individuals and PACs were usually larger sources of funding than parties.

Public subsidies are available for some state elections. Twenty states have some form of public financing of campaigns. Some states channel funds to parties, others make the donations to individual candidates. States which direct funds to parties include Iowa, Rhode Island, North Carolina and Oregon. The uses that parties make of public funds vary between the states, in part a consequence of the differing legal regulations. In Rhode Island funds are used for maintaining a party headquarters and paying staff. In Oregon funds are passed on to county-level parties where they are used to fund organization and individual candidates. In Iowa funds have been channelled to candidates for federal elections (Jones 1984).

THE CAMPAIGN

On several occasions in this chapter we have noted the forces stimulating the development of candidate organizations separate from parties. Though this trend has gained strength in recent years it is not new. A round-table discussion of members of Congress in the late 1950s evoked the widely endorsed comment: 'If we depended on the party organization to get elected none of us would be here' (Clapp 1963: 397). Subsequent developments have enhanced candidates' independence from parties. The parties' control over resources has diminished while that of non-party structures has grown. The parties' electioneering capabilities have suffered from the decline in activists (discussed in Chapter Six). The spread of television has facilitated the transmission of campaign information by means other than party organization. Innovations in campaign technique such as direct mail and television advertising have led to the commercialization of these services. Freelance professionals are now an alternative to parties in the provision of campaign services.

Incumbents have used office to promote their personal electoral security, diminishing their dependence upon parties. In Congress and many state legislatures the number of staff assistants to members have proliferated since the 1950s. The scope of constituent casework, press relations, monitoring of constituency opinion and other services has expanded in consequence. Members of Congress have increased the number of trips they make to their districts paid by public funds. These innovations in incumbent resources have facilitated 'permanent campaigns' in which name recognition and a favourable image are developed to such a degree that re-election is almost inevitable (Fiorina 1977).

Professional expertise and technology in campaigns originated in the inter-war period. Radio advertising was first employed in the 1928 presidential election. It spread to state contests in the east in the early 1930s. A public relations firm, Whittaker and Baxter, later to become the first commercial political consultancy, was employed on the Republican side in the 1934 California gubernatorial campaign. George Gallup conducted probably the first opinion poll for a candidate, his mother-in-law, in Iowa in 1932 (Salmore and Salmore 1985).

Further innovations took place in the post-war years, most conspicuously in presidential contests. Eisenhower's 1952 campaign was informed by public relations techniques. A television advisor was employed, and television advertising concentrated in critical areas. A personal organization mounted John Kennedy's bid for the 1960 Democratic nomination. Relatives, friends and long-term political associates comprised most of the leading figures in the campaign organization. Pollster Louis Harris was contracted to the campaign.

In 1968 Nixon's personal organization conducted both the nomination and election campaigns. The latter effectively excluded the Republican National Committee. Professionals from television and advertising worked to fashion the image of a new Nixon to displace the negative associations of the old (McGinniss 1969). Four years later the bloated Committee for the Re-election of the President (CREEP) conducted Nixon's campaign. Concerned only with the presidential contest, the CREEP empire included fund raising, polling and get-out-the-vote operations.

Commercialization of campaign services spread rapidly in contests below the presidential level in the 1960s. In 1962 professional consultants were used in 168 campaigns, rising to 658 in 1968 (Rosebloom 1973). Reliance on professional expertise and technology freed candidates from dependence on labour-intensive party campaigns. New style campaign methods possessed a sophistication and apparent effectiveness unmatched by parties. For example, opinion polls enabled candidates to ascertain their prospects of victory, measure voters' reactions to them and test the response to various campaign themes with more precision than the impressionistic assessments of local party officials. Computerized lists of detailed voter profiles delivered a more precise pool of likely supporters and financial donors than a canvass. Television advertising could deliver a more potent message to a wider audience than leaflets or public meetings.

None of the new campaign services are necessarily anti-party. For example, it was the Republican party that used a television advisor in the 1952 campaign. In many other western democracies these techniques have been appropriated by parties, as in the contracting of polling organizations to the national headquarters of various British parties. In the US, however, the new campaign techniques have largely developed around candidates rather than parties. In part, they developed because they offered apparently more effective electioneering methods than parties could provide (Ware 1985). Additionally, parties were slow or financially incapable of utilizing the new methods. For candidates there was an additional attraction to adopting the new techniques – they freed them from obligations to parties.

Capital-intensive campaigning contributed to the escalating cost of elections. For example, between 1976 and 1984 spending on elections rose at three times the rate of inflation. Cost is one of the most serious limitations on the use of the new techniques. Many candidates cannot afford them. They are most widely used in the most costly elections – but they are not exclusive to them. A sample of 1978 House candidates found that advertising media specialists were the most frequently employed type of consultant but even they featured in only a minority of campaigns. Incumbents were less dependent upon consultants than challengers. The former rely more upon full-time campaign employees (Goldenberg and Traugott 1984). It is probable that these employees are drawn from the members' congressional staff, exemplifying the use of incumbent resources to electoral advantage.

The relative infrequency of consultants, even in the high cost House contests, is an indicator of the nature of most candidate organizations. They centre on friends, relatives and associates. They are more personal than professional coalitions. Note, for example, the prominence even in presidential campaigns of the candidates' long-term allies. Carter's campaigns featured a 'Georgia Mafia' including Hamilton Jordan and Jody Powell whose association with the candidate originated during his time in state politics. Similarly, Reagan's campaign staff included associates from his governorship in California, including Edwin Meese, Michael Deaver and Lyn Nofziger.

Candidate-centred organizations often run non- or even anti-partisan campaigns. Neither George McGovern nor Jimmy Carter named the party whose nomination they were seeking when they announced their presidential candidacies in the 1970s. These statements made no reference to heroes of the Democratic past nor the party's need to win the election. Both campaigned against a Washington Establishment of which their own party was a part through its control of Congress.

Aloofness from party connections is also evident in congressional campaigns. Only a quarter of the 1978 House candidate sample rated partisan affiliation as an important theme in their campaign materials. The candidates' characteristics, issues and constituency service were given greater prominence. Half of Republican incumbents and a third of their Democratic counterparts never mentioned their party affiliation (Goldenberg and Traugott 1984).

Despite the development of candidate organizations, parties continue to be involved in electioneering. Elections remain the centre of party activity in many locales. County parties, for example, distribute literature, posters and signs, place newspaper advertisements, issue press releases and seek to co-ordinate candidate campaigns in their area. Revealingly, the newer campaign methods such as polling, television and radio advertisements are rarely utilized by county parties. Roughly half of the state parties offer assistance to candidates in the form of research, polling and literature distribution. Many more provide seminars on campaign techniques (Cotter *et al.* 1984).

Extensive though local party activity is in campaigns, its impact is modest. The 1978 House candidate survey found that a majority (52 per cent of incumbents, 68 per cent of challengers) rated party organization as a somewhat important or important impact on the vote (Goldenberg and Traugott 1984). A House survey in 1984 found state and local parties given a low rating by candidates for most aspects of campaigning. They were not seen as making significant contributions to campaign management, issue development, mass media advertising and gauging local opinion. Where local parties were significant was in registration, get-out-the-vote efforts and the recruitment of volunteers. Republican organizations enjoyed a near monopoly of the highest ratings (Herrnson 1986).

The perceived strength of local party organizations conditions the nature of the campaigns that candidates run. Where 1978 House campaign managers saw local parties as weak, they devoted three-quarters of the budget to mass media. Where local parties were viewed as strong, mass media accounted for 54 per cent of the campaign budget (Wattenberg 1986).

In the last decade national party structures have assumed an unprecedented degree of involvement in campaigns below the presidential level. The Republicans have shown the greater innovativeness in this sphere. Their funding of candidates has already been mentioned. They also provided many 'in kind' services to candidates. Where parties were ascribed a significant role in the 1984 House campaign survey it was commonly Republican national structures that earned this description (Herrnson 1986).

Reconciling parties with commercial consultants, the Republican national party committees buy blocks of campaign services from campaign professionals such as pollsters. These services are then given to chosen candidates as a co-ordinated expenditure or sold at below the market rate. The RNC also has its own staff which provide campaign expertise. For example, guidance is given on the conduct of polls. Interviewers are trained, data interpreted and recommendations made for campaign strategy. Both the RNC and the National Republican Congressional Committee have prepared television advertisements for candidates. Scripts have been written, filmed, edited and prepared for transmission. The RNC has also compiled a databank of voting records and population characteristics for the entire country. This information is used to advise candidates and parties on the targeting of registration, get-out-the-vote and candidate recruitment efforts.

The Republicans have also used 'generic advertising' to promote the entire party ticket. In 1980 (drawing on the example of the British Conservatives' 1979 campaign) the RNC sought to generate a more positive image for the party. Organized around the slogan 'Vote Republican. Time for a Change', media advertising worth $9.4 million dollars was broadcast. The Republican successes below presidential level may indicate that this campaign worked to the advantage of the party's candidates throughout the ticket. Lacking both staff and funds, the efforts of the national Democratic party have been insubstantial in comparison. Imitation of the Republican been attempted but shortage of resources has produced a more modest performance. For instance, the DNC electoral data set consisted in 1980 of past results from parts of only twenty states.

Heightened national party involvement in elections has been read as a sign of party rejuvenation. In this view, the national structures are recapturing functions previously lost by state and local organizations to re-establish a role for parties in the electoral process (Kayden and Maye 1985). But this view should be treated with caution. It is yet to be shown that heightened activity translates into long-term influence. National party activity has been a lopsided development, concentrated on the Republican side. Moreover, the electoral revival of the Republican party in the early 1980s, possibly attributable to heightened national party activity, proved short-lived. The party lost control of the Senate and several state legislatures in 1986, confirming its minority status below presidential level.

Other evidence, such as the progressive decline of party contributions as a proportion of candidate income, suggests that some negative trends for parties continue. Presidential primaries revived in number in 1988 and that year the Democrats opted to reduce the complement of super-delegates for the 1992 national convention. The announcement that parties are alive and well in the electoral process may yet be exaggerated.

CONCLUSION

In this chapter we have discussed the attenuated role of parties in the electoral process. Most candidates are not recruited by parties. Nor are most candidates selected by parties. Nominations, including the presidential level, are largely voter-dominated. Most party organizations make no concerted effort to influence the nominating process. In some jurisdictions where influence is attempted, its impact is less decisive than it was. Party contributions are a negligible proportion of candidates' income. The financial influence of parties is enlarged beyond contributions by co-ordinated expenditures and the 1988 election saw a vast increase in the spending of 'soft money'.

Parties are still active in election campaigns. They continue to perform many of their traditional functions. But these functions are also performed by candidate organizations, and local parties rarely use the newer style campaign techniques.

National party structures are involved in sub-presidential campaigns to an unprecedented degree. Particularly on the Republican side, they provide services to candidates and the sub-national parties. Whether heightened national activity presages a revival of party electoral influence is still to be demonstrated.

8 Party and voters

From the early years of the republic parties became a way of connecting voters to government. In so doing they provided regularized mechanisms through which public opinion has permeated and energized the constitutional system. Elections, in particular, have blown draughts of public opinion into the institutions of government, bringing fresh, and fresh combinations of, principles and interests to bear on decision-making processes. Periodically, in critical election eras, these draughts have been of storm force, redistributing influence between and within the parties. More often election results have been light breezes which have only slightly disturbed the political order.

In this chapter we are concerned with the ways contemporary parties structure the electoral world for voters. In our analysis we are sensitive to the distinctive properties of the contemporary era, which condition the manner in which the parties perform their electoral roles and which distinguish that performance from the past. First, the prolonged absence of a critical realignment has deprived the parties of sharpness in the principles and interests which they represent and which distinguish them from each other. Secondly, and in part the explanation for the foregoing, periodic reforms have circumscribed the capacity of today's parties to shape the electoral order as thoroughly as their predecessors did. None the less the parties continue to shape voters' perception of the political world and their behaviour in it. It is this influence that we examine in this chapter. We begin by assessing the degree of voters' attachment to parties, employing the concept of party identification (partisanship). Secondly, we examine the impact of parties on two phases of electoral participation, registration and voting. We then assess the influence of party on the vote in presidential and congressional elections. Finally, we depict the social and geographical bases of the two parties.

PARTY IDENTIFICATION

Support for the two parties is pervasive among the American public. Close

Table 8.1 Party identification in the United States, 1952–88 (in percentages)

	1952	1956	1960	1964	1968	1972	1976	1980	1984	1988
Strong Democrats	22	21	20	27	20	15	15	18	17	17
Weak Democrats	25	23	25	25	25	26	25	23	20	18
Leaning Democratic	10	6	6	9	10	11	12	11	11	12
Independent	6	9	10	8	11	13	15	13	11	11
Leaning Republican	7	8	7	6	9	10	10	10	12	13
Weak Republicans	14	14	14	14	15	13	14	14	15	14
Strong Republicans	14	15	16	11	10	10	9	9	12	14
Apolitical, don't knows	3	4	2	1	1	1	1	2	2	2
Total	101	100	100	100	101	99	100	100	100	101

Source: Harold W. Stanley and Richard G. Niemi (1989) *Vital Statistics on American Politics* (Washington, DC: Congressional Quarterly Press)

to 90 per cent of the electorate think of themselves as either Republicans or Democrats. These affiliations extend into periods between elections suggesting that they involve a commitment more than simply current voting preference. These affiliations are commonly known as party identification, a psychological attachment entailing some sense of belonging. Identifiers are attracted to a party and have a positive view of it. First formulated at the University of Michigan in the 1950s, party identification is sub-divided by degrees of attachment. Identifiers are classed as strong, weak or leaning (or independent) in their affiliation (Campbell *et al.* 1960). Non-identifiers are classed as independents, apoliticals or don't knows (Table 8.1). The great bulk of non-identifiers are the independents. Subsequently the term independent has had two interpretations. Either it is used restrictively to mean independent, non-identifiers (sometimes known as pure or independent independents). Alternatively, it has had a broader interpretation embracing the pure independents plus the leaning (or independent) Republicans and Democrats. In this study we adopt the former, restrictive usage.

In the Michigan model party identification derived from childhood socialization. Parental influence was profound. Most identifiers were attracted to the party their parents supported. Where a parent was politically active the socializing experience was particularly powerful. Households without a consistent partisan affiliation were more likely to produce a new generation of independents than where parents were unchanging in their support of a party.

In this view partisanship was durable. It developed before voting age was attained and lasted for life. Few voters (around 20 per cent) reported ever having altered their party identification, seeming to confirm the formative influence of early socialization. Changes were attributable to either personal of social stimuli. The former were changes in individual circumstances such as marital status or occupation. New environments generated new partisan stimuli. Such stimuli create pressures for conformity, resulting in changes in partisanship. Social stimuli refer to society-wide experiences such as civil war and economic depression. Such experiences temporarily give politics a salience and intensity that it usually lacks for most voters. Amidst social upheaval the parties are re-evaluated, old loyalties shaken and new ones forged.

More recent studies have challenged the Michigan formulation of the stability and sources of party identification. Changes over time in the direction, volume and strength of party identification indicate considerable fluidity. Fluctuations around elections suggest a responsiveness to the stimuli generated by a particular campaign. For example, landslide losses in the presidential contests were accompanied by reductions in Republican identifiers in 1964 and Democrats in 1972. Panel studies (where the same individuals are interviewed at several points in time) reveal a degree of fluidity unexpected from voters' claims to constancy. Approximately one voter in six changed partisanship between consecutive elections 1956–58–60. Most switches were between a party and independence rather than between parties. Even among voters who retained their loyalty to the same party there was considerable fluidity in the strength of their attachment (Dreyer 1973).

Evidence of fluctuations in adult partisanship prompted a re-evaluation of its sources. In the Michigan formulation the sources of identification were largely non-political. Revisionist theories argued that party identification is responsive to short-term, political influences. But revisionists dispute what the relevant influences are. For some, issues are decisive. Voters attracted by the policy stances adopted in a particular presidential campaign forge an attachment to the party which persists (Jackson 1975, Franklin and Jackson 1983).

A second view emphasizes the primacy of attractive candidates in fostering identification with parties (Page and Jones 1979). A third variant pivots partisanship upon the past performance of parties in office. Socialization is a major source of identification but subject to constant modifications in the light of experience of parties in power (Fiorina 1981). Despite the controversy, party identification is a concept of considerable utility. It is associated with – and this leaves open whether it is cause or effect – a range of voter activities, evaluations and preferences. On several dimensions partisans differ from independents, Republicans from Democrats.

In this chapter we will show the association of partisanship with electoral participation and voting behaviour. But it serves to differentiate voters on other dimensions, such as interest in politics, ideology and evaluations of presidents. Interest in election campaigns and concern about their outcomes is higher for partisans than independents (Campbell *et al.* 1960). Republicans are predominantly conservatives while Democrats are ideologically hete-rogeneous (Levitin and Miller 1979). Partisans are more favourable in their evaluations of presidents of their own parties than of their opponents. Democrats are more positive about Democratic presidents than Republicans and vice versa (Edwards 1984).

ELECTORAL PARTICIPATION

The term 'turnout', as frequently used in the context of US elections, is a calculation of those who vote as against all those who are old enough to do so. For example, the 'turnout' in the 1988 presidential election was 50 per cent (of the total population of voting age). The turnout of registered voters – the standard measure in other countries – was over 70 per cent. In non-presidential years turnout is even lower, barely more than a third of the voting age population vote in mid-term congressional elections. A smaller proportion of the American public votes in elections than their counterparts in nearly any other western democracy. Only in Switzerland do as small a proportion of the adult population vote as in the United States.

In understanding why voting is low, turnout in the US usage is unhelpful for it obscures the huge shortfall in registration. To avoid confusion following from the idiosyncratic use of the term turnout, we employ the phrase electoral participation to cover both registration and voting in elections. Several authors have attributed low electoral participation in the US to the character of the parties. Bland pragmatic parties have been seen as a disincentive to participation. Where parties fail to offer alternative principles voters cannot use elections to determine the shape of future government activity. Where the stakes of elections are low the stimuli to participation are weak (Duverger 1959). A second variant of the low stakes argument is that which connects party support to major social cleavages. In Europe, for example, parties have been electoral expressions of class or religious conflicts. In contrast, US parties are heterogeneous in their support. In the former, where parties represent distinctive, conflicting interests the stakes of elections are high. Moreover, socially distinctive parties provide voting cues which can be utilized by voters low in political interest and information (Powell 1980). A more specific variant of the preceding argument maintains that working-class parties promote participation (Alford 1963, Burnham 1980). Where working-class parties are present there are organized efforts to mobilize the stratum of the electorate most prone to non-participation. Such efforts counteract the deficiencies of information, interest and sense of individual political efficacy that lead to non-participation. Lacking such parties, the US has exceptionally low levels of participation in the lower echelons of the social structure.

The legal impediments to register to vote also depress voting. The US is one of the few western democracies in which the initiative for registration rests with the voter rather than the state. There is no household survey or use of government data such as census returns to compile registers. Neither registration nor voting is required by law. Though there are many variations between the states in registration procedures, most require the voter to appear in person at a registration office to enrol. The inconvenience of time and travel deters some voters from enrolling. Though some states do allow registration by post, the initiative for obtaining the appropriate form usually has to come from the voter. Some registers are closed a month or more before election day, disenfranchising new residents or those voters whose interest is stirred by an election campaign. Registers are periodically purged (updated) by removing the names of those who have failed to vote in recent elections. While this procedure cleanses the rolls of those who have died or moved away it also removes those who have abstained for several elections and remain in other respects qualified to vote. The onerousness of registration requirements contributes to the 30 per cent of American adults who are not enrolled to vote, by far the largest percentage of unregistered voters in the western world.

Parties contribute to the restrictiveness of registration requirements. Registration laws are enacted by partisan governors and legislatures. Efforts to enact uniform, accessible registration procedures have failed in Congress in the face of largely Republican opposition and Democratic disunity. A bill requiring all states to offer voter registration by mail and at the offices of state agencies – specifically, when obtaining driving licences (the 'motor voter' provision) – passed the House with almost unanimous Democratic support and strong Republican opposition in February 1990. But blocking tactics by senate Republicans prevented the bill being enacted.

Restricting the electorate confers advantages differentially between parties. Two types of party are associated with onerous state registration laws – the Democratic-dominated south and the former machine strongholds in the urban-industrialized states of the north. The former was once notorious for an array of devices such as poll taxes, understanding and literacy tests designed to disenfranchise blacks. As late as 1960 only 6 per cent of blacks were registered in Mississippi. In some areas poor whites were disqualified by these methods. For example, in 1960 less than half of white voters were registered in Texas and Virginia. The effect of these devices was to consolidate the hegemony of the Democratc party and of conservative elements within it by suppressing the possibility of inter-racial class alignments. Many of these devices were outlawed by the 1965 Voting Rights Act and the Twenty-Fourth Amendment. But restrictive, if not overtly racially discriminatory laws persist in the south. Registration in the south is below the national average. In every southern state blacks are registered in smaller proportions than whites.

In northern states onerous registration laws were part of the attack conducted against party machines around the end of the nineteenth century. Laws were written to dry up the supply of immigrant voters on which the machines thrived. Registration requirements eliminated some voters who lacked the necessary motivation or knowledge to enrol. But immigrants were more directly the targets of some devices, such as the abolition of votes for aliens and the imposition of literacy tests to qualify for the franchise. It was often Republican-controlled state governments that wrote registration laws whereas most big-city machines were Democratic. That some laws only applied to the large cities within the states is another hint of the target they were aimed at (Erie 1988).

Within the confines of restrictive legislation, parties assist voters to overcome the hurdles to registration. First, partisanship increases the likelihood of registering. Identifiers are more likely to register than independents. Strong partisans are more likely to register than weak ones. Second, party organizations mobilize voters to register. In a survey of county parties approximately half reported undertaking registration drives (Cotter *et al.* 1984). Congressional candidates in the 1984 election rated registration and get-out-the-vote drives one of the most significant election activities undertaken by parties (Herrnson 1986). This involvement in registering voters is a distinctive characteristic of American parties (though not a unique one). In most other western democracies state initiative dominates the registration process. A role for parties is confined to the margins such as securing postal ballots for absentee voters.

Most recent Democratic presidential campaigns have funded registration drives on the premise that the party has most to gain from expanding participation. In 1984 the party aimed to register 10 million new voters. Three million dollars were devoted to the effort by the Democratic National Committee. Subsequent claims of 4 million new registrations are probably exaggerated. Registration efforts were also conspicuous on the Republican side that year. Aimed at counteracting the Democratic and non-party efforts

Table 8.2 Self-reported registration and voting, 1988

Group	A: Registered	B: Voted	Difference (A – B)
Whites	67.9	59.1	8.8
Blacks	64.5	51.5	13.0
Hispanics	35.5	28.8	6.7
Northeast	64.8	57.4	7.4
Midwest	72.5	62.9	9.6
South	65.6	54.5	11.1
West	63.0	55.6	7.4
Employed	67.1	58.4	8.7
Unemployed	50.4	38.6	11.8
Eight years school or less	47.5	36.7	10.8
1–3 years high school	52.8	41.3	11.5
4 years high school	64.6	54.7	9.9
1–3 years college	73.5	64.5	9.0
4 years college	83.1	77.6	5.5
All	66.6	57.4	9.2

Source: *Statistical Abstract of the United States, 1990* (Washington, DC: US Bureau of the Census, 1990)
Note: The use of self-reporting inflates the participation rate

to register blacks, the RNC, state parties and the Reagan-Bush campaign sought to mobilize new registrations. Targeted groups included fundamentalist Christians, Miami-based Cubans (the most conservative fraction of the Hispanic vote), military families, the elderly and white-collar workers. The RNC alone spent $10 million on registration. As with the Democrats, the Republican claim of 4 million new voters registered is suspect. In fact, the combined efforts of over 200 different organizations increased registration by 4 million, under 3 per cent of the electorate.

Voting by those who are registered is also assisted by many party organizations. Around two-thirds of state parties have some form of voter mobilization programme and campaign activity is widespread among county parties (Cotter *et al.* 1984). Party activity can increase participation. Studies have shown that campaign activity by parties makes few converts but enhances the participation rate of existing supporters (Kramer 1970–1).

Low rates of electoral participation are commonly viewed as a Republican advantage. Pro-Democratic groups such as blacks, Hispanics and those with the least formal education are below average in their propensity to participate. They are below average in registration, and often above average in failure to vote when registered (Table 8.2). If more of the Democrats' natural constituency participated, so the conventional wisdom runs, the party's vote would rise.

The actions of partisans in office suggests they subscribe to this wisdom. Congressional Republicans have been in the forefront of blocking efforts to liberalize registration laws. The Nixon and Ford administrations opposed easier registration legislation introduced by Democrats in Congress four times in the 1970s. In 1977 the Carter administration proposed election-day registration but opposition mainly from Republicans saw the measure fail in Congress. As previously mentioned, the 1990 House vote on the 'motor voter' bill divided very strongly along party lines.

Several dissents against the conventional wisdom that high participation is a Democratic asset can be entered. Analysis of registered voters suggests little difference between their partisanship and that of the voting-age population as a whole. The Democratic lead among the entire electorate is similar in magnitude to that among registered voters (Finkel and Scarrow 1985). In the states that register voters by party, Democrats have the advantage in the great majority. In some southern states such as Florida, Republicans are closing the gap in enrolment but the deficit remains considerable.

A projection of the impact of more liberal registration procedures revealed little Democratic gain. Uniform adoption of the then current most accessible procedures would have boosted the vote by 9.1 per cent in 1972. Democratic identifiers would have constituted an additional 0.3 per cent of the vote, a difference statistically equivalent to zero. In no recent presidential election would such a shift in participation have altered the outcome (Rosenstone and Wolfinger 1978).

Analysis of participation levels in past elections suggests no correspondence between high rates and Democratic success. In the period 1932–76 participation in presidential elections was on average slightly higher when Republicans won (Fenton 1979). Democrats have won when participation was low (1948) and lost when it was high (1952).

Those with 'Democratic social traits' cannot be assumed to be supporters of the party. Non-voters are less interested in politics and less concerned about election outcomes than voters. They are less well informed, less partisan and less likely to have political opinions. Given these disparities between voters and non-voters it cannot be assumed that the latter would reproduce the behaviour of the former if they voted. Non-voters are particularly susceptible to short-term influences because they bring fewer predispositions to campaigns. Short-term influences accrue to one side disproportionately in each election but to neither party consistently. Polls of non-voters 1956–76 reveal a lopsided preference for the winning candidate (Petrocik 1981).

But in two elections, 1952 and 1980, non-voters' preferences did differ from voters'. In both years non-voters preferred the Democratic candidates while voters favoured the Republicans. In the former year 100 per cent participation would have narrowed Eisenhower's margin of victory. In the latter, Reagan's lead might have been reversed (Petrocik 1987). In the latter year the Electoral College vote might have been altered sufficiently to re-elect Carter, though the increase in participation necessary to achieve such a change would have been enormous. Such calculations suggest that in some contests, though not all, higher participation would aid Democratic candidates.

VOTING

Partisanship is the single most important guide to voting behaviour. Most voters are party identifiers and cast ballots consistent with their identification. In the 1988 presidential contest 82 per cent of identifiers voted in accordance with their partisanship.

Though most models of voting behaviour include party identification its impact on the vote is disputed. As discussed in the first section of this chapter, scholars differ over whether partisanship is a cause of the vote, an effect or a mix of the two. In the Michigan model partisanship is effectively the cause of the vote (Campbell *et al.* 1960, Goldberg 1966). For others it is closer to being an effect (Page and Jones 1979). For a third set of authors partisanship is a mix of causes and effects of the vote (Franklin and Jackson 1983).

In the Michigan model partisanship has both direct and indirect influences on the vote. In the former partisanship determines many votes. In the latter it colours perceptions of the candidates and issues of particular campaigns. It acts as a 'perceptual screen' providing a more favourable image of the candidates and issues of the voter's preferred party compared to those of the opposition.

In this interpretation party identification is a powerful but not omnipotent influence on the vote. It can be disrupted by the short-term forces of candidates and issues. For example, both contributed to Eisenhower's victories in the 1950s despite the minority status of the Republican party among identifiers. Candidates have been the principal factors disrupting party loyalties as too few voters exhibited knowledge about issues for them to influence many votes (Stokes 1966).

The validity of the Michigan model of voting was undermined by new methods and new evidence. Methodologically, the Michigan model was faulted for under-representing the impact of issues on the vote. In the early studies issues consisted of a set 'menu' prepared by the researchers. There were three criteria to be satisfied to qualify as an issue voter: awareness of the issue, an opinion on it, ability to differentiate the stances of the parties.

Table 8.3 Voting defections by party identifiers, 1952–88 (in percentages of identifiers)

Office					Year					
	1952	1956	1960	1964	1968	1972	1976	1980	1984	1988
House	20	18	20	21	26	25	28	31	30	26
Senate	21	20	21	21	27	31	31	29	28	28
President	23	24	21	21	31	33	26	32	20	18

Source: Martin P. Wattenberg (1990) *The Decline of American Political Parties, 1952–88* (Cambridge, Mass.: Harvard University Press)

Under these conditions there were few issue voters. But using an alternative formulation their numbers multiplied. Where voters could set their own issue agenda – as in answering a question about the most important problem facing the government in Washington – many more exhibited the necessary knowledge and discrimination for issue voting (Re Pass 1971). Criticisms were also entered against a unidirectional (recursive) conception of causation of the Michigan model. Partisanship influenced perceptions of candidates and issues but not vice versa. Subsequent non-recursive models of the vote have shown that partisanship is both cause and effect. Candidates and issues shape partisanship and vice versa (Jackson 1975, Page and Jones 1979).

The new evidence consisted of a decline in partisanship in the electorate. Known as dealignment, this waning of partisanship entails a depletion of the volume and strength of party identification and of its impact on the vote (Burnham 1970, Nie *et al.* 1976). The shrinkage of party identification is evident in Table 8.1 and also in the decline in strong identifiers. Voting defections from partisanship multiplied from the late 1960s, reaching a peak in 1972 when a third of identifiers, almost entirely Democrats, deserted their party's presidential candidate (Table 8.3). The diminished impact of party on the vote is also evident at the aggregate level in election outcomes. From 1968 to 1988 the electorate simultaneously elected a Republican president and Democratic House of Representatives in five contests out of six. Voters were also more likely to be neutral about both parties than in the past. The candidates and issues are now rarely perceived in partisan terms (Wattenberg 1986).

Issues were advanced as a strengthened influence on the vote as partisanship waned. Several authors detected a rise in issue voting but disagreed about its magnitude. In one view, parties became more coherent in their stances in the 1960s. The Democrats were seen as more liberal than the Republicans on a range of issues whereas no such clarity had been evident in the 1950s (Pomper 1972). New issues that had not been salient in the New Deal era, such as the Vietnam War, crime and drugs, concerned voters from the late 1960s onwards. Voters exhibited a greater consistency in their ideological position across issues, and between issue positions and the vote (Nie *et al.* 1976). One interpretation of the 1972 election attributed as much significance to issues as to partisanship to explain the vote (Miller *et al.* 1976).

The magnitude of issue voting varies across elections. Voting on issues is facilitated by candidates who define distinctive positions. The paucity of issue voting in the 1950s is partly attributable to the consensus politics of the period. On subsequent occasions, as in 1968 on policy over the Vietnam War, undifferentiated candidate positions depressed issue voting (Page and Brody 1972).

Retrospective models are another variant of issue voting. Here issues are conceived of as the effects of policy rather than as stances or positions. Voters are concerned about the ends of policy, not the means. Voters employ their past experience, and expectations about the future, which are conditioned by past experience, in deciding how to vote (Fiorina 1981).

Some authors, including a member of the original Michigan school of writers, now attach prime importance to candidate factors as determinants of the vote. Most voters opt for the candidate to whom they feel closest. Evaluations of candidates are conditioned by influences such as their personal characteristics, issues and partisanship. There is a correspondence between voters' issue positions and their preference for a candidate. But candidate factors are at work in producing this consistency. Voters are persuaded by the policy stances of their preferred candidates. They adjust their issue positions to align with their favoured candidate. Alternatively, voters project (infer) that their preferred candidate shares their issue stances. Here it is the perceptions of the candidates' positions that are adjusted to conform to those of the voter. These forces also operate in reverse to distance voters from the issue positions of disfavoured candidates (Markus and Converse 1979, Page and Jones 1979). Where such perceptual adjustments are not made, negative candidate evaluations can overwhelm the impact of issue proximity in influencing the vote. McGovern in 1972 lost votes among his natural issue constituency to doubts over his competence (Popkin *et al* 1976).

Studies of voting behaviour have been concerned overwhelmingly with presidential elections. However, the last decade has seen a growth industry develop in analysis of voting in congressional elections. Two concerns have been central to these studies: explaining individual voting behaviour and accounting for aggregate outcomes in mid-term contests. In the Michigan studies partisanship provided the answer to both questions (Campbell *et al* 1960). Presidential elections are high in salience for voters, stimulating a surge in turnout. The volume of information available in presidential campaigns facilitates the use of voting cues other than partisanship. In addition, participation is swollen by voters lacking attachments to parties. Support for winning presidential candidates extends down the ticket to produce coattail effects of gains for his party in lower level contests.

The subsequent mid-term election is lower in salience, resulting in a lower participation. Information is also in shorter supply. Partisanship is discarded by fewer votes and fewer non-partisans vote. Taking account of variations in participation across different categories of identifiers, mid-term elections are a more accurate representation of the long-term distribution of party loyalties than presidential contests. They approximate more closely the normal vote. The regularity of coattail effects in presidential years and losses by the president's party at mid-term was explained by the surge and decline of participation and partisanship.

Subsequent scholarship has sought to account for the magnitude of losses suffered in mid-term elections. Many authors have emphasized the state of the economy. One found that mid-term losses correlated with the annual change in per capita income and presidential approval ratings in Gallup polls (Tufte 1975). An alternative thesis of economic voting stresses the role of 'strategic politicians' rather than voters to account for mid-term losses. Politicians believe that voters' perceptions of the economy affect their votes. When conditions are favourable to the president's party, incumbents seek re-election, able candidates offer themselves in open seats and contributions are sufficient to provide for adequately funded campaigns. In less favourable circumstances the president's party is debilitated by shortages of funds, experience and quality in candidates. Expectations of electoral strength or weakness become self-fulfilling prophecies (Jacobson and Kernell 1981).

In elections to the House, incumbents enjoy enormous rates of success in winning reelection. In every congressional election year since 1974 the success rate of incumbents has been at least 90 per cent, reaching a peak of over 98 per cent in 1988. Close contests involving incumbents are almost as rare as incumbent defeats. Compared to their opponents, incumbents are well known and well financed, and have records of achievement in constituency service (Mann and Wolfinger 1980, Fiorina 1977). At the level of Congressional districts there are also still numerous one-party areas to give a partisan underpinning to the other electoral advantages of incumbents.

Senate incumbents have fewer advantages. Their policy positions have more visibility, making them objects of greater controversy and facilitating issue voting in Senate elections (Abramowitz 1980). Their opponents are often well known and well financed. Most Senate incumbents who seek reelection succeed but usually at lower rates than their counterparts in the House.

Table 8.4 Demographic groups and party identification, 1984

Group	Democratic lead over Republicans (%)
Northeast	+9
Midwest	+1
South	+14
Mountain west	−7
Pacific	+7
White Protestant	−14
Catholic	+23
Jewish	+42
Under 30	+4
30–59	+8
Over 60	+9
Income percentile	
0–10	+36
11–30	+29
31–60	+6
61–90	0
91–100	−33
White	0
Black	+72
Union	+27
Non-union	+2
Nation	+9

Source: Martin P. Wattenberg (1986) *The Decline of American Political Parties, 1952–84* (Cambridge, Mass. and London: Harvard University Press)

SOCIAL BASES OF PARTY SUPPORT

The pivotal stages in forging connections between social groups and parties have been electoral realignments. Each major realignment reassembled the electorate into demographic blocs uneven in their support for the two parties. Bloc cohesion tended to be greatest in the immediate aftermath of realignment. As the years since the realignment increased so the experience waned in its impact on the electorate. For subsequent generations the realignment era was not the formative experience that it was for those who lived through it (Beck 1974). Over time bonds between demographic blocs and parties loosened, facilitating victories for the minority party of the realignment. Eventually the proportion of the voting-age population without strong party loyalties multiplies until another realignment reshapes the electorate.

Table 8.5 Group support for Democratic candidates in presidential and house elections, 1988 (%)

Group	A: Presidential	B: House	Difference (B − A)
Professional/			
managerial	40	49	9
Other white collar	42	50	8
Blue collar	50	60	10
Unemployed	62	65	3
Union household	57	63	6
Education:			
Less than high school	56	63	7
High school graduate	49	57	8
Some college	42	53	11
College graduate	43	50	7
White	40	50	10
Black	86	88	2
Hispanic	69	76	7
White Protestant	33	44	11
Catholic	47	55	8
Jewish	64	68	4
Northeast	49	54	5
Midwest	47	55	8
South	41	54	13
West	46	49	3

Source: *New York Times*, 10 November 1988 and 8 November 1990

In the prolonged absence of critical realigning elections since the New Deal, dealignment has become the vogue term in the scholarly literature. Where the electorate is undergoing dealignment, depicting the social bases of party support is complicated by their variability. There are fewer party identifiers than there were. Voting across presidential elections is volatile. Split-ticket voting in simultaneous elections is substantial.

We provide three types of evidence to define party support. Table 8.4 records party identification. Table 8.5 shows the vote in presidential and House contests respectively in 1988. Table 8.6 shows the fluctuations in support for the parties' presidential candidates 1952–84 among the blocs that formed their original New Deal coalitions.

Table 8.6 Voting loyalty of New Deal demographic coalition blocs in presidential elections, 1952–88 (%)

| | \multicolumn{7}{c}{Democrats} |
	Poor	Blacks	Union families	Non-Protestants	South and border	Central cities	Nation
1952	47	83	59	57	55	51	44
1956	47	68	55	53	52	55	42
1960	48	72	66	82	52	65	50
1964	69	99	80	75	58	74	61
1968	44	92	51	61	39	58	43
1972	45	86	45	45	36	61	38
1976	67	88	63	57	53	61	50
1980	71	88	50	44	47	69	41
1984	66	81	55	47	44	70	41
1988*	NA	86	57	49	NA	58	46

| | \multicolumn{7}{c}{Republicans} |
	Non-Poor	White	Non-union families	Protestant	North	Non-central cities	Nation
1952	56	57	61	61	57	57	55
1956	59	59	63	62	60	60	57
1960	50	51	55	63	50	52	50
1964	40	42	45	44	38	40	39
1968	44	47	46	49	47	45	43
1972	61	66	63	65	60	63	61
1976	49	52	52	53	49	49	48
1980	52	56	54	54	51	53	51
1984	61	65	63	62	60	61	59
1988*	NA	59	59	60	NA	55	54

Source: Robert Axelrod, 'Presidential Election Coalitions in 1984', *American Political Science Review*, 80 (March 1986); *New York Times*, 10 November, 1988.
*Data for 1988 obtained from different polling organization.

Despite the passage of half a century many residues of the New Deal realignment remain. Democrats continue to have more identifiers than Republicans. The partisan profile of many demographic groups is similar in direction (though not magnitude) to that of the New Deal era. The Democrats continue to draw from the have-nots, the Republicans from the haves, though some groups (such as Jews) have retained their partisan loyalty despite their upward social mobility. Core elements of the Democratic coalitions of the 1930s – the working class, trade unionists, Catholics, Jews, blacks, big city residents, the white south – continue to favour the party in most instances.

The major exception is the white south, which has been predominantly Republican in recent presidential elections, and which began showing slight margins in favour of Republican identification in the mid-1980s. The smaller Republican coalition – the middle class, northern whites, Protestants, non-unionized workers, rural residents – also persists.

As the New Deal alignment has weakened so the cohesiveness of most of the blocs that defined it has eroded. Except for blacks there has been a movement away from the party preference established in the realignment era as evidenced in both identification and voting. Blacks are the exception to the rule, having accentuated their identification and electoral support for the Democratic party. Other social cleavages show a decline in their relevance to partisanship and voting. Class (the manual/non-manual cleavage), religious and regional differences are more muted than they once were. In the presidential elections of the early 1980s class differences in voting remained barely visible.

In many groups majorities are not consistent supporters of either party. Rather, split-ticket voting is sufficiently widespread for majorities of most groups to vote Republican in presidential contests and Democratic in House elections (exemplified in Table 8.5). The result of such divided loyalties is the two-tier or split-level electoral system prevalent since 1968, in which Democrats seemingly always control the House and Republicans usually control the presidency.

A striking feature of this split-ticket voting is its regularity, frequently producing a Republican president and a Democratic House simultaneously, but never *vice versa*. The Democrats' hold on the House is attributable to the benefits of incumbency. Entering elections with vast advantages in visibility, finances and records of constituency services, incumbents (most of whom are Democrats) are almost invincible. The Democrats' hold on the House is also reinforced by the persistence of Republican presidents. For mid-term elections almost inevitably result in losses for the president's party, so Republican efforts to whittle away the Democratic advantage receive a quadrennial setback when seats are lost in non-presidential years and a new cohort of Democratic incumbents is implanted.

Yet in presidential elections Democrats are disadvantaged by internal disunity and, relatedly, by their liberalism on issues. As members of the more socially and ideologically heterogeneous party, the Democrats are more exercised by the task of welding their components together for a national election. Lengthier and more public contests resulting from the post–1968 reforms of the presidential nominating process have aggravated the problems of achieving reconciliation within the party (Polsby 1983). Party unity is less of a problem for the more homogeneous Republicans in national contests, and for Democrats at the level of the Congressional district.

In part Democratic disunity has resulted from policy conflicts, particularly on foreign and soical issues. The intensity of internal controversies over issues like the Vietnam War in 1968 and 1972 produced an irreparably divided party in the election campaign. In addition, the perceived liberalism of Democratic nominees on foreign and social issues has been at odds with the conservative disposition of the electorate, alienating voters, including Democratic identifiers. Republican presidential candidates benefit from more conservative stances, and a more homogeneously conservative party. Whilst many Democratic candidates for Congress are liberals they suffer no handicap because issues have so little prominence in House elections.

Table 8.7 Electoral College coalitions, 1968–88 (1988 Electoral College votes in parentheses)

Party	States carried six times	States carried five times
Republicans	Alaska (3)	Connecticut (8)
	Arizona (7)	Delaware (3)
	California (47)	Florida (21)
	Colorado (8)	Kentucky (9)
	Idaho (4)	Maine (4)
	Illinois (24)	Michigan (20)
	Indiana (12)	Missouri (11)
	Kansas (7)	North Carolina (13)
	Montana (4)	Ohio (23)
	Nebraska (5)	South Carolina (8)
	Nevada (4)	Tennessee (11)
	New Hampshire (4)	
	New Jersey (16)	
	New Mexico (5)	
	North Dakota (3)	
	Oklahoma (8)	
	South Dakota (3)	
	Utah (6)	
	Vermont (3)	
	Virginia (12)	
	Wyoming (3)	
	21 states (187)	11 states (131)
Democrats	District of Columbia (3)	Minnesota (10)
	DC (3)	1 state (10)

ELECTORAL COLLEGE COALITIONS

Stable alignments of the electorate in the past have been accompanied by a durable winning coalition of states in the Electoral College. An example is the combination of the Midwest, West, New England and Pennsylvania in the Republican majorities of the post-Civil War era. This was superseded by the alliance between the south, east and west in the New Deal realignment favouring the Democrats.

Regions such as the south have had a distinct history and culture which has had a formative influence on the political attitudes of its natives. In addition, demographic groups are unevenly distributed across the nation. Concentrations of ethnic, religious, and occupational groups contribute to distinct regional political profiles. For example, the eastern states contributing to the New Deal coalition reflected the numbers of Catholics, Jews, industrial workers, Irish, southern and east European ethnic groups located there.

Table 8.7 reveals the strength of Republican candidates in recent presidential elections. The west and south (1976 excepted when a southerner was the Democratic presidential nominee) have been Republican strongholds at presidential level. Collectively these two regions represent 98 per cent of the vote required to win an Electoral College majority. The Republican benefit from strength in these regions has been magnified by population growth which has increased their representation in the Electoral College and thus their influence over presidential contests. Continued population growth in these regions will enlarge the representation of these Republican strongholds in the Electoral College when seats in Congress are reallocated following the 1990 census.

What is striking about the Republican presidential coalition is the discontinuity with elections for other offices. Of the thirty-two states favouring the Republicans at presidential level, only ten do so in state contests. Twelve of these states lean towards the Democrats in state elections. Whilst there is one reliably Democratic state in presidential contests, there are twenty-seven in state elections (see Table 5.1, p. 81).

CONCLUSION

In this chapter we have reviewed the influence of parties within the electorate. We have noted that this influence has declined since the 1950s which has given rise to discussion of dealignment. But the evidence of change and decline should not obscure the evidence of stability and strength of party in the electorate. The overwhelming majority of the electorate are party identifiers. Partisanship remains a reliable guide to electoral participation and voting behaviour. Dealignment entails, so far, the weakening of partisan forces, not their disappearance.

There are some indications that dealignment was a phase rather than a trend. The 1980s witnessed a resurgence in the volume and strength of party identification. In presidential voting in 1988 the rate of defection from partisanship was the lowest yet recorded. Many traces of the New Deal realignment remain visible. The Democrats retain their plurality in identification and, rather frayed at the edges, the voting blocs on which their strength was founded. These New Deal legacies persist despite the incorporation of successive waves of new voters into the electorate who had no experience of the 1930s. Party systems and loyalties persist long after the historical circumstances that gave rise to them have passed. But if dealignment is a trend the New Deal system will progressively crumble. Whether modern parties possess the political relevance to facilitate a new realignment must be doubted.

9   Party in government

As Chapter Two recorded, the electoral competition between the parties which began in the 1790s has been a contest over which interests and which policies will have primacy in government. Each successive party system witnessed changes in the substance of political conflict and the purposes to which power was put. The transition from one party system to another registered changes not only in what elections were about but also in what government did in their aftermath.

But the capacity of American parties to shape the purposes of government has been limited, particularly in contrast to parliamentary systems. Even in these systems, parties' uses of power face obstacles such as bureaucratic inertia and the inadequacy of forecasting techniques. The American parties have been beset by additional obstacles deriving from the political context of the Constitution, laws and culture. We discuss these obstacles in the opening section of this chapter. Then we establish where parties and partisans do nevertheless feature in American government and the roles that they perform there. Finally we describe the impact of realigning eras in producing the temporary approximation to government by party that is possible in the American context.

OBSTACLES TO PARTY GOVERNMENT

A party affiliation is a prerequisite for obtaining a vast range of positions in American government. In part this follows from the number of offices that are elective. At national level only Congress, the president and vice president are elected but in state and local government a total of over half a million offices are filled by election. Some heads of departments in state and local government, some judges and district attorneys are chosen by voters. Unless these elections are non-partisan, as many for judicial and local government offices are, then these positions are currently a virtual exclusive preserve of the Republican and Democratic parties. Partisanship is also a criterion for selection to many appointive positions in government. Where elected officials appoint say, judges or heads of executive departments, they usually select their fellow partisans.

The range of appointments dependent upon the appropriate partisanship is now smaller than it once was. The Jacksonian era saw the establishment of the spoils system (from the maxim: 'To the victor belong the spoils') which produced a turnover in government personnel whenever power changed hands. Jobs ranging from senior administrative positions to US postmasters and manual workers in state and local government were included in the spoils of victory. Whilst the turnover of personnel was often smaller than was legally permissible, the consequence of the spoils system was that continued employment depended upon the support of the party hierarchy. As late as 1963 the governor of Pennsylvania was entitled to appoint 53,000 of the state's 80,000 employees. In Chicago in the 1970s the Democratic machine was fuelled by control of over 30,000 jobs on the city payroll.

The scope of patronage has been eroded by over a century of reforms extending the career civil service principle (alternatively known as the merit system), giving officials a security of employment independent of partisan control. In addition, the Supreme Court decision in *Elrod* v. *Burns* in 1976, a case involving employees of the Chicago sheriff's department, ruled that officials could not be discharged solely for partisan reasons as this infringed First Amendment protections of freedom of association and political belief. The Court did, however, accept that partisan criteria were permissible in making appointments to policy-making positions. In a subsequent case (*Branti* v. Finkel, 1980) the Court required that evidence of the desirability of partisanship for effective job performance had to be supplied by officials wanting to dismiss existing staff. In 1990 the Court imposed further restrictions on patronage, deciding that it is unconstitutional to hire, promote or transfer most public officials unless "party membership" is "an appropriate requirement" for the job. "To the victor belong only those spoils that may be constitutionally obtained," wrote Justice Brennan for the Court (*Rutan* v. *Republican Party of Illinois*, 1990).

Thus, to date, there has been a substantial penetration of government by partisans in America, extending much farther than in countries such as Britain where norms of neutrality and career service have prevailed in recent times. In this sense party in government is considerable in the US. The European parallels are the Italian parties' colonization of the public sector and the 'party state' in West Germany (Spotts and Wieser 1986, Smith 1986).

Despite the pervasiveness of partisans in office they do not exhibit a disciplined unity around party policy. Thus the widespread presence of partisans provides only limited cohesion and coherence to the work of government. Though the United States has parties in government, the parties do not govern. Party government (alternatively, responsible party government) has had its advocates, particularly among academics, but has never come close to realization in practice (American Political Science Association 1950, Ranney 1954).

For political scientists, party government involves both the staffing of government and the making of policy by parties (Rose 1974, Katz 1986, La Palombara 1987). In Katz's formulation there are three conditions for party government. First, governmental decisions are taken by people chosen in elections conducted along party lines or by individuals appointed and responsible to parties. Second, policy is decided along party lines either within a governing party or between the parties in a coalition. Third, the highest officials are selected by their parties and are responsible to the people through their parties.

Whilst the United States may approximate to the first condition, it fails on the second and third. Policy is often not made along party lines. On many issues there is no party policy. Rather, policy is the outcome of bargains struck between the different branches of government, factional coalitions across party lines and non-party actors such as interest groups and career bureaucrats. Nor are the highest officials chosen by their parties. Rather voters in primary elections decide nominations and, through general elections, the leaders in office.

Many constitutional and legal impediments stand in the way of party government in America. The Constitution fragments power between the federal government and the states, and between the institutions at each level. Devices such as federalism, the separation of powers and the system of checks and balances divide power between institutions and foster conflict between them (Ranney and Kendall 1956).

The federal system contributes to the internal diversity of the parties by fostering their decentralization. The substantial regulation of party affairs is effected largely through state laws. As the foregoing chapters reveal, there are variations between state laws concerning matters such as party structure and methods of nomination. Similarly, election law consists principally of state statutes and all elections, including those for president, respect state boundaries. This patchwork of laws encourages parties to adapt to their state environments. When partisans from different states meet, as in Congress and national conventions, the differences between them become apparent, hindering agreement.

The large volume of elective offices, particularly in local government, encourages the organizing efforts of parties to be concentrated at that level. Even where elections are, by law, non-partisan this may be only a formality which obscures a party role in recruiting candidates and mounting campaigns. Moreover, it is in local and the less prestigious state office contests, where constituencies are smaller and expenditures lower than in federal or gubernatorial elections, that parties continue as important mechanisms for running campaigns.

The volume of elections impedes party government in two ways. First, except in one-party strongholds, elective offices are likely to be shared between the parties. This qualifies the degree to which government can be conducted along party lines. Second, the number of election contests, and their frequency, fosters a preoccupation with electioneering. The immediate needs of election campaigning – recruiting candidates, raising funds, registering voters, campaigning – take precedence. Policy debate and the formulation of programmes are neglected in comparison. Issue development, if it is undertaken at all, is attuned to the demands of a particular election rather than being a continuing process. Issues are developed by individual candidates which impedes collaboration between the victors in office.

The separation of powers obstructs party government by diffusing authority between the executive and legislative branches, and between the two chambers of the latter. The constitutional prohibition on overlapping membership militates against the domination of one branch by the other or their representation of common interests. Checks and balances underwrite the independence of the branches from one another. For example, separate elections work against the domination of all branches by the same interests. This institutional demarcation, in concert with voter dealignment, has made the divided control of federal government between a Republican president and Democratic House of Representatives the contemporary norm. In the states divided control obtains now in a majority of cases and is more common than in the past.

Office-holders' desire to protect institutional prerogatives from intrusion is also underwritten by the different constituencies that elect them. Executives are chosen by larger, more heterogeneous units than legislatures. Legislative upper houses are chosen by larger, more heterogeneous constituencies than lower houses. Thus the electoral pressures operating on the various institutions differ, resulting in differences between them, including which party is in control. Until the 1960s such divided control could also result from the unequal sizes of constituency electorates in state legislatures. In some states constituency boundaries had been drawn before the urbanization of the twentieth century occurred, resulting in the over-representation of rural voters compared to their numbers in state electorates. Outside the south such malapportionment of seats was usually a Republican advantage, precluding Democratic control despite majority support among voters. New York exemplified this tendency, the Democrats often able to win the governorship but not both houses of the legislature. Gerrymandering still continues, often maintaining the majority party's status, but since the Supreme Court decisions of the 1960s (beginning with *Baker* v. *Carr* in 1962) constituencies have to be of approximately equal size, ending the rural domination of urban state legislatures and the divided control it produced.

Even where one party controls both legislative and executive branches, cohesion in government is often lacking. Southern states, once a Democratic monopoly, were poor examples of party government. State Democratic parties were riddled by factional, territorial and personality conflicts, obstructing unity in government.

Fixed terms of office remove a possible device for imposing party discipline in office. Federal and state constitutions decide when elections will be held, not the office-holders. Neither branch can unilaterally force the other to face the electorate. Executives cannot dissolve legislatures nor can the latter terminate the life of the former by a vote of no confidence. Thus threats which may enforce deference and co-operation between branches in parliamentary systems are absent under the separation of powers. Not only are the terms of office fixed, they are also of different durations so they are not elected simultaneously. For example, at federal level the presidential terms last four years, those for representatives for two years. Even where the terms are of the same length the election dates often do not coincide. In the states most governors and legislators now serve four-year terms but they are not chosen on a single election day in many cases. In consequence, unified party control of government is regularly exposed to possible disruption by a new set of elections. For example, since the Civil War, unified control at federal level has been terminated nine times as a consequence of mid-term elections. From 1880 to 1955 all presidential elections produced single party control. It was only mid-term elections that disrupted it. Since 1955, however, presidential election years have produced six instances of divided control, featuring a Republican president and one or both houses of Congress with Democratic majorities (Table 3.1).

All of the above effects tend to produce fractures within parties across the institutions of government. Another set of constitutional and legal influences tend to channel competition into but two major parties. This, inevitably in such a heterogeneous nation, produces great diversity within the parties (for greater detail see Chapter Five).

The Electoral College encourages broad party coalitions by requiring an absolute majority to win the presidency. Presidential electors are almost universally allocated on a winner-take-all principle by the states. To win the presidency parties must manufacture an appeal to win popular majorities in at least a substantial minority of states or all of the large, most heterogeneous states. Under this requirement an appeal to a narrow demographic, ideological or territorial constituency is insufficient to win the presidency.

The Electoral College is a counterweight to federalism in that it deters the internal diversity of America from finding expression in several, regionalized parties. Rather it forces this diversity into a small number of parties. Such inclusiveness precludes ideological rigidity and tight discipline. Only internally permissive parties can enable a broad coalition to survive intact, and only broad coalitions can win the presidency.

Primary elections also encourage convergence within a small number of parties and prevent them from being strictly disciplined. The permeability of the major parties makes them accessible to previously unrepresented political forces thereby discouraging the formation of new competitors. Such accessibility through the primaries removes control by party officials of selection and de-selection as a means of enforcing cohesion around a programme. Other pressures emanating from the primary system, such as the incentives to create candidate organizations and forge individual voter coalitions in order to win nominations, also foster atomized parties.

PARTIES IN THE FEDERAL GOVERNMENT

For all the disruptive influences of laws and the Constitution, parties are a source of linkage between officials in government. The disruptive forces limit the firmness and the extent of cohesion that parties provide but they do not eliminate it. In a system beset by institutional fragmentation, parties are the most consistent source of alliances across and within the branches of government. It is perhaps a testimony to the need for such a link that Madison, who expected there to be no national parties when he was defending the Constitution before its inception, nevertheless was a formative influence upon the creation of the alliance of notables known as the Jeffersonian Republican party which dominated government in the early nineteenth century.

Since that time, parties have provided alliances within and between the legislative, executive and judicial branches of government. The upper echelons of the executive branches are populated by supporters of the president's party. Most appointees share the president's party identification (Brown 1982). Such reliance on common partisanship indicates its value as a source of shared attitudes, concerted action and mutual obligations. By making partisan appointments, presidents pay off old debts, incur new obligations and assemble a team with some common goals.

However, we need to distinguish a reliance on party identification in making appointments from recruiting through party organizations. Whilst the former is the norm, the latter is no longer. Until the 1960s, state and national party organizations were the channels through which entry into the executive branch was reached. Potential appointees established their worthiness by party service (such as working in campaigns, or helping to fund them). Requests for jobs were made through party organizations or needed their approval to qualify for appointment. In the past the number of jobs was large and the chairman of the national committee processed applications at the beginning of a new administration.

Party organizations no longer serve as executive branch recruitment agencies. From Kennedy onwards presidents have established their own personnel departments to staff the administration. The national party committees may be consulted over appointments but they are less likely to be a source of recommendations. In 1977 the Democratic National Committee was critical of the Carter administration for failing even to consult them over appointments.

The altered role of parties in the appointment process is partly a reflection of the growth of independent identifiers, narrowing the range of potential appointees that can be found through party structures. More importantly the change reflects the character of modern presidential appointees. The large number of low status jobs once at the president's disposal have disappeared under the extension of the merit system. Of the appointments under presidential control, now many are in managerial and policy-making positions in the highest ranks of the federal administration: departmental secretaries and their immediate subordinates, ambassadors, heads of agencies and commissions. Such posts often require experience and expertise in sometimes arcane policy areas. The specialists who possess such skills are rarely active in party affairs. Thus party organizations are not able to recruit the calibre of personnel to fill those positions which remain under the president's appointive authority (Mackenzie 1981). Among cabinet-level appointees experience in elective or party office is now rarer than in the past. Managerial experience and policy specialization take precedence over previous service as public or party officials (Polsby 1978).

Common partisanship is one of the few attributes linking together most presidential appointees. The upper echelons of the executive branch have been called 'a government of strangers', consisting of individuals who know neither each other nor the president on taking office (Heclo 1978). They have not been elected together on a common party ticket. Nor have they worked together in the past. They have little sense of collective responsibility on coming to office, and the constitutionally fixed terms of office which allow the executive to persist despite internal disunity do not engender it subsequently. Most appointees are not career politicans so loyal service to president and party are not likely to be of value in obtaining employment in the future.

In office additional pressures disrupt what unity and loyalty to the party a president may provide an administration at the outset. Competing influences on policy-making and implementation fragment the executive branch.

Table 9.1 Congressional support for the president's position on votes, 1954–88

Years	President (party)	President's party		Other party	
		House	Senate	House	Senate
1954–60	Eisenhower (Rep.)	68	80	54	52
1961–63	Kennedy (Dem.)	83	75	41	47
1964–68	Johnson (Dem.)	81	71	49	56
1969–74	Nixon (Rep.)	73	73	53	50
1974–76	Ford (Rep.)	65	72	41	48
1977–80	Carter (Dem.)	69	74	42	52
1981–88	Reagan (Rep.)	64	74	31	41

Source: John F. Bibby (1987) *Politics, Parties and Elections in America* (Chicago: Nelson-Hall); *Congressional Quarterly Almanacs* (Washington, DC: Congressional Quarterly)

Bureaucratic inertia militates against innovation. Interest groups, career civil servants, congressional committees and the courts provide alternative cues to those emanating from party platforms. Progressively the administration dissolves into largely autonomous policy arenas over which the president struggles to impose a common purpose.

In dealing with Congress, party provides the most durable block in presidential efforts to build support. Temporarily public opinion or some sense of mandate or crisis may bind the branches together across party lines. But such consensus is transient. Partisanship is the consistent source of presidential allies in Congress. The president's position on votes is supported by an average of two-thirds of his own party in Congress, by 40 per cent of his opponents. Whilst these figures evidence the absence of polarization in Congress, they do show that party makes a difference in how members respond to presidential stances (Table 9.1).

Shared partisanship indicates some traditions and perspectives that presidents have in common with their fellow partisans in Congress. They are also bound together by some interdependence in electoral fortunes. Presidential coattails are now short but a few members may owe their election to the ability of their presidential candidate to attract votes to the party ticket. Presidents who can enact their programmes are likely to strengthen their own prospects for re-election by having their policies translated into law. The success and, related to this, the popularity of the president, also has a bearing on his own party's performance in mid-term elections. Though losses in the House are virtually inevitable for the president's party, their magnitude varies according to his popularity. Popular presidents confer fewer disadvantages on their party's incumbents than unpopular ones (Kernell 1977, Tufte 1975).

Presidents are leaders of their parties in only a qualified sense (Ranney 1983). Party organizations and leaders exert virtually no influence in choosing presidential nominees. The manner of winning the nominations does not imply support from party notables such as the members of Congress and in some cases, McGovern in 1972 is an extreme example, such backing was conspicuously absent. The president is also short of formal resources with which to impose his leadership on the party. He lacks the power to discipline members of Congress or to control who represents his party there.

To exert leadership over their parties, presidents depend on symbolic, organizational and policy resources more than formal powers. For the public the president is the most visible representative of his party, and at election time, perceptions of parties are still coloured by voters' attitudes to their presidential candidates (Wattenberg 1986). His party's national committee is an organizational resource for the president. He appoints its chairman and influences the activities it undertakes. To varying degrees, presidents also assert organizational leadership by promoting the welfare of state and local parties. They visit party gatherings, help to raise money and campaign in elections for party candidates.

Presidents are major influences on party policy. Colloquially, the president's programme and party policy tend to be synonymous. More accurately, national party policy consists of the platform adopted at the national convention in presidential election years. Platforms are conditioned by the preferences of the nominee. Where a candidate is the obvious nominee in advance of the convention the platform (written by the platform committee) is tailored to his wishes. Where the nomination is still to be resolved the front-runner may make concessions on the platform to assuage opponents, such as Carter's agreement with Kennedy at the 1980 convention that unemployment and high interest rates would not be used to curb inflation.

Platforms have often been derided as electioneering devices, irrelevant to government. But research into the fate of the winning party's platform after the election suggests that they do have a bearing on government. Presidents do try to fulfil many of the pledges made in platforms. Of those pledges that are introduced into Congress, the great majority are enacted, suggesting a shared commitment by the president and his congressional party to the promises made during the election (Fishel 1985, Pomper and Lederman 1980).

In securing enactment of their programmes presidents concentrate their lobbying efforts on the members of their own party. They meet regularly with their party's congressional leaders to plan the legislative timetable and gauge sentiment on impending bills. Though the congressional leaders work with the president they do not work for him. They ensure that the president's programme is considered by congress but they do not always give it their

Table 9.2 Success of president's position on votes in Congress under unified and divided control, 1953–88

President (Party)	Years	% Success	
		Unified control	Divided control
Eisenhower (Rep.)	1953–54	85.9	
	1955–60		67.7
Kennedy (Dem.)	1961–63	84.5	
Johnson (Dem.)	1964–68	82.8	
Nixon (Rep.)	1969–74		67.0
Ford (Rep.)	1974–76		57.7
Carter (Dem.)	1977–80	76.4	
Reagan (Rep.)	1981–88		61.8

Source: *Congressional Quarterly Weekly Report*, 19 November 1988

support. Most leaders diverge from the president on some issues, as Democratic Senate leader Mike Mansfield did in opposing the Johnson administration for its conduct of the Vietnam War. Congressional leaders are chosen by their legislative parties, not by the president, and they are also sensitive to protecting institutional prerogatives against the executive branch. They are intermediaries between president and Congress rather than subordinates of the former.

In cultivating individual members, presidents can offer help to their congressional partisans in securing re-election. They may make personal appearances with candidates, offer endorsements, provide materials for inclusion in campaign literature and help to raise funds. Assistance in serving constituencies is made by channelling resources such as government contracts, new hospitals and roads to the districts of favoured incumbents (so-called 'pork barrel' legislation). The prestige of incumbents (and their egos) can be enhanced by tokens of recognition such as invitations from the president to attend official functions (Edwards 1984). These resources help to bind the president's party in Congress into a supportive coalition. In general, Congresses controlled by the president's party are more supportive of presidential initiatives than where control is divided (Table 9.2).

If the president's party is a minority in Congress he is forced into greater dependence on the other party to construct majorities for his proposals. This necessitates liaison with the majority leadership to adjust the timing and content of legislation to maximize the likelihood of success. The majority leadership accept that the initiative for most major legislation emanates from the White House and they ensure that the president's proposals receive consideration in Congress. They may even help to pass presidential proposals they support. The effectiveness of collaboration between president and majority leadership across party lines has varied over time, dependent largely upon the president's commitment to co-operation. During the last six years of the Eisenhower administration Democratic leaders such as Senate majority leader Lyndon Johnson collaborated with the administration to forge a bipartisan consensus. On the other hand, Democratic House leaders were rarely consulted or accommodated during the Reagan presidency, producing a partisan polarization on votes with resultant defeats for the administration.

As the discussion of presidential-legislative liaison reveals, parties are vital to the operation of Congress. Both chambers are organized along party lines. The Speaker of the House is the elected leader of the majority party. On all the committees and sub-committees that conduct the detailed business of Congress, places are allocated by party. Thus each committee and sub-committee is controlled by the majority party. Votes on procedural matters

Figure 9.1 Party unity votes in Congress, 1968–88

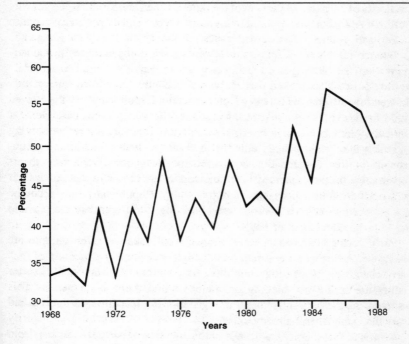

concerning who will control business are highly partisan, reflecting how crucial they are to party interests.

Party is the single most accurate guide to how members of Congress vote. But partisan voting is much more limited than in many parliamentary systems. In Congress party unity votes (generously defined as where more than 50 per cent of one party votes in opposition to more than 50 per cent of the other) occurred on approximately half of all votes in each chamber in the later 1980s. This represents a marked increase over the late 1960s and early 1970s when party unity votes were around one-third of the total (see Figure 9.1, which records the mean between the party unity votes in the House and the Senate). Using a more rigorous standard of party unity, 90 per cent of one party opposing 90 per cent of the other, only 7 per cent of all House votes and 3 per cent of all Senate votes were party votes in 1988.

Individual members exhibit great variations in their association with party majorities. Some members vote with the majority on virtually every party vote. Others, often conservative southern Democrats or liberal eastern Republicans, are regularly at odds with their party's majorities. For example, in 1988 Senate Republican Lowell Weicker of Connecticut was opposed to a majority of his party 73 per cent of the time. On the Democratic side, Howell Heflin of Alabama was opposed to his party majority on 47 per cent of votes.

Partisan voting varies across issues. In the 1980s President Reagan's preference for higher defence and lower domestic expenditures produced many partisan cleavages on budgetary issues. Environmental and social welfare policy also evoked partisan votes. In contrast, votes on foreign aid showed few differences between Democrats and Republicans. By the 1980s civil liberties votes were registering partisan differences. In the past, Democratic divisions between northern and southern blocs on civil rights issues, on which the former usually allied with the Republicans, had muted partisanship in this sphere. But now southern Democrats, reflecting their dependence on the expanded black electorate, are closer to the stances of their northern fellow partisans. Simultaneously, Republicans have become less supportive on civil liberties votes, serving to differentiate the parties from one another (Sinclair 1985).

Party voting is a product more of shared outlooks and interests than of discipline. A formal party line is rare though occasionally a meeting of the party caucus or its steering committee may endorse legislation. But such endorsements are not binding on members and there is no penalty for disregarding them. Endorsements of legislation are less attempts to produce unity than signs that it already exists.

Efforts to foster unity are usually at the initiative of party leaders but they have few resources to impose discipline. They have no control over members' nominations and there is no equivalent of a British party whip that can

can be withdrawn to expel dissidents from the congressional party. To produce unity leaders rely more on positive inducements than punishments. They can schedule business to conform with other demands on members' time. They can provide help in advancing legislation that a member favours. They can use their influence to secure appointments to legislative committees for members seeking to serve their constituencies or pursue their interests. They can assist re-election by personal appearances and help in raising funds.

The most punitive action taken by congressional parties against dissidents is to deprive them of their status on legislative committees. Either members are removed from a committee or reduced in seniority (relegating them in the line of succession to the chairmanship of the committee). Democratic Representative Phil Gramm of Texas was disciplined in the former fashion in 1983 for his active support of the Reagan budgets. Gramm's response of winning re-election as a Republican and subsequently gaining election to the Senate suggests that such a penalty did not damage his political career. Examples of such discipline are rare. Independence of party is widely accepted among members because every member benefits from the freedom to respond to constituency or interest group pressures or personal preferences.

In the last quarter of a century changes within and outside Congress have been mixed in their implications for parties and party leadership. In the 1970s trends both centralizing (towards parties and party leaders) and decentralizing (towards individual members) were apparent. Examples of the former were the reduction in the powers of committee chairs in the House, and their dependence on the support of the caucus (a meeting of the party's House membership) to remain in office. The unseating of three chairmen in 1975 signalled the power of the Democratic caucus, resulting in chairs more responsive to party members thereafter. The assertiveness of the caucus was also reflected in an enhancement in the powers of the speaker. Members of the Rules Committee were to be chosen by the speaker, subject to caucus approval, strengthening the influence of the party leadership over the committee that controls the agenda of the House.

Offsetting these centralizing trends was a tendency towards atomization of power in Congress. Sub-committees and sub-committee chairs proliferated, multiplying the number of power centres. The assertiveness of individual members was also aided by the expansion of staff numbers. In an era of electoral dealignment members capitalized on the widened opportunities for influence, activism and self-advertisement to promote their electoral security. Individualism – at the expense of leadership from president, party or committee – flourished.

In the 1980s these conflicting trends were resolved in favour of centralization, to the benefit of party leaders. The pivotal development stimulating this change was the primacy of deficit reduction as the objective of congressional activity. Opportunities for individual members to deliver constituency benefits were constricted. The imperatives of cutbacks and selecting priorities required co-ordination, a role which the party leaders assumed as they manufactured legislative compromises (Davidson 1988).

In the federal judiciary partisan influences are evident in both the selection of judges and the decisions made in court. Federal judges, including the justices of the Supreme Court, in the great majority of cases, share the party identification of the president who nominates them. Despite their common partisanship some justices have been seriously at odds with the presidents who appointed them. Eisenhower came to regard his nomination of Earl Warren as Chief Justice as his greatest mistake and Truman reached the same conclusion about his appointment of Tom Clark.

Partisanship has also been employed to explain the decisions judges make. Democratic judges tend to be liberals on economic matters, supporting government regulation of business and workers over management. Republicans tend to be more conservative in such cases. In civil liberties cases Democrats again tend to be liberal, siding more frequently with minorities and accused persons than Republicans (Tate 1981, Goldman 1975).

PARTIES AND STATE GOVERNMENT

Many of the obstacles to party government at the federal level are replicated in the states. Principles such as the separation of powers and checks and balance are reproduced in state constitutions with similarly disruptive effects for party government. State laws, far more than federal ones, intrude into party affairs, prescribing the rules of their internal operations. Some state laws and constitutions impose further impediments to party government. Nebraska law requires non-partisan elections to the state legislature and in most states several executive branch positions are elective, militating against single-party control.

Different laws and constitutions contribute to the variations between the states in the approximation to party government. Other influences include the degree of electoral competitiveness of the parties, the heterogeneity of electorates and the nature of the state political culture. In areas of one-party domination, such as parts of the south, a party role in government is meagre. Elective office is a virtual monopoly for one party but it lacks cohesion. Rather, splits between factions, institutions and personal cliques produce fractures in the dominant party.

In other states, party is a greater source of cohesion and programmatic coherence. The industrial states of the northeast and midwest have traditionally been the centres of the strongest party role in government. States such as Connecticut and Illinois are electorally competitive between the parties.

The parties draw votes from different sections of the electorate and their role is underpinned by a culture which accepts partisanship as legitimate. In the following paragraphs we seek to delineate some of the principal variations between the states in the governmental role of parties.

State executives, as already mentioned in passing, differ from their federal equivalent in the greater number of officials who are elected. Elections for governor are universal. Elections for lieutenant governor occur in all but a handful of cases. Secretaries of state, attorney generals and state treasurers are also commonly elected. In some states, Louisiana is an example, the number of elected executive branch officials runs into double figures. Whilst some states provide for a single ticket of governor and lieutenant governor, the norm is that executives are elected separately. The consequence is an executive branch consisting of individuals with disparate electoral bases and even different party affiliations.

In making appointments the discretion of the governor varies. At one extreme, New Jersey, all heads of departments are appointed at the discretion of the governor. However, this is an untypical example. Control over appointments shared between the governor and one or both houses of the legislature (and some positions filled by election) is the norm. At the other extreme to New Jersey are states such as Florida and Mississippi where control over appointments is a legislative branch monopoly. Governors' inability to control the composition of the upper ranks of the state bureaucracy qualifies their capacity for imposing their objectives. A survey of serving governors found that lack of control over appointments was cited as the most serious obstacle to effective performance of their responsibilities (Beyle 1968).

Patronage appointments vary greatly in number between the states. In 1975 approximately a third of all state employees were not under the merit system. In states such as Oregon and California only a handful of senior appointments are dependent upon political preferment. In states such as Indiana and West Virginia large numbers of patronage appointments remain though the *Rutan* decision may lead to a reduction in the future.

In making patronage appointments the contemporary parties are not usually strong influences on decisions. Many governors rely on their own or the official personnel recruitment mechanisms rather than parties. Surveys in the 1970s of state party chairmen found that a majority were not consulted by governors about appointments (Huckshorn 1976, Gibson *et al.* 1984). Where party officials are consulted their comments are not necessarily binding and they are not invited to propose names for consideration. The reasons for the reduced role of parties over appointments in the states are the same as those relevant to the federal level. There are both fewer party identifiers and patronage appointments. Of those appointments which remain, many require skills that are not usually found among party activists.

Except for Nebraska, most state legislatures are organized along party lines. The majority party controls the agenda and provides the presiding officers and the majorities on committees. Bipartisan coalitions have organized some legislatures when the majority party is divided, but such instances are uncommon (Jewell and Patterson 1986).

Legislative party leaders in the states are generally stronger than their counterparts in Congress. The seniority system is rarely employed. Instead, party leaders designate the chairs and the members of committees, giving them a leverage over the membership. In addition, the high turnover rate of state legislators, producing many inexperienced members, may enhance the dependence upon leadership cues.

The degree of partisanship in legislative voting varies according to the political and economic environment in which the legislature operates. Industrial, electorally competitive states produce the highest rates of partisanship, often exceeding that found in Congress. More rural, electorally one-sided states produce lower partisanship. Legislatures that are one-party monopolies usually lack unity. The dominant party is divided by institutional, geographical and ideological splits, and personal cliques. In such states affiliation to the dominant party is a precondition of entry into the legislature rather than a guide to behaviour in office.

The party role in state judicial selection varies along both legal and informal dimensions. State laws define how judges will be chosen. Some permit partisan elections and some prohibit them, requiring non-partisan contests. Where appointive systems are employed some confer the responsibility on partisans such as governors and state legislators. Others follow the Missouri plan in which a special commission devises a short-list of candidates from which the governor chooses. Under this system judges are appointed for one year, then stand in a retention election which has no opponents but voters decide whether to retain or dismiss the incumbent.

There has been no systematic study of state judicial selection so the role of party in practice cannot be gauged accurately. Undoubtedly some legal formalities disguise the role that party plays in some instances. Michigan, for example, by law runs non-partisan elections for judges. But in practice the parties recruit the candidates and mount their campaigns. An impressionistic assessment suggests that non-partisan procedures often obscure informal partisan influences: 'In general, judges are chosen (no matter what the formal method of selection) from among lawyers who have been actively engaged in politics and who enter the judiciary with a recognized, partisan political background' (Morehouse, 1981: 317).

Some studies of judicial decision-making in the states have revealed differences between Republican and Democratic judges similar to those found at federal level. Democrats tend to be liberals in supporting minorities, employees, unions and defendants. Republicans tend to be more supportive of the authorities, management and the prosecution. Where partisan differences have not been found this has been attributed to the judges' working conditions, such as periods away from home on the judicial circuit when they are in each others' company which fosters a common outlook, depressing partisan difference (Nagel 1961, Ulmer 1962, Adamany 1969, Dubois 1988).

REALIGNMENT AND PARTY GOVERNMENT

The potential for party government is heightened by critical electoral realignment. Each realigning era has produced long periods of unified party control of the federal government. In realignments national issues are to the fore and the differences between the parties assume a moral intensity as the politics of principle displaces bargaining over interests. Large numbers of new members are elected to Congress, mainly on the majority side: they are particularly sensitive to the political climate that produced the realignment. The durability of one-party control of the presidency and Congress also facilitates the penetration of the bureaucracy and the judiciary so that they are reshaped to conform to the policy agenda of the new majority.

Thus realignment removes some of the obstacles to party government in the US. One party controls all the branches of government, helping to overcome the impact of the separation of powers. The primacy of national issues subdues the fragmenting effects of federalism and parochialism. The national policy agenda also counters the decentralized decision-making system in Congress and the fragmentation of the bureaucracy. Even during realignments, parties are not policy-making institutions but there is an untypical cohesion around programmes, particularly on those issues on which the realignment pivoted (Clubb *et al.* 1980, Brady 1988).

We can illustrate these influences at work by examining the impact of the Civil War and Great Depression realignments. In both eras partisan voting in Congress increased. The divergence between the parties was greatest on the realignment issues of slavery in the Civil War era, of government intervention and social welfare during the Depression. But other issues also became sources of partisan cleavages where they had not been in the past. In the former period votes on the federal role in public works, constructing railroads, supervising trade and the banks became more partisan than they had been before the realignment. In the Depression aid to agriculture emerged as a new partisan issue (Brady 1988, Sinclair 1982).

The behaviour of the Supreme Court towards the new policy agenda differs between the two periods. In the Depression the Court, composed principally of Republican appointees, ruled several items of New Deal legislation unconstitutional in the early years of the realignment. In time the

Court's hostility waned. The judges' greater receptivity towards the New Deal occurred prior to any alteration in the Court's membership, perhaps a reflection of deference to the continued Democratic successes in elections. Although Roosevelt threatened to increase the number of justices to mould the Court more in his own image, the signs of greater receptivity by the judges appear prior to the announcement of the Court-packing plan (Nelson 1988). In time, vacancies opened up on the Court and Roosevelt appointed justices sympathetic to his outlook. In contrast, in the realignment of the Civil War era, the Court's invalidations of legislation emerged several years after the establishment of the new electoral majority. It was after 1865, by which time a majority of judges were Republicans, that conflicts between Congress and the Court became intense. The divergence is attributable to the different perspectives of Republicans in the two branches. In Congress, Radical Republicans committed to vigorous Reconstruction in the south and punitive action against former confederates were in the ascendant. But the Radicals were not a majority on the Court. As in the New Deal era, the Court did become more deferential to Congress in the longer term. But, in addition, Congressional radicalism receded, helping to restore peace between the two branches.

The continued absence of realignment helps to explain some of the salient characteristics of contemporary American government. Divided control is now the norm at federal level where formerly it was the exception. Membership turnover in Congress is low and incumbency, especially in the House, an almost irresistible asset in securing re-election. Lacking an agreed national policy agenda, power in Congress is decentralized and its members parochial in their preoccupations. The continued activism of the Supreme Court may also be underpinned by the absence of consistent guidance from voters and the elected branches over what policies enjoy support. Deference to the elected branches is impossible where they are unable to signal what policy decisions should be deferred to.

Lacking forces for coherence, the pressures for inertia are powerful. Agreed solutions to major problems such as budget and trade deficits cannot be forged in the American system where pressures from the electorate to compel agreement and consistency are lacking. Inertia can be overcome by the shock of particular events, and election results (Reagan's 1980 victory is an example) but such contingencies are short-lived in their impact. Over time their impact wanes. Either inertia returns or policy is again buffeted by a new set of forces. The fluctuations in post-Vietnam foreign policy from a 'retreat from Empire' to resurgent Cold War to contemplation of the end of both the arms race and the division of Europe are examples of short-term responses. Where policy is so susceptible to transient forces consistency and predictability are impossible. Policy is a stream of ad hoc reactions rather than the pursuit of agreed objectives by agreed means.

CONCLUSION

In this chapter we have shown the relevance of parties to American government. Partisanship, if not necessarily activity within a party organization, provides access to government via election or appointment. But parties do not govern. They are not policy-making institutions, rather they are internally diverse and incohesive. These characteristics we attribute to the divisive effects of laws and the Constitution which propel the political forces of a heterogeneous nation into but two parties, while also fracturing them with institutional rivalries and different electoral bases.

But the divisive impact of the institutional framework in which parties operate is not omnipotent. Party is the strongest adhesive force in American government, linking office-holders between and across the branches of government. Moreover, party cohesion varies over time, suggesting some autonomy from the disruptive effects of the Constitution and legal regulations. Events and particular election results can provide an impetus to party unity but the most consistent and enduring force for cohesion is realignment. Periodic critical elections have reconstituted the parties into more coherent blocs than they were before.

Now more than fifty years since the last major realignment, the prospects for party government are again meagre. Parties are still not policy-making bodies. The abandonment of mid-term Democratic conventions denotes a retreat from the cautious and, as it proved, ineffectual efforts to generate a party policy other than in presidential election years (see Chapter Six). Split-ticket voting, the resulting divided control of government, the diffusion of power in Congress and the individualism of members all seem likely to persist. In the continued absence of realignment we anticipate no regeneration of party in government.

10 The decline of party

Repeatedly through the last five chapters we have noted losses of party influence over the last quarter of a century or so. As organizations, in elections, among voters and in government, parties have become less effective and less dominant in the performance of their traditional functions such as recruiting personnel for public office, linking voters to officials, and providing the electorate with cues with which to differentiate candidates from one another. Since the early 1960s party capacity to perform these functions has weakened. In addition, non-party structures have emerged as alternative performers of formerly party functions.

In this chapter we assemble the evidence of party decline that has been dispersed across the preceding chapters. Secondly, we seek to explain why decline has occurred. Lastly, we assess the argument that emerged in the mid–1980s that a revival of party was underway.

PARTY DECLINE

Parties have never been strong in America compared to their more comprehensively organized and programmatic counterparts in Europe, particularly those on the left of the political spectrum. As we have frequently observed, American parties have operated in a hostile environment produced by constitutional and legal impediments, and an antagonistic culture. But a role for parties, albeit a restricted one, has gained acceptance in America. Most modern political scientists have been advocates of parties and by the middle of the twentieth century the anti-party strain had disappeared from the academic literature. To the contrary, parties were seen as essential to American democracy. In one famous formulation, 'political parties created democracy and modern democracy is impossible save in terms of the parties' (Schattschneider 1942: 1). In 1950 a committee of the American Political Science Association recommended a strengthened role for party, advocating a shift towards responsible parties in America (American Political Science Association 1950).

Within twenty years of the report's appearance the tone of academic writing about parties had become alarmist. The conventional wisdom came to see party functions being undermined. A flurry of book, article and chapter titles attest to the perception that a new, possibly terminal phase of party history was underway: 'The end of party politics', *The Party's Over*, 'The political parties: Reform and decline', and *Parties in Crisis* are examples (respectively Burnham 1969, Broder 1972, Ranney 1978, Hrebnar and Scott 1979). In the following paragraphs we collate the evidence that has so exercised academic thinking about parties in the last two decades. To ensure continuity with the previous chapters we retain the four forms of party – organizations, electioneering, voters, government – to present our evidence. Our aim here is to summarize evidence, much of which has already been presented. Greater detail and references to sources can be found in the relevant chapters.

Organization

The decline of parties as organizations is apparent in the fall in the number and calibre of activists they attract. Faced with a diminished workforce parties are less effective in performing labour-intensive electioneering activities than they once were. Candidates have recruited their own teams of campaign workers and used capital-intensive electioneering methods.

Amateur clubs, which stressed purposive (policy, ideology) incentives to participation, are fewer in number. Membership has fallen and a smaller proportion of members are active than they were twenty-five years ago (Ware 1985). Machines have continued the decline they were already experiencing by the early 1960s. Defeats in the mayoralty primary in 1979 and 1983 seem to signal the last hurrah of the longest surviving big-city machine in Chicago. The quality of activism among those dependent upon material incentives to participate has also deteriorated. Many patronage workers engage in little or no activity for the party in elections, apparently without penalty, suggesting the absence of a reserve army of labour for parties to draw upon (Johnston 1979).

Elections

Organizational decline is reflected in the diminished role of parties in elections. They lack the workers, finances and skills to deliver modern election campaigns. Candidate organizations are now the norm based on friends and relatives, interest group members, issue activists and, if finances permit, contracted professionals. That electioneering has become profession-alized is a demonstration of party failure to monopolize campaign activity. Rather, pollsters gauge voter opinion, political consultants manage cam-paigns, media specialists devise commercials for broadcast, direct mail firms generate funds for which individuals and political action committeees are the principal suppliers.

Party control over nominations has also weakened in the last twenty-five years (the decline period). Before decline, primaries co-existed with conti-nued control of the nomination by party organization in some locales. But that combination is rarer now as parties' abilities to mobilize electorates behind preferred candidates have diminished, the failings of the Chicago machine providing an outstanding example.

Presidential nominations have registered a sharp fall in party influence over the decline period. As late as 1968 state party organizations supplied the great majority of delegates to national conventions. They could (and in 1968 the Democrats did) disregard the evidence of opinion polls and the few primaries to nominate a candidate who had entered no primaries and lacked public popularity but was acceptable within the party organizations. Now primary victories are the essential route to the nomination. Even in the non-primary states control of delegate selection by parties is slight. In most areas party organizations do not attempt to exert control. The national convention now ratifies the winner of the primaries, irrespective of whether he enjoys support within the party organizations (and McGovern in 1972 and Carter in 1976 conspicuously lacked it).

Voters

The term dealignment expresses the diminished influence of parties on the electorate in the last quarter of a century. During that time there has been a depletion in the quantity and strength of voters' attachment to parties, and in the latter's impact on the vote. Electoral participation, partisanship and voting behaviour all record diminished party influence. Voter registration fell successively as a proportion of the eligible electorate from 1964 to 1976. Turnout in elections fell by 10 per cent of the adult population between 1960 and 1988. In the latter year half the potential electorate did not vote.

The incidence and strength of partisanship receded in the decline period. In part, this explains the fall in participation. Pure independents doubled as a proportion of the electorate in the decade 1964–74. In the same period strong identification waned, falling from over a third of the electorate at the earlier date to a quarter at the later one.

Voting behaviour is less constrained by partisanship than it was before decline. Votes cast contrary to party identification are now more common.

Before decline the defection rate averaged one identifier in seven in presidential elections and one in eight in Congressional contests. In some subsequent elections defection has characterized a quarter of identifiers. Increased ticket-splitting provides another indicator of weakened party influence on the vote. In the immediate pre-decline period ticket-splitting in presidential–House voting accounted for an average of 14 per cent of the vote. In the subsequent five elections it was never less than 25 per cent. In state and local contests split-ticket voters are now the majority.

Greater oscillations in voting preferences over time are another reflection of an electorate less anchored by party loyalties than formerly. Greater aggregate volatility is evident within one election and across several contests. An example of the former is the five times that the lead in the polls changed during 1980 and the swing from a more than 15 per cent lead for Dukakis to a similar advantage for Bush in the 1988 contest. Oscillation across elections is evident in the alternation from landslides to close contests at presidential level 1964–80. Individual voters are also more fluid in their preferences than they were before decline. In the 1950s two-thirds of voters claimed only to have ever voted for one party. By the 1970s less than half the electorate claimed such constancy. The timing of voting decisions also reflects the diminished anchorage to parties. Before the decline most voters decided how to vote before campaigns were even begun. In 1980 over half the voters made up their minds during the campaign and 9 per cent on election day. Such delays in the making of the voting decision reflect an electorate with greater susceptibility to short-term influences compared to the more secure party loyalties of the past.

Voters became less positive in their attitudes towards parties after the early 1960s. In this change we can detect shifts toward both negativity and neutrality. The former is evident in the growth of public disenchantment towards the parties. Fewer people saw strong party competition as a necessary ingredient of an effective democracy and more saw parties as self-interested (Dennis 1980). Signs of neutrality are evident in the increase in the number of voters who have neither positive nor negative attitudes towards the two major parties. Such voters doubled as a proportion of the electorate between 1960 and 1980 from 17 to 36 per cent respectively. Evaluations of presidential candidates and election issues are less informed by association with party than before decline. Candidates are now largely perceived free from partisan affiliations. Issues are associated more with candidates than with parties (Wattenberg 1986).

The absence of durable attachments to parties is consistent with the transitory character of much of Americans' lives. Frequent changes of residence, of jobs, of partners, indicate that lasting commitments are difficult to sustain and even discredited. If such central human experiences lack durability it is unlikely that politics, tangential to most lives, will generate greater depth and constancy (Reilly 1987).

Government

The weaker attachment of voters to a party has increased the incidence of divided control in Washington and the states. In the former, the particular American variant of coalition government is now the norm rather than the exception (Sundquist 1988–9). The decline period coincided with the deterioration in relations between president and Congress of the 1970s. Whilst divided control probably accentuated this conflict it was not the cause of it. Relations between the two branches when they were controlled by the same party during the Carter presidency were also more antagonistic than they had been in previous periods of unified control. Carter failed to evoke the same volume of support that Johnson and Kennedy had extracted from Democratic Congresses. All the major items of Carter's domestic agenda – hospital cost containment, the energy programme, restructuring of the tax and welfare systems – were defeated or heavily amended despite the comfortable Democratic majorities in Congress.

In both the executive and legislative branches the impact of party waned during the decline period. In the former, party recruitment of executive branch officials was displaced by a presidential personnel division. In the latter, party cohesion on votes reached its nadir in the late 1960s and early 1970s. In the House only one vote in three in those years divided a majority of Democrats against a majority of Republicans compared to one vote in two a decade earlier. A less precipitous decline, but one starting from a lower base, occurred in the Senate. Power in Congress became diffused throughout the sub-committee system, multiplying the numbers with influence while diminishing its concentration in individuals like the party leaders.

SOURCES OF CHANGE

There is no consensus among academics about why party decline occurred. A variety of explanations have been offered and few are mutually exclusive of one another. Given that decline has occurred in all four forms of party, and that sudden change in something as complex and durable as parties is uncommon, it seems plausible to think that several factors were at work, if not of equal weight.

We have identified six categories of causes that have been employed to account for decline. In the main these causes identify forms of change which occurred outside the parties but had a destructive influence upon them, undermining their capacity for performing their traditional functions. These changes occurred in: the nature of society; technology and mass communication; attitudes; institutions; generations; and the content and management of political controversy. We review each in turn.

Social change

The altered nature of Western societies since the Second World War has been characterized as an evolution from industrialism to post-industrialism. Relevant to the role of parties in this development are the changes in the class structure, the nature of work and the standard of living. These changes, it is argued, undermined the New Deal voting alignment that had emerged in a mature industrial society. The blocs that made up that alignment altered in size and character. For example, manual workers fell in numbers while improving their living standards. Ceasing to be have-nots, manual workers and other components of the New Deal coalition such as Catholics became less supportive of the redistributive programmes of Democrats. The growth of white-collar professionals produced a more variegated, less Republican middle class than its smaller, pre-war predecessor (Ladd and Hadley 1975).

Generalized affluence also undermined activism in party organizations. Near full employment and a welfare state reduced the power of material incentives as a stimulus to activism. In an earlier era economic insecurity had encouraged participation in parties to obtain patronage jobs and other material benefits. Amidst affluence, patronage jobs lost their attractiveness. They were usually too poorly paid to be competitive with non-patronage employment which was plentiful and available without the requirement of party activism.

Other social changes also reduced the supply of party activists. The 1960s and 1970s witnessed an acceleration of the longer-term trend of growing female employment outside the home. As more women were incorporated into the paid workforce so their time available for party activity diminished.

Technology and mass communication

Technological change transformed the conduct of elections and the transmission of political information to the detriment of parties. Capital-intensive methods of mobilizing votes and gauging their preferences became available. Computers came to perform functions previously undertaken by the party workforce. They facilitated mass mailings, the precision targeting of potential supporters and the rapid analysis of survey returns. Television commercials provided an alternative method of reaching voters to personal contact by party activists.

Adoption of these new techniques by candidates enabled them to gain independence from party organizations in electioneering (Sabato 1981). In consequence, campaign organization, voting cues and political information in general derived increasingly from non-party structures. Candidates freed from dependence on parties in campaigns emphasized their own issues and personal attributes rather than their party affiliation. In office the successful exploiters of these new methods pursued a similar independence from party.

Attitudes

Many of the changes in public attitudes that occurred in the decline period are concomitants of the evolution of post-industrialism described above. As society altered so new priorities and novel political styles displaced the old. Three sets of attitudinal changes have been connected to party decline. The development of both post-material attitudes and the purist styles are linked to post-industrialism. The third, political cynicism, appears to be largely independent of these societal changes.

Post-material values were an outgrowth of the affluent society. Economic security lost its primacy for voters amidst prosperity. As a result the electorate in general, and young voters socialized in the affluent society in particular, shifted their concerns away from the welfare state–economic management issues on which the New Deal alignment pivoted. Rather, post-material concerns about the quality of life gained in importance. Salient post-material issues of the decline era included civil rights for blacks, environmental protection and women's rights (Inglehart 1977). For voters concerned with these issues the New Deal party cleavage was neither a relevant voting cue nor a stimulus to partisanship.

The new issue agenda was embraced by white-collar professionals who grew in influence in the Democratic party from the 1960s. They espoused liberal stances on socio-cultural issues and anti-imperial positions on foreign policy. But their attitudes were not shared by traditional Democrats. When the new professional strata captured the party, as in McGovern's nomination for the presidency in 1972, the unrepresentative minority alienated the party's electoral base, producing a landslide defeat (Kirkpatrick 1975, 1976, Miller *et al.* 1976, Ladd 1976–7).

A distinctive political style also characterized the new professionals. Variously labelled 'purists' or 'amateurs', they rejected the politics of bargaining and compromise. Instead they wanted parties based on moral principles that appealed to a like-minded coalition. They wanted their own preferences translated into election programmes rather than modified to maximize support (Kirkpatrick 1976, Polsby and Wildavsky 1976, Soule and Clarke 1970). The purist style undermined the coalitional nature of the parties, alienating those whose preferences had not been accommodated.

Third, and apparently unrelated to post-industrialism, the decline period witnessed progressive falls in public confidence in political institutions. The sources of this growing disenchantment have not been established with precision but it seems plausible to suggest that a combination of divisive issues like civil rights, intractable problems like Vietnam and the corruption in high office of Watergate were contributory forces. All major institutions, including the parties, experienced a loss in public confidence. Growing disenchantment is unconducive to promoting loyalty to and participation in the parties (Beck 1984).

Institutions

Institutional change consists of the political reforms of the 1960s and 1970s which diminished party influence. Some of these reforms took place within the parties, as in the Democrats' restructuring of the presidential nominating process. Most were external to the parties though they were not immune from their effects. Reforms were articulated through internal party rules, federal and state laws, judicial decisions, the procedures and working practices of Congress. It was not the manifest intent of reform to weaken parties. Rather parties fell victim to the reforms' unintended effects (Ladd 1978, Kirkpatrick 1978, Polsby 1983).

Reforms of the Democrats' presidential nominating process were designed to reinvigorate the party by promoting participation within it. Enlarged citizen involvement and influence necessarily reduced the control over the outcome exerted by party elites. The magnitude of the reduction was increased by the proliferation of presidential primaries which the McGovern–Fraser commission and its successors did not intend to promote. The switch from low turnout party-run meetings (caucuses) to mass turnout, election-like forums demolished the prospects for elite control to survive. Caucuses might have been susceptible to elite leadership, primaries were not. Party organizations lacked the numbers and the influence to control primaries. The delegate selection process became a succession of state intra-party election contests. Candidates adopted election-style campaigns, they assembled personal organizations, recruited paid consultants and appealed to votes through the mass media. National convention delegates were candidate supporters additionally bound by the voters' mandates delivered in the primaries rather than party elites prepared to bargain to obtain benefits for themselves and their parties.

Reforms of campaign financing aimed at eliminating electoral corruption. Contributions were to be restricted in size and publicized. By including parties in the restriction candidates' financial dependence upon them was also curbed. The trend towards candidate financial independence from party was also accentuated by the promotion of alternative sources of funds. The federal government, for the first time, and political action committees, to a greater extent than formerly, moved into the funding gap vacated by party.

Within Congress, changes to promote the effectiveness of individual members undermined the collective influence of party. Devolution of decision-making into sub-committee fragmented power, rendering it less susceptible to the centralized control exerted by party leaders. The increase in members' personal staffs and constituency offices allied with devolution to heighten the scope for individuals to serve their localities, strengthening their re-election chances. The exploitation of these opportunities enhanced the electoral security of incumbents. Electoral security became more personal and less partisan. In consequence the incentives for incumbents to emphasize party in Congress or in campaigns diminished.

The reduction in multi-member constituencies eroded a role for party organizations in elections to state legislatures. In the 1950s a majority of states used multi-member districts to elect at least a quarter of the lower house of the state legislature. By the 1970s most states relied exclusively on single-member constituencies. Partly a response to Supreme Court demands for the principle of 'one man, one vote' in apportioning constituencies, partly a response by minority parties seeking to counteract the advantage of the majority in multi-member seats decided by pluralities, the growth of single-member seats diminished party organization influence in elections. Multi-member districts were geographically large. In a large area few candidates could mount sufficiently effective individual campaigns to win the primary votes necessary to qualify for the general election. Candidates were forced instead to rely upon party organizations to solicit primary voters on their behalf. In the general election the reliance on plurality victories to decide contests allowed one party to sweep all the seats in a multi-member district. In consequence, the candidates of particularly the majority party had an incentive to mount a collective campaign effort by which they could all benefit. The natural agency of such collective efforts was the party organization. When multi-member districts receded so too did the disincentives to the creation of individual campaign organizations.

Generations

Generational explanations of party decline stress the qualitative differences between the new voters of the 1960s and 1970s compared with older members of the electorate (Abramson 1976, Beck 1974). New voters grew to political maturity when the socializing impact of party was waning. Candidate-centred campaigns were growing more common, and the last six years of the Eisenhower presidency entailed divided party control in national government. Partisan influences in elections and government were both weak.

New voters of the decline era were distant from the experience of the Depression and New Deal, the events which had been formative political experiences for the new voters of the 1930s, being so profound as to lock many of them into a party identification for life. By the 1960s young voters were two generations removed from the realignment era. Neither they nor their parents had lived through a period that forged political affiliations durably. Neither personal experience nor family socialization tended toward partisanship for the new generation of voters in the decline period. For the presidential elections 1968–80 pure independents outnumbered strong partisans by an average of 8 percentage points among newly eligible voters. In elections 1952–64 strong partisans had an average lead over independents of 19 percentage points among those able to vote for the first time.

The impact of generational change was exaggerated by the expansion of young voters in the electorate as a result of the post-war baby boom, and the passage of the Twenty-Fifth Amendment in 1971 lowering the voting age to eighteen. In consequence, young voters were an untypically large segment of the electorate in the decline period. Thus, to a greater degree than normal, young voters shaped the character of the electorate as a whole, depressing the strength and quantity of partisanship.

Political controversy

Politics was more divisive and conflictual in the late 1960s and the 1970s compared to the placidity of the earlier years of the post-war consensus. Urban riots, the disruption of university campuses and mass protests against the Vietnam War signalled a more contentious political climate. New issues emerged to dominate the political agenda of the period such as race relations, law and order and the Vietnam War. These issues had played no part in the forging of the New Deal alignment and undermined it as a cue to voting choice and partisan loyalties.

The parties took stances on these issues which either failed to forge new attachments or disrupted existing loyalties. The Vietnam War is an example of the former where, except in the 1972 presidential election (when American troop withdrawals were already under way, lessening the issue's public salience), the parties were not consistently distinguishable from one another. On race relations the parties did come to diverge as the liberal-dominated Democratic party continued to advocate positive measures to improve conditions for blacks while Republicans pursued a southern strategy of attracting white conservatives. As a result, the Democratic coalition in presidential elections was transformed. Many white southerners deserted the party while newly enfranchised southern blacks were attracted to it (Nie *et al.* 1976, Petrocik 1981).

The new issue agenda also fractured the parties in Congress. Established lines of cleavage between the Congressional parties fragmented as the content of legislation embraced new issues. For example, social welfare programmes targeted at the very poor (as in Johnson's battery of programmes under the War on Poverty) were more disruptive of party unity than the more established programmes of the New Deal–Fair Deal era such as Social Security and public housing (Deckard 1976).

New controversies undermined the activist base of at least the Democratic party. Intense internal party conflict over the Vietnam War alienated activists motivated by purposive incentives. The escalation of the war by a Democratic administration deterred participation in the party in two ways. First, it weakened loyalty to the Democratic party. Second, it encouraged activists to find non-partisan methods of opposing the war, stimulating resort to interest groups, direct action and support for individual candidates who adopted anti-war stances.

WEIGHING THE SOURCES OF CHANGE

Little attempt has been made to weigh the explanatory power of the various sources of party decline. The only efforts we know of are concerned exclusively with dealignment among voters (Norpoth and Rusk 1982, Wattenberg 1986). We attempt such an effort here. To guide our evaluation we use two comparative methods, the historical and the cross-national. The former prompts us to look at the timing of decline. It has occurred since the early 1960s. Thus the historical method encourages us to find sources of decline in forces emerging or sharply gaining in strength after the early 1960s. Whilst long-term, evolutionary forces of party decline may be relevant they cannot, independently, account for the sudden deterioration of party influence. Remember that the period preceding decline was one of stability and relative strength for parties. The years 1952–64 have been described as the 'steady state period' for party identification (Converse 1976). Party organization in the early 1960s has been said to have been enjoying an 'Indian Summer' (Ware 1985). We think, therefore, that 'period specific' forces for decline were particularly powerful.

Cross-national comparisons are useful because party decline is not a uniquely American phenomenon (Mair 1984). Whilst party decline is not universal in Western Europe, nor as severe or as multi-faceted as in the US, it has nevertheless occurred in some countries. Decline is evident in Europe in each of the four forms of party that we have considered it in America: in organization, in elections, in the electorate and in government. Organizational decline is evident in the fall in party membership, either absolutely or in relation to electoral supporters (Bartolini 1983, von Beyme 1985). Decline in elections is evident in the increased reliance on television rather than the party workforce to communicate the campaign. Signs of dealignment are apparent in several forms such as falling party identification and turnout, increased volatility and fragmentation of the vote (Mair 1984, Dalton *et al.* 1984, Crewe and Denver 1985). In government, party decline has occurred in a form distinctive from that of the US. In Europe party-dominated institutions have been displaced from control over policy-making by corporatist or neo-corporatist arrangements of intermediation involving bureaucrats and interest group representatives (Lehmbruch 1977).

Where common effects are found we have reason to think that common causes are at work. As party decline is evident in both the US and in Europe we suspect that some common forces are at work. Thus those explanations for decline which rely on uniquely American sources of change are insufficient.

Employing both historical and cross-national comparisons leads us to attach particular importance to new political controversy as a source of decline. New issues emerged both in the decline period, and in other democracies. Though the content of the new issues was not necessarily the same, they did appear in many countries, thawing out the party systems of Europe which were said to have been frozen in a mould established in the inter-war years (Lipset and Rokkan 1967). New issues, allied with incapacity to produce responses satisfactory to their electorates, diminished parties as voting cues, sources of loyalty and forums for political activism. Existing voters became detached from parties while new cohorts never forged the attachments that their predecessors had done. In government, parties were weakened by their incapacity either to organize or to resolve the major controversies of the day. We conclude that political issues were a potent force for party decline.

In the US the failure to resolve major controversies in an electorally appealing manner was reflected in the continuing absence of a major realignment. Though anticipated by some scholars by the later 1960s, no realignment occurred despite such apparently propitious conditions as the waning of the New Deal alignment, an influx of large numbers of new voters into the electorate and an abundant supply of intense issue conflicts. With the failure of realignment so departed the prospect of replenishing the parties as sources of cohesion in government, agencies of political participation and objects of voter loyalty.

The intractability of the issues and their very profusion may help to account for the absence of realignment. But the actions of political leaders are also pertinent to explaining the failure of realignment to materialize.

Political leaders were unable or unwilling to polarize the parties and the electorate on the major controversies, or to devise a policy agenda attractive to a new majority. Given the social discord of the period, the absence of electoral polarization can be seen as responsible statesmanship aimed at mitigating conflict. In 1968, for example, Nixon campaigned on the slogan 'Bring Us Together'. He championed the cause of the *Silent* Majority rather than one vociferously demanding a transformation of policy.

Other aspects of leadership behaviour also served to eschew realignment. Presidential elections of the period witnessed personal rather than party quests for victory. Both of Nixon's successful campaigns were mounted by personal organizations independent of the Republican party. No effort was made to translate personal support for Nixon into converts for the Republican party in general. Similarly, by 1984 Reagan was preoccupied with his own re-election rather than encouraging the shift towards the Republican party that he had articulated four years earlier.

By the later 1960s the condition of parties and voters was less conducive to major realignments than in the past, even had the appropriate action been forthcoming from political leaders. Here the long-term sources of party decline mesh with the more immediate shocks of political controversy to militate against realignment. Campaigning beyond the presidential level was becoming individualized, organizational atrophy was underway and voters' independence from parties for voting cues was growing. Under these conditions a programmatic response by *a party* was less plausible than in the past. Rather electoral individualism impeded a collective response. The major policy conflicts were fought out within rather than between parties which were diminishing in their resources to mobilize voters who, in turn, had less need of them as cues to the vote and as objects of durable loyalty.

Political controversy ramified into several of the other categories that we used to identify the sources of decline. For example, the Vietnam War probably contributed to the attitudinal, generational and institutional changes. First, the failure to find a consensual policy on the war, the 'credibility gap' which emerged over successive administrations' handling of information about its conduct, and the social divisions aggravated by the unevenness of the sacrifices made to prosecute it, discredited political institutions, contributing to the disenchantment of the decline era. Second, these effects were most marked on those whose attitudes to parties were most malleable, the new political generation. Their lack of prior political experience rendered them particularly susceptible to period effects. The time lapse since the New Deal would also have weakened the impact of parental socialization in forming partisanship. But more than the weakening of socializing effects is at work in explaining the non-partisanship of the new generation. A panel study of adolescents beginning in 1965 found that non-partisans had multiplied by the time they were young adults in 1973 (Beck 1984). Such a drop-off must be attributable to the events of the intervening eight years in which the dissension and dissatisfaction over Vietnam were politically salient.

Third, the Vietnam War was a spur to institutional change. It prompted both reform of the presidential nominating process and internal change in Congress. In the former case, the inaccessibility of the delegate selection process in 1968 to anti-war forces mobilized behind McCarthy discredited the existing machinery. Accessibility became one of the principal goals of the reformed procedures. In Congress the efforts to rein in the executive branch and to redistribute internal power both gained impetus from the war. The reassertion of congressional power in the 1973 War Powers Act, the proliferation of sub-committees to enhance institutional capacity, the greater dependence of committee chairs on party support to increase their responsiveness, are all examples of the war's ramifications.

In stressing the importance of new political controversy we do not reject the influence of other sources of decline. The circumstances in which politics was being conducted were undergoing multiple qualitative changes. Voters were more affluent, more educated and more geographically mobile than ever before. Political information – derived from television – was more abundant and delivered in a more arresting manner than in the past. Campaigning was more expensive and more sophisticated. But we see these forces as evolutionary influences upon the party system. They did not suddenly appear and therefore were unlikely to have had a sudden impact on the parties. For example, over 70 per cent of American households had televisions by 1956. Novel campaign methods were adopted gradually not suddenly. Moreover, the trend towards dealignment registered across the whole electorate. It was not the responsibility only of the new political generation but rather a response by all age groups. We suggest that this common response was the consequence of a common experience of the content and management of the political controversy of the later 1960s and 1970s. Political controversy provided the short-term 'shocks' to depress party influence rapidly. Without such shocks party decline would still have occurred because the other forces were in themselves sufficient to effect it. Without these shocks we assume that the decline would have been a more gradual one. Party influence would have eroded rather than collapsed.

Whilst institutional change was a short-term force we do not regard it as a major contribution to decline. First, it fails the test of cross-national comparison. Though party decline occurred elsewhere, institutional reforms do not loom large in accounting for it. Second, we believe that reform sapped party influence where it was already weakening. For example, parties only provided 17 per cent of the funds to congressional candidates before the major reforms of campaign finance law were introduced.

Reform of the presidential nominating process did terminate party control of presidential nominations but opinion polls and primary results were already reducing the discretion available to national conventions. This evidence could be neglected, as the 1968 Democratic convention exemplified, but only at the cost of nominating a demonstrably unpopular candidate. Moreover, the impact of this change was confined to the role of parties in the presidential nominating process and did not contribute to other facets of decline. In a decentralized party system the presidency had never been a consistent focus of party activity. Rather, presidential politics was of concern to state and local parties usually only for a short time every fourth year. Concern was stimulated by parochial considerations for a coattail effect in the election and access to patronage thereafter. But both had shrunk to meagre proportions before presidential nominations were reformed. The absence of a counter-reform movement from party organizations betokens both their already weakened condition and also the marginality of presidential elections to their activities.

Reform of the presidential nominating process was a response to decline already underway. The need for change was widely acknowledged in the Democratic party in 1968 following the loss of the presidency, the turmoil and discord that surrounded the delegate selection process and the national convention. In that year the party had failed to respond to demands emanating from the public. According to the Preface of the reform commission recommendations, change in the party's rules was necessary to guarantee its responsiveness in the future. Without reform political demands would be articulated outside the Democratic party, either through other parties or in direct action (Commission on Party Structure and Delegate Selection 1970).

PERSISTENCE AND RENEWAL

An academic preoccupation with decline has obscured the many continuities in party history. Emphasis upon the demise of party influence neglects both how much of it still survives and what the limits to it were before decline started. It is worth reciting the signs of persistence to keep the degree of change in perspective.

In outline the American party system retains the same features that it has exhibited for a century or more. It is a two-party system. The organization of the party is dominated by the cadre-caucus type and power is decentralized. Parties are treated as public institutions, subject to extensive legal regulation (Ware 1988). During the last quarter of a century some of these attributes have gained in strength rather than declined. As we noted in

Chapters Three and Five, the electoral stranglehold of the two major parties is now stronger than ever. It was some of the institutional reforms of the decline period, such as the provision for the public funding of the major parties' presidential campaigns in advance of the election, that have strengthened the Republicans and Democrats against smaller competitors.

Where change has occurred, the decline is a relative one. Most voters continue to be party identifiers, pure independents never constituting more than 16 per cent of the electorate. In presidential and Congressional elections most identifiers continue to vote for their party's candidates, indicated by a defection rate which peaked at 27 per cent in 1972. In other words, the proportion of voters casting a vote consistent with their identification never fell below 73 per cent. Unchanged also is the predominance of Democrats among party identifiers, an advantage which has lasted for half a century.

Durability of party influence remains evident in government. As we noted above, partisanship is virtually an essential prerequisite for access to major public office. In partisan elections the hold of the two major parties is almost complete. Though the ability to dismiss personnel on partisan criteria has been circumscribed, appointment as often required the appropriate party identification, though the effect of the *Rutan* decision may be to weaken it in the future. In Congress, partisanship remains the best guide to how members vote and who the president's strongest allies are.

Local party organizations show many continuities with the past. National surveys show that the type and volume of activity that they undertake remains much as it was before decline. Most county parties continue to distribute literature, stage events, raise money, produce publicity and conduct registration drives. Where change has occurred it is generally in the growth of activity rather than its decline (Gibson *et al*. 1985, Gibson *et al*. 1989).

By the mid-1980s some authors proclaimed a recovery in the performance of parties. Heightened party activity or influence was evident in some facets of organization, electioneering, the electorate and government. Proponents of revival argued that parties had adapted to the new environments in which they operated to find new niches where they assumed new functions or performed traditional roles by novel methods (Kayden and Mahe 1985). We now assemble the evidence of party recovery mentioned in passing in earlier chapters and assess its persuasiveness.

The clearest signs of resurgence are in the form of party organization. The novelty in this development is that it has been most marked at the national and state levels whereas formerly the most organized layer of the party was the local one. Organizational resurgence is concentrated on the Republican side. The Republican national committee has undergone a marked increase in staff, funding and activity since the early 1970s. State parties have also developed as organizations, particularly on the Republican side. They have a larger, more specialized staff and a wider range of activities than in the pre-decline period.

Organizational resurgence also finds expression in the revival of a party role in elections. Again, the change is most marked on the Republican side. Republican national party structures (the National Committee, the Senate Campaign and Congressional Committees) identify winnable seats, recruit candidates, train, finance and link them to political action committees. State party activity has been promoted by assistance from the National Committee through the secondment of staff and the provision of services such as polling. Whilst parties in general account for only a small percentage of candidate contributions, Republicans receive much greater assistance than Democrats. Both parties make substantial contributions to candidates in the open-seat, competitive races which are the most fiercely contested. In 1988 there was also a surge in party expenditures in the form of 'soft money', that is the spending by state parties on activities like get-out-the-vote drives which have been free from legal limits since the FECA amendments of 1979.

Partisanship among voters recovered in the 1980s. In 1984 pure independents numbered 11 per cent, the lowest total since 1968. Voting was also more consistent with partisanship after 1980. The defection rate in the 1988 presidential election of 18 per cent was the lowest for thirty years. Split-ticket voting also diminished, falling in state and local contests to its 1968 level. Electoral participation also revived in the early years of the decade. The elections of 1982 and 1984 reversed a twenty-year decline in turnout in mid-term and presidential elections respectively.

More positive attitudes to parties were exhibited in the 1980s. Political institutions in general enjoyed a revival in public confidence as Reagan's policies appeared to deliver economic recovery and international respect. Parties probably benefited from this general restoration of trust. By 1984 parties were seen as sources of conflict and confusion by fewer voters than at any time for twenty years (Dennis 1986).

Partisanship in Congress revived during the 1980s. In 1981 House Republicans were almost unanimous in support of Reagan in crucial votes on his budget- and tax-cutting proposals. But in the longer term, it was the Democrats who exhibited the greatest cohesion. The degree of unity achieved by House Democrats in 1987 set a thirty-year record. In that year two-thirds of all votes in the House involved a majority of Democrats opposed to a majority of Republicans, the highest proportion for over thirty years.

These various indicators suggest that the trend of party decline may have stopped but we are cautious about how much of a recovery has occurred. Our reservations centre on the impact of the parties, and the durability and magnitude of change. The evidence of organizational resurgence and the enhanced role of party in elections consists more of activity than of influence.

Parties provide more services to candidates than they did during the decline era but the value of these assets has yet to be demonstrated. For all its organizational development the Republican party remains locked in minority status below the presidential level. After a surge of support at the beginning of the decade Republicans ended the 1980s electorally weaker than they began it. By 1989 they had fewer seats in Congress, and controlled fewer governorships and state legislatures than they did in 1980. Thus the long-term benefits of heightened party organizational capacity and influence are as yet invisible.

Concentrated in the 1980s, the modest signs of recovery are as yet too short-lived to be described as a trend. In some spheres recovery was attributable to period effects which are already over or whose continuity is doubtful. For example, Congressional party unity owes a lot to Reagan. He polarized the parties by pursuing a controversial programme of cutting budgets, increasing defence expenditures and aiding the Contra rebels in Nicaragua. He was also partisan in his approach to the House, declining to cultivate the Democratic leadership in his quest for bipartisan support. In the last two years of his presidency Reagan encountered in House Speaker Jim Wright a Democratic leader prepared to mobilize his party to curb presidential influence. But these forces for partisanship are now absent. Reagan and Wright have left office. President Bush has championed a bipartisan approach to the nation's problems and has a less divisive programme for alleviating them.

We are sceptical of the argument that more active national organizations have produced party unity in Congress (Kayden and Mahe 1985). Though such mechanisms have the potential to produce cohesion, we do not think they have been employed so as to achieve such an outcome. First, while it is the Republican party that has been most active in aiding candidates, it is the Democrats who exhibited the greatest unity in the late 1980s. Secondly, in identifying candidates to recruit and aid there is no evidence that Republican national structures employ ideological or programmatic criteria (Salmore and Salmore 1985, Herrnson 1988). To the contrary, a concern for winning is paramount. Candidates' politics are considered only insofar as they influence their electability.

The greater partisanship of presidential voting behaviour is probably attributable to the nomination of centrist Democrats in the last two elections. Both Mondale and Dukakis were New Deal Democrats nominated by an ostensibly united party. Previous Democratic candidates 1968–80 suffered at least one of the handicaps of being non-centrists, insurgents or the nominees of a divided party. But there is no guarantee that the conditions pertaining in the last two elections will recur. In fact, given the continued failure of the Democratic party to reconstitute the New Deal electoral coalition there must be incentives for future nominees to change strategy. A coalition there must be incentives for future nominees to change strategy. A possible alternative is to target the western states rather than the south. As Republican identifiers are more numerous in the west than in the south, the success of this strategy requires defections to the Democratic nominee, depressing the impact of partisanship on the vote once again.

The increase in electoral participation also proved to be a transient recovery. The increased turnouts of 1982 and 1984 were not sustained. Instead the following elections witnessed sharp falls in voting, resuming the downward trends which had been in progress up to 1980. In 1986 turnout was the second lowest for a mid-term election in the twentieth century, little more than a third of the voting age population (37. 1 per cent) participated. Outside the south, the turnout was lowest at mid-term since the eighteenth century. In 1988 only half the eligible electorate (50.1 per cent) voted, the lowest turnout since 1924. In the mid-term elections of 1990 approximately one third of the electorate voted.

On several indicators there has been a recovery but only from the nadir of the mid-1970s not a restoration of the position existing prior to decline. Pure independents and ticket-splitters remain more numerous than they were 1952–64. The perception of presidential candidates and issues in party terms remains lower than in that earlier era. Whilst the decline may have ended, parties have yet to recapture the influence they exhibited a quarter of a century ago.

CONCLUSION

In this chapter we have reviewed the case for party decline. We accept that decline has occurred but we are cautious about its magnitude. It is necessary to appreciate both the limitations to party influence prior to the onset of the decline process and the signs of continuing vigour when it was underway.

In accounting for decline we attribute particular importance to the political controversy of the later 1960s and 1970s. This period effect is of value in explaining the timing of decline. Its occurrence coincided with the proliferation of divisive issues outside the New Deal cleavage over government intervention issues that politicians did not manipulate so as to fuel a major realignment. The modest evidence for party revival in the 1980s reinforces our view that the decline era was a phase attributable to period effects rather than a trend brought on by forces which persist, such as professionalized campaigning. Some aspects of party revival are also attributable to period effects (such as the Reagan presidency) which have already passed. Whether this heralds a resumption of decline, a period of stability or continued revival driven by a new set of forces we consider in the final chapter.

11 Conclusion: looking to the future

In this chapter we speculate about the future shape of the American party system. Is the salience of party politics within the political system likely to rise, to remain stable, or to decline? We draw on our analysis of the party system in the previous chapters, in order to consider some future possibilities. We attempt to distinguish among the likely, the unlikely, and the extremely unlikely. We look at a few straws in the wind, less in order to draw attention to these as the basis of future developments (for some of these straws may well have disappeared by the time this book is being read), than to gauge the direction and speed of the wind.

THE DEATH OF THE PARTY SYSTEM?

The least likely scenario for the future of the party system is the absence of any future, the more or less gradual decline unto death. As we have just seen (in Chapter Ten), even at its lowest depths, the decline of party has been limited. A large majority of voters continue to identify with one of the major parties. First-time voters are turning towards Republican-party identification (however tentatively and instrumentally) rather than towards independence. (From 1976 to 1988 the percentage of independent and 'don't know' identification among voters old enough to vote for the first time dropped from 47 per cent to 37 per cent [Norpoth and Kagay 1989].) Even granting that party identification now comes less from long-term socialization and habituation, and more from conscious choice, and is therefore perhaps more easily changeable, it may for the same reason prove to be more meaningful to identifiers. Conscious choice of partisan identity may not always carry with it the zeal of the convert, but it would seem to imply recognition and encouragement of the political relevance of partisanship. And even granting that citizens' neutrality towards parties is still prominent, this attitude would seem to imply toleration of parties rather than opposition to them. No one is crusading for a return to the opposition to party systems characteristic of early nineteenth-century American attitudes.

We have also seen that local and national party organizations remain active. The recent bureaucratization of parties that may be stifling their creativity can also be seen to be preserving them as organizations. In terms of money and personnel the parties have more resources than ever before. Bureaucratization provides a layer of officials who are committed to promoting the parties' causes and whose careers interest them in the parties' success. This can work for the preservation and even the enlargement of party organizations, as long as public attitudes towards parties generally remain positive or neutral, rather than actively hostile. Legal deregulation of party organizations – which (as we shall suggest below) is unlikely massively to revive parties – nevertheless has not been proposed in areas that might undermine the duopoly of Democrats and Republicans. While this means that the party system is denied the opportunity for revival through the activities of third parties, it also means that the two existing parties *are* propped up.

In government, party still structures legislatures, and it remains relevant to the election and appointment of officials, and by no means irrelevant to their behaviour in office. Political careers still require partisanship. Successful political careers often require other methods, too: partisanship is no longer sufficient, but it is still generally necessary. Just as the decline of American hegemony in world politics since the 1950s can be seen as a *relative* decline – a consequence of the rising importance of other countries – the decline of the party system can be seen as a consequence of the rise of rival – but not all-conquering – campaigning and governing devices. This decline in the hegemony of parties does not point towards their ultimate demise. The USA is not on the verge of demonstrating how representative democracy can function without a party system.

THE LIMITED CALL FOR LIMITED REFORM

If survival on the current plateau seems more likely than further drastic decline, what about the prospects for further revival, building on and going beyond the slight revival of the 1980s? Can the vitality and influence of parties rise from the plateau towards pre-decline levels or even beyond? For many commentators party revival remains an urgent necessity. In party decline they perceive the debilitation of American democracy by means of government immobilism and growing susceptibility to pressures from special interests. A restoration of party influence, it is argued, would reverse these damaging effects, restore public accountability and enhance the capacity of government to address social and economic problems. As we have suggested, the American party system has served as an institutionalized form of the right to revolution; it seems worth preserving in order to preserve that right.

In spite of the strong feelings that party revival would be desirable, it is significant that the most frequently discussed proposals for strengthening parties omit some obvious possibilities. Many reforms that could have a major impact on parties are not seriously discussed. There are, for example, no proposals to abandon the direct primary. There is no proposal to provide national parties with a veto over local nominations. There are no proposals for making parties the sole sources of election funds or to sell television advertising only to parties. So alien and unrealistic are these innovations in an anti-party culture that even the proponents of stronger parties do not advocate them. Whilst the reforms they do propose are more acceptable, they would be correspondingly more modest in their effects if adopted.

Throughout this study we have emphasized the recurrence of conscious efforts to remake American parties to bring their form and operation into line with idealized conceptions of what they should be and do. American attitudes towards parties have found expression in the legal regulation of parties and elections and in the internal reforms to which the parties – especially the Democratic party – have submitted themselves. In the 1980s the reform impulse was relatively quiescent. There was no reform on the scale undertaken in the 1960s and 1970s. However, there remain several problems that reformers continue to address, among them the problem of party decline traceable in part to previous reforms. Moreover, even if the more grandiose reform schemes that are sometimes aired seem unlikely to be adopted, the party system continues to be changed in small ways, often with unforeseen results. The most likely areas in which potentially reviving, if modest, changes are likely to occur are finance, television advertising, presidential selection procedures and legal regulation. We will discuss these four in turn.

FINANCIAL REFORMS

This is an area in which reformers are still struggling to define feasible objectives. However, it may well be a realistic area in which to seek party-reviving measures, because such changes have already begun here. As we have seen in Chapter Seven, amendments to the campaign finance legislation in the later 1970s sought to enlarge the party role in financing elections.

The common assertion that American elections are simply too expensive may be misplaced: it has been argued that the cost of American campaigns actually compares rather favourably with what little is known about the costs per voter in other democracies (Penniman 1984), and that in any case vigorous spending correlates well with greater citizen participation and voter education (McConnell 1987). And it is often pointed out that candidates who spend more than their rivals do not always win; the Machiavellian observation that power attracts money (rather than money determining who has power) seems to apply. However, there remain many legitimate concerns about the ways in which the money is raised, distributed and spent. In particular there is growing concern about the increasing dependence of Congressmen on PAC money (a phenomenon that we noted in Chapter Seven). According to Common Cause, between 1978 and 1988 PAC contributions as a percentage of the average House candidate's campaign funding increased from 28 per cent to 45 per cent. In recent years, this increase has been even more noticeable among Democratic incumbents than among Republican incumbents. (Between 1982 and 1988, the proportion of funding received from PACs increased among House Democrats from 38 to 52 per cent, among House Republicans from 35 to 40 per cent.) Some Democrats think their increasing dependence on business PAC funding threatens to distort the ideological purity and image of the party. Until now, legislative attempts to limit the role of PAC money in congressional campaigns have been handicapped by the Democratic congressional majority's recognition of its relatively greater dependence on that money. Indeed, the present situation arises out of attempts by Democratic party organizations to try to match the Republican party's fund-raising capacity. A pragmatic attitude towards increasing the financial health of the party and its candidates has prevailed over reformers' scruples about the sources of finance. This attitude has helped boost the campaign chests of Democratic incumbents in both House and Senate. In the 1988 elections, Democratic senatorial candidates raised more money than Republican ones.

However, if the Democrats' growing dependence on PACs becomes so great that it is perceived as a real disadvantage by Congressmen and senators themselves (because fund-raising takes up so much time as well as because it restricts their legislative independence) or by significant numbers of voters (because they feel their representatives are sacrificing their interests to those of the organized contributors), there is some chance that new legal regulations will be introduced. In 1989 these chances were boosted by the revelation that five US senators (four Democrats, one Republican) had received large campaign contributions from the owner of the failing Lincoln Savings and Loan Association in California, in return for their intervening on the Association's behalf against regulative measures contemplated by the Federal Home Loan Bank Board. The senators involved were able to claim – plausibly – that this was just another instance of the now well-established practice of legislative representatives acting as ombudsmen to protect their constituents from the bureaucrats. But the case seems to have focused an unusual amount of public attention on this practice at least in so far as it is connected to campaign contributions, and therefore it helped to keep campaign finance reform on the legislative agenda.

Many bills designed to reform campaign finance were introduced in Congress in 1989. Several of these, including the bill initiated by President Bush, aimed to raise the ceiling on party contributions to candidates. Under the Bush proposals party contributions were to be increased to 150 per cent of their current level while donations from 'connected' PACs (connected to corporations, trade unions, trade associations) were to be eliminated. These changes would disadvantage incumbent Democrats, who would lose funds from PACs and would probably find their party less able than the Republican party to contribute up to the higher ceiling. So such legislation was unlikely to pass. Before Congress adjourned in October 1990, the Senate had passed a bill outlawing PAC donations, but a parallel bill in the House was easier on incumbents, proposing merely to scale down PAC donations. No bill emerged from the House–Senate Conference Committee. Moreover, even if such legislation were enacted, it would not significantly enlarge the party role in elections and government. A 150 per cent increase in party contributions would still constitute only around a quarter of the cost of a competitive House campaign. Candidates would still rely primarily on non-party sources of funds, whether from PACs or from individuals. As long as party funds continue to be a small portion of total campaign funds their effects on recipients are likely to be modest.

Nor would a higher party contribution necessarily promote partisanship among the beneficiaries. Under current Republican practice no ideological or policy tests are imposed as a condition of qualifying for funds, so they do little to promote a more homogeneous party. The greater party unity of Congressional Democrats compared to Republicans in the later 1980s demonstrates that current funding practices are not a major stimulus to cohesion. More stringent conditions to qualify for party funds are unlikely to be introduced. The electoral prospects of neither party are likely to be enhanced by requiring candidates to have a particular political complexion before they receive funds. Both parties prefer to back winners rather than ideological conformists.

Legislation in this area could take the form of producing different sources of finance, rather than merely increasing the proportion of finance provided through parties. These different sources would not have to take the form of direct government subsidies. For example, it has been suggested that cheap or free air time for political broadcasts (in effect, a subsidy for campaigns) could be made a condition for the granting or renewal of a television company's broadcasting licence, and that tax credits could be given to individual citizens for small donations (around $50) to parties or to candidates (Sabato 1987). In March 1990, both the Democratic and Republican national party chairmen endorsed the call for free television time, for the two major parties as well as for individual candidates. Such indirect public subsidies might have the effect of boosting the resources of challengers relative to those of incumbents, as well as of reducing the role of PAC money. For that reason, direct public funding seems to be the reform preferred by some Democratic Congressmen, although the party as a whole has not adopted this position. And while the Democrats remain of two minds on the desirability of public financing, Republicans generally oppose it, since it seems like yet another way of publicly subsidizing the Democratic majority's incumbent status. So stalemate on this issue (as occurred when the Senate debated it in 1987 and 1988) may recur. Even if there is some new legislation, there is likely to be a continued tendency for a divided system of campaign finance (public funds for president, private funds for Congress) to underpin that exaggeration of the separation between presidency and Congress that has been such a notable feature of the American political system in the last quarter century.

THE USE AND ABUSE OF TELEVISION

Similar rather speculative comments can be made about responses to the growth of negative campaign ads on television. Numerous reforms have been proposed – for example to abolish paid ads altogether, to force them to be longer than the standard fifteen or thirty seconds (presuming that this would improve the content), and to require candidates or their identified representatives to appear in them (to make them more responsible for the content, so at least they cannot leave the mud slinging to others).

It is possible that negative ads reduce voter turnout, and that there is at least in that limited sense a backlash against them. And while there were several pungent negative broadcasting campaigns in 1989 and 1990, beginning with the primary campaigns in 1990, there have also been a few cases (for example the Minnesota and Rhode Island gubernatorial races) where candidates have won partly because they have publicly eschewed negative ads. Some electors are becoming repelled by negative ads to the extent that they not only reject the messages that they convey but also vote for the other candidate instead of merely not voting at all. If this trend continues then the effectiveness of negatives ads will decline and their use will decrease without the need to impose legal regulation. In March 1990 David Broder, noting the current unease with empty, negative campaigns, hopefully called 1990 'the year a genuine rebellion against the cheapening of US politics may take place' (Broder 1990). Short of such a widespread rebellion, it is difficult to envisage negative ads disappearing from election campaigns.

When they do become less prominent there remain two deeper problems.

One is that the attacks on 'old-style negative campaigning' themselves constitute a new style of negative campaigning. The second is that if negative ads, old- or new-style, are replaced by a return to the cooler style of campaign ads that prevailed before the rise of negative ads in the 1980s, this might actually have the counter-effect of making partisanship even less salient in the minds of the electorate. What is needed for a revitalization of partisanship is not cool image politics, but the use of 'negativity' – heated denunciation of opponents' weaknesses – on partisan and general policy grounds, rather than personal or nit-picking ones, so that Americans' political cynicism is lowered and their partisan consciousness raised. Otherwise the reaction against negative ads could simply form part of the continuing general distaste for politicians and parties.

FURTHER REFORMS OF PRESIDENTIAL SELECTION

In addition to money and television, the reform agenda also covers the better-trodden ground of the rules and procedures governing presidential selection. The most important of the recent changes in this area has been the southern regional primary. In the years between the presidential elections of 1984 and 1988, Democratic party leaders in the south arranged for the primary elections in fourteen southern and border states to take place on the same day, the second Tuesday in March (which came to be known as 'Super Tuesday', a term first used in 1984 to describe the day on which the greatest number of presidential primaries occur). The purpose of co-ordinating these contests, and of arranging for them to take place early in the primary season, shortly after the first contests in Iowa and New Hampshire, was to make the Democratic candidates give greater attention to the sensibilities of southern voters. The aim was to produce a moderate candidate, perhaps also a southerner, to lead the Democrats to victory.

The event disappointed these hopes. Albert Gore, a centrist candidate from Tennessee, succeeded in boosting his delegate count to competitive-looking numbers, and won the primaries in five southern states. But Jesse Jackson won more votes (27 per cent) than any other Democratic candidate on Super Tuesday. He won the primaries in four southern states; this was hardly what the architects of the southern regional primary had in mind. Michael Dukakis (from Massachusetts) was already the front-runner, and the southern primaries did little to stop him from going on, as he did, to become the Democratic nominee. The first contests – the Iowa caucuses and, even more, the New Hampshire primary, although electing relatively few delegates to the nominating conventions, remained enormously important. Proponents of the southern regional primary claimed that all of the Democratic candidates moderated their rhetoric more than in previous years, because they were more aware of the importance of the south. But it could be argued that the southern primary merely magnified the effects of the choices made by voters in Iowa and New Hampshire. Besides, six non-southern states also held their delegate selection contests on Super Tuesday, making it more like a national than a southern primary.

Although the southern regional primary was a Democratic idea, the Republican party was also generally affected by the changes in the dates of primary contests. Some have argued that, when (as in 1988) there is a nomination battle in the Republican party as well as the Democratic party, Republican candidates actually stand to gain more strategic advantage from the southern primary than Democratic candidates do. An interesting contest in the Republican primaries can attract moderate or conservative voters away from the Democratic primaries and into the Republican ones, possibly attaching them to the Republican party as a result. Some of the growth in Republican registration in the south in 1988 may be traceable to this feature of the southern regional primary. Super Tuesday does seem in that year to have clarified and thereby assisted the nomination process in the Republican party at least as much as in the Democratic party. Following an impressive victory in the South Carolina primary on the previous Saturday, George Bush won a large majority of delegates in all of the sixteen states with Republican contests on Super Tuesday, thus practically clinching the nomination. The Democratic choice was not yet so clear.

There remain within the Democratic party many misgivings about the way that presidential candidates are selected. Some have argued in favour of the adoption of a national primary – national at least in the sense that all of the individual state contests would be held on the same day. But this degree of change is highly unlikely, partly because its effects are rather unpredictable. (For example, would it make the presidential contest more sensitive to domestic welfare issues, so that Democrats might expect to do better, or would it instead increase the influence of the activists who have made presidential elections turn more on cultural and foreign policy issues [Shafer 1989]?) Smaller changes look somewhat more plausible. Many have argued that the weight given to the first contests, in Iowa and New Hampshire (where the choices are made by the middle of February), gives an unrepresentative slant to the whole process. The idea of a series of regional primaries is catching on in some quarters; a proposal for eight regional primaries emerged from a Senate committee in 1989. One prominent suggestion (made by – among others – Bruce Babbitt, a former governor of Arizona, and one of the losers in the presidential race in 1988) has been to divide the country into four regions, and to hold the first primaries in small states selected at random within each region. It is argued that this would conserve the advantages of the present system – most importantly, the relative ease and economy of mounting campaigns in small states for relatively unknown and under-resourced candidates – at the same time that it removed some of the existing bias introduced by always starting in Iowa and New Hampshire. Another, somewhat less ambitious idea in the air is to rearrange primary dates in order to move more systematically from primaries in small states like New Hampshire at the beginning, to middle-sized ones in the middle, to big ones at the end of the primary season. Florida, Texas, Illinois, New York and Pennsylvania would have to delay their primaries, joining California and Ohio at the end of the season.

However, events do not seem to be moving in this direction. The Democrats now propose to move California's presidential primary to early March in 1992, a week before Super Tuesday. This clustering of contests at the front end of the primary season makes the nomination process more and more like a national primary, although one that perhaps (as with Super Tuesday in 1988) will produce little clarity of electoral choice. In any case, it is difficult to see the Democratic party actually managing to adopt such a complicated set of reforms as a systematic rearrangement of primary dates. It would require a strong desire to produce an electable candidate (and it is not always clear that this desire is uppermost in the minds of all Democratic officials and partisans), a widespread conviction that some such change would actually help produce such a candidate, and an energetic and well-managed effort to make the necessary changes in the laws of each of the relevant states. For the moment there seems to be a lingering scepticism within the Democratic party that even such relatively minor tinkering with the primary system or other selection procedures would be worth the effort, and a strong suspicion that stability and predictability of the procedures would now be more useful than further reforms on however modest a scale.

Nevertheless there are some marginal changes currently being made by the Democratic party in its presidential selection procedures. At the insistence of Jesse Jackson, the Democrats have agreed to reduce the number of super-delegates at their nominating convention, and to disallow the winner-take-all-by-district type of primary.

The percentage of the nominating convention consisting of super-delegates is to be reduced from 15.5 per cent of the total in 1988 to less than 10 per cent in 1992. (Democratic governors and most Democratic members of Congress will still be *ex officio* delegates, but members of the Democratic national committee will not.) In 1988 Jackson ended up with a much smaller proportion of super-delegates than his proportion of popular vote in the primaries. Therefore he argued that the inclusion of super-delegates violates the reform principle of proportional representation. It does, of course – that was its purpose – but (as we have noticed in Chapter Seven) this device has actually had very little impact on the nomination outcome, so reducing the number of superdelegates or even eliminating them altogether might not change much.

Winner-take-all-by-district primaries are those in which the principle of strictly proportional representation in delegate selection can be violated at the Congressional district level, without violating the letter of the rule that abolished winner-take-all primaries at the state level. This 'loophole' primary was first used in 1976, to get around the Mikulski Commission's abolition of the winner-take-all-by-state primary. The 1976 Democratic National Convention voted to close the loophole, but it was reopened by the Winograd Commission rules adopted before the 1980 election (because it was felt that the loophole would help the renomination chances of Jimmy Carter). Four states – Illinois, Pennsylvania, Maryland and West Virginia – had loophole primaries in 1988. Jackson argued that this arrangement works against those candidates whose support is very strong in some districts and very weak in others, thus violating the principle of choosing convention delegates so as to represent as precisely as possible the strength of candidates among the party primary voters.

Both of these rules changes constitute adherence to the reform principle of proportional representation established by the McGovern-Fraser Commission in 1972. This principle has been challenged – by the loophole primary from 1976 to 1988, and by the reintroduction of *ex officio* delegates since 1984 – but never removed from the Democratic party's presidential nomination procedures, nor ever decisively weakened in its operation, so these most recent changes are not revolutionary. It is worth noting that they have been introduced in a consciously unrevolutionary fashion, too, with no recourse to a reform commission. Perhaps the most notable recent change in the reform process in the Democratic party is this ending of the long line of reform commissions, which had been established after every presidential election from 1968 to 1984. The dominant view among Democratic leaders now is that their attention must be focused on the party's message, rather than on the mechanics of the nomination process.

DEREGULATION

Complementing the quiescence of party reformism is the tendency towards legal deregulation of parties at the state level (noted in Chapter Six). Over the last twenty years judges have relaxed the legal restrictions on parties. Continued deregulation would be consistent with judicial decisions that have given the parties primacy in regulating delegate selection to national conventions, in creating open primaries, in endorsing candidates and in structuring party organization. This judicial counter-movement against the earlier (and still living) judicial approval of heavy regulation has stemmed partly from the belief that party decline could be reversed by deregulating the parties.

The counter-movement has proceeded in a piecemeal fashion, and it is probably too early to see where it will lead. It seems promising that it concentrates on reviving parties at the state and local level, whereas many reforms and renewal efforts have concentrated on the national level. However, it must be emphasized that greater legal discretion does not necessarily result in stronger parties. There are many beneficiaries of weak parties in government and elections, including incumbents, legislative bureaucracies and political consultants. Parties are gradually learning to use the new campaign techniques and consultancy services, but these rivals to parties in the political system are likely to impair the capacity even of more legally autonomous parties to assert themselves beyond their own internal affairs. Nor is deregulation necessarily advantageous to parties. Some laws have sought to protect the integrity of parties which is threatened by deregulation. For example, the opportunity to create open primaries may widen participation in the party but by people who lack allegiance to it and are unconcerned for its long-term future. Openness is acquired at the expense of cohesion and organizational integrity – a point that proponents of stronger parties have often made about the direct primary in general.

Nor do parties necessarily exploit the opportunities afforded by deregulation. Only in a handful of states has even one of the parties opted out of the closed primary that was formerly compulsory. In California the state Republican party not only declined the opportunity to make primary endorsements, but also threatened sanctions against any county party that made use of its discretion. The state party went to the lengths of successfully sponsoring a state law that prohibited Republican county parties from making endorsements.

As these examples reveal, there is only patchy enthusiasm for deregulation within the parties. Were partisans committed to deregulation they could effect it without the aid of judicial decisions. State legislatures could simply repeal regulatory legislation. But we see no indication that this is likely to occur. Proponents of deregulation may win additional victories in the courts. But the parties reflect rather than resist an anti-partisan culture. They are unlikely to press for deregulation or even to capitalize on the opportunities for autonomy that judicial decisions grant them.

Party deregulators may be neglecting the need to give parties something to do, because of their preoccupation with giving them room to do it in. The way in which the parties handle or fail to handle political issues, and the way in which they succeed or fail in representing durable coalitions of interests, might determine their fate more than either their legal status or their campaign practices will.

REALIGNMENT ISSUES AND PARTY COALITIONS

In the past, critical realignments have been a source of party revival. But they have been revolutionary events in American politics, reshaping the party system, the political agenda and the boundaries of government activity. They have been more than changes in voting behaviour. Thus, recent changes in voter loyalties, such as the rise of Republican identification and the shrinkage of the lead enjoyed by the Democrats, do not constitute a full critical realignment. Not only is there reason to doubt that such a realignment is under way, we also think that it is unlikely to occur in the immediate future.

American politicians and citizens have learned to live in a political world where parties are but one among many organizing forces. Parties as intermediary organizations between voters and governments, as sources of voter cues and loyalties, as mechanisms for organizing government, are less visible and less potent than in the past. Parties now play supporting parts rather than leading roles in American government. Political elites do not construct the world for voters in partisan terms. Unsurprisingly, voters do not perceive elites or issues in terms of partisanship.

Critical elections require *partisan* controversies. But conflicts are now unlikely to be presented or perceived in partisan terms. Candidate-centred campaigns depress partisan themes. A more partisan politics would imperil many current elites such as the congressional incumbents who benefit from extensive ticket-splitting. Presidents, pivotal in past realignments, have fewer incentives to make elections critical. They are selected by a largely non-partisan nominating process, in which party notables play only a small role. Their campaign organizations are usually separate from those of their parties. For the general election their funding is entirely independent of party. Moreover, one consequence of the Twenty-second Amendment (limiting presidents to two terms of office) may be a shortening of presidents' time perspectives, diminishing their interest in long-term party building. Electorates are unlikely to embrace durable party loyalties where the partisan stimuli from political elites are so weak.

From different angles in Chapters Two, Four and Ten, we have seen that the new partisan issues that have emerged since the 1960s have tended rather to complicate and to weaken party loyalties than to realign and to strengthen them. At the level of political elites, there is much more evidence than there is in the electorate, of partisanship being boosted by the forces normally associated with critical realignment. Thus, conservative Democratic politicians continue to move into the Republican party, and liberal Republicans retiring (e. g. Senator Jacob Javits in 1980) or defeated at the polls (e. g. Senator Lowell Weicker in 1988) are often replaced by conservative Republicans (D'Amato for Javits) or by liberal Democrats (Lieberman for

Weicker). With the anomalous bits of each major party thus moving into the other one, these parties can be seen to be more coherent than at any time since the Civil War. Nevertheless, party decline rather than party realignment has resulted from the injection of social and foreign policy issues into the partisan arena. The greater ideological coherence of the leaders in each party may actually make the parties less relevant to the electorate. Party activists may have realigned along the new social or cultural issues, at least in presidential elections, but voters in general have not polarized along these lines. The selection of two rather managerial candidates by primary voters in both major parties in the 1988 presidential election reflects this generally rather cool electoral response to the social issues (which, as the actual election battle showed, are potentially quite hot issues).

This does not mean that there is an end of ideology looming up in American party politics. As we have argued, party politics is an inherently ideological phenomenon, in the United States as elsewhere. If it were not, parties would find survival much harder. For both major parties, ideology remains relevant. The Democratic party continues its years-old search for an ideological position that will distinguish it from the Republican party's conservatism without diminishing its presidential electoral chances. However, the moderate or centrist wing of the party continues to be frustrated in presidential politics. In 1984, the moderate candidates (Askew, Glenn, and Hollings) were easily defeated in the primaries; in 1988 moderates like Sam Nunn and Charles Robb – both perhaps more authentically centrist than Albert Gore – did not even run. The Democrats seem to be wedded to distinctive and non-centrist positions both in foreign policy and on certain social issues such as affirmative action and abortion. These positions both reflect and magnify the inversion and the crumbling of the New Deal coalition that we noted in Chapters Two and Eight. Democratic presidential nominations have displayed the diminishing influence of the foreign policy and social conservatism of some of the original groups in that coalition. A defection of Democratic working-class whites to the Republicans, which has affected big city elections as well as presidential elections, is connected to the Democratic party's social liberalism, especially perhaps its position on affirmative action (Edsall 1988).

For their part, the Republicans too have difficulty in striking a comfortable ideological posture. The party's social issue conservatism, even when it is not connected with religiosity, does not always harmonize with its economic conservatism. The most promising group of new recruits to Republican party identification and voting are younger voters, but this group, although they have also been shifting from liberalism to conservatism, tend to embrace economic – and possibly also foreign policy – rather than social conservatism. This is one of the reasons that Republican leaders have resisted the urge to use the social issues to help establish a major partisan realignment. Even the new economic conservatism of young Americans may prove to be unreliable if there is a strong reaction against the glitz and the yuppie hero of the 1980s.

The Republican position on the abortion issue illustrates their ideological problem. In retrospect, perhaps it can be seen that the controlling strategy all along has been to appear not more principled but more moderate than the Democrats on this issue. At any rate, there has clearly been a pragmatic strategy emerging during the Bush administration. From 1980 to 1988, the Republican party officially opposed the principle that abortion should be completely unrestricted, and questioned the wisdom of the Supreme Court's liberalizing initiative in this area (the 1973 *Roe* v. *Wade* decision). But George Bush himself had great difficulty defining his position on abortion during the 1988 campaign, perhaps aware that his 'vacillations put him squarely in the centre of American opinion' (McWilliams 1989: 190). Following the Supreme Court's July 1989 *Webster* decision, which countenanced greater restrictive legislation by individual states, American public suspicion about government interference in this area began to be redirected away from federal courts towards state governments. In October 1989 the Florida state legislature (controlled by Democrats) refused calls by the (Republican) governor to exercise the *Webster* option of tightening the availability of abortions; the following month, gubernatorial elections in Virginia and New Jersey turned partly and unexpectedly on the successful portrayal of the Republican candidates as too inclined to governmental interference with women's rights to choose whether or not to have an abortion. As the conservatives on abortion have come to be seen as more extremist than the liberals – who are learning to portray themselves as merely upholding the traditional healthy American suspicion of government intervention – Republican leaders have begun backing away from their hard line. Bush – who had switched to that line in 1980 to make himself compatible with Reagan – seemed relieved to be able to retreat to a softer line, stressing the personal nature of the abortion issue and the ability of the Republican party to accommodate diverse views.

This open Republican party turn towards pragmatism and away from the conservative extremes that it had seemed to embrace under Reagan has been visible from the outset of the Bush administration, on economic and foreign policy as well as on social issues. One of the most prominent developments highlighted by the elections of 1990 is the re-emergence of "moderate" politicians in the Republican Party. This development goes along with current shifts in American public opinion away from strong conservative sentiments on domestic and foreign policy; it does not fight against these shifts. Bush himself had come from the mainstream of Republican pragmattists, and he appointed such politicians to key positions (including his secretaries of state, treasury and commerce). In a world in which both international politics and the American and world economies have become more imponderable, the pragmatic posture may seem desirable. The lack of policy clarity in the early Bush years, as compared to the early Reagan years, corresponds to a greater perception of complexity in the larger political world. However, pragmatism also entails the problem of the fuzzy image. During the Reagan years, the argument against the Democratic party's 'me too' strategy in presidential nominations was always that voters, offered the choice between a real conservative and a fake one, would choose the real (Republican) one. If the Republican party under Bush comes to be seen as a party of the pragmatic muddle, voters might prefer a Democratic muddler to a Republican one. Ideological clarity is risky, but so is the lack of ideological clarity.

As we have suggested in previous chapters, the likeliest scenario for the immediate future is the continuation of divided party control of American government. Many Democrats seem to have given up hopes of capturing the presidency, as many Republicans despair of capturing Congress. Current Republican hopes for an increase in their Congressional seats in 1992 are based on technical developments such as reapportionment and incumbents' retirements, rather than on renewed partisanship. Bipartisanship has been the watchword of the early Bush years, even though it has been evident – for example, in budgetary negotiations between President Bush and Congressional leaders – that partisan posturing often remains as the controlling context that limits what bipartisanship might accomplish. Voters individually might be increasingly attracted to the notion expressed in several quarters in 1990, that Congressmen's incumbency advantages should be reduced, and that incumbents should be examined suspiciously at every election, or even limited by constitutional amendment in the number of times they may be reelected. (In 1990, three states decided to limit the tenure of their state legislators.) Such anti-incumbent sentiment could cut into Democratic control of Congress if it were translated into votes. However, this translation would have to overcome the classic problem of the first performer (the 'collective action' problem): no individual Congressional constituency has a rational interest in forgoing the benefits provided by its Congressional incumbent until it can be sure that other Congressional constituencies will do the same.

The continuation of divided government probably means a continuing uncertainty in policy directions, with policies decided one day and reversed the next, and it is likely to be accompanied by further debate among political observers as to whether this marks the failure or the success of American democracy. All this is not fore-ordained. The deeds and words of party events. For example, Democrats might cohesively and aggressively exploit the prospect of a post-Cold War 'peace dividend' to propose new domestic programmes, perhaps thus boosting their presidential fortunes. However, the actual emergence of a peace dividend, however much it might help to unify the Democratic party in the electorate, could equally lead back to a more intense fragmentation of the Democratic party in Congress, the situation that existed in the days before deficit reduction politics tended to concentrate Congressional Democrats' minds. Likewise, one might speculate that if the political and strategic rivalry of the Cold War were to be replaced by international economic rivalry – as seems to be anticipated by some currents of American public opinion – Republican presidential candidates might prove to be less electorally attractive, and the Democratic party a more plausible presidential force. On the other hand, such a development might favour the Republicans – who in the 1980s succeeded in making themselves appear to be the agenda-setting 'sun' party on economic issues – or it might simply make voters more apathetic about parties, and more inclined to support the status quo. Thus the current uncertainty of economic and political developments outside the political parties, and outside the United States, as well as the unpredictability of party leaders' actions and voters' preoccupations, leaves open the possibility of dramatic shifts in the ideological and coalitional shape of the parties, and in their electoral fortunes.

CONCLUSION

Even such dramatic shifts might well not do much to revive the political parties. The atomized condition of American politics and government, in part a consequence of party decline, remains an impediment to party revival. The individualism of candidate-centred politics obstructs both the critical realignment and the piecemeal reforms that might effect party revival. Critical realignments are unlikely where parties lack electoral salience. Pressures for party-inspired reforms are weak where so many elected officials benefit from atomized politics and are strongly positioned to resist innovations that would curb their autonomy. For these reasons, in spite of the new uncertainties of American and world politics in the 1990s, and leaving to one side the possibility of catastrophes on the scale of the Civil War or the Great Depression, we foresee a continuation of the situation prevailing for the last two decades, with realigning forces working more powerfully on elites than on voters, on presidents than on Congresses, and towards economic more than social conservatism. This partially realigning politics should be enough to keep partisanship simmering and the party system thus maintained on its present plateau, but it seems insufficient to heat up the party system to the degree that would be necessary to produce serious party revival and a thoroughly new arrangement of partisan alignments.

A possibly comforting final observation: as long as divided party control of American government persists, it may well be desirable to have rather weak parties. Divided control is a reflection of party decline but it is also a workable form of government when parties are weak. If divided control and strong party cohesion were to occur at the same time, one might see complete political deadlock. In the absence of a major realignment that establishes united party control of government, weakened parties would seem to be necessary. The system of separated powers does not function at its best in such circumstances, but neither does it function at its worst.

References

Abramowitz, Alan I. (1980) 'A comparison of voting for US senator and representative in 1978', *American Political Science Review* 74: 633–40.

Abramson, Paul R. (1976) 'Generational change and the decline of party identification in America: 1952–1974', *American Political Science Review* 70: 769–78.

Adamany, David W. (1969) 'The party variable in judges' voting: Conceptual notes and a case study', *American Political Science Review* 63: 57–73.

Adams, John (1823) Letter of 27 September 1808, *Correspondence Between the Hon. John Adams and the Late William Cunningham, Esq.*, Boston: E. M. Cunningham.

Adrian, Charles R. (1959) 'A typology for non-partisan elections', *Western Political Quarterly* 12: 449–58.

Alford, Robert R. (1963) *Party and Society: The Anglo-American Democracies*, Chicago: Rand-McNally.

American Political Science Association (1950) 'Toward a more responsible two-party system', Report of the Committee on Political Parties, *American Political Science Review* 44: Supplement.

Anderson, Kristi (1979) *The Creation of a Democratic Majority: 1928–1936*, Chicago: University of Chicago Press.

Armstrong, Philip, Glyn, Andrew and Harrison, John (1984) *Capitalism since World War II*, London: Fontana.

Aronowitz, Stanley (1973) *False Promises: The Shaping of American Working-Class Consciousness*, New York: McGraw-Hill.

Banfield, Edward C. (1961) 'In Defense of the American party system', in Robert A. Goldwin (ed.) *Political Parties, USA.*, Chicago: Rand McNally.

Banfield, Edward C. and Wilson, James Q. (1963) *City Politics*, Cambridge, Mass.: Harvard University Press.

Bartholomew, Paul (1968) *Profile of a Precinct Committeeman*, Dobbs Ferry, NY: Oceana.

Bartolini, Stefano (1983) 'The membership of mass parties: The Social Democratic experience 1889–1978', in Hans Daalder and Peter Mair (eds), *West European Party Systems: Continuity and Change*, London: Sage.

Bass, Harold F. (1984) 'The president and the national party organization', in Robert Harmel (ed.) *Presidents and Their Parties: Leadership or Neglect*, New York: Praeger.

Beck, Paul Allen (1974) 'A socialization theory of partisan realignment', in Richard Niemi *et al.*, *The Politics of Future Citizens*, San Francisco: Jossey Bass.

_____ (1979) 'The electoral cycle and patterns of American politics', *British Journal of Political Science* 9: 129–56.

_____ (1984) 'The dealignment era', in Russell J. Dalton, Scott C. Flanagan and Paul Allan Beck (eds) *Electoral Change in Advanced Industrial Societies: Realignment or Dealignment,?* Princeton: Princeton University Press.

Beyle, Thad (1968) 'The governor's formal powers: A view from the governor's chair', *Public Administration Review* 28: 540–45.

Von Beyme, Klaus (1985) *Political Parties in Western Democracies*, Aldershot: Gower.

Bibby, John F. (1979) 'Political parties and federalism: The Republican national committee involvement in gubernatorial and legislative elections', *Publius* 9: 229–36.

_____ (1980) 'Party renewal in the national Republican party', in Gerald M. Pomper (ed.) *Party Renewal in America*, New York: Praeger.

Binkley, Wilfred E. (1947) *American Political Parties: Their Natural History*, New York: Alfred A. Knopf.

Black, Earl and Black, Merle (1987) *Politics and Society in the South*, Cambridge, Mass.: Harvard University Press.

Bone, Hugh A. (1949) *American Politics and the Party System*, New York: McGraw-Hill.

Bowman, Lewis and Boynton, G. R. (1966) 'Activities and role definitions of grassroots party officials', *Journal of Politics* 28: 121–43.

Brady, David W. (1988) *Critical Elections and Congressional Policy Making*, Stanford: Stanford University Press.

Bridges, Amy (1984) *A City in the Republic*, Cambridge: Cambridge University Press.

Broder, David S. (1972) *The Party's Over: The Failure of Politics in America*, New York: Harper & Row.

_____ (1990) 'Americans are demanding change', *International Herald Tribune* 28 March: 9.

Brown, M. Craig and Halaby, Charles N. (1987) 'Machine politics in America, 1870–1945', *Journal of Interdisciplinary History* 17: 587–612.

Brown, Roger G. (1982) 'Party and bureaucracy: From Kennedy to Reagan', *Political Science Quarterly* 97: 279–94.

Burnham, Walter Dean (1969) 'The end of party politics', *Transaction* 7: 12–22.

_____ (1970) *Critical Elections and the Mainsprings of American Politics*, New York: W. W. Norton and Company.

_____ (1980) 'The appearance and disappearance of the American voter', in Richard Rose (ed.) *Electoral Participation: A Comparative Analysis*, Beverly Hills: Sage.

Burns, James Macgregor (1963) *The Deadlock of Democracy*, Englewood Cliffs, NJ: Prentice-Hall.

Campbell, Angus, Converse, Philip E., Miller, Warren E. and Stokes, Donald E., (1960) *The American Voter*, New York: Wiley.

Campbell, James E. (1985) 'Sources of the new deal realignment: The contributions of conversion and mobilization to partisan change', *Western Political Quarterly* 38: 357–76.

Cavanagh, Thomas E. and Sundquist, James L. (1985) 'The new two-party system', in John E. Chubb and Paul E. Peterson (eds) *The New Direction in American Politics*, Washington, DC: Brookings Institution.

Ceaser, James W. (1979) *Presidential Selection*, Princeton: Princeton University Press.

_____ (1980) 'Political change and party reform', in Robert A. Goldwin (ed.) *Political Parties in the Eighties*, Washington, DC: American Enterprise Institute.

Chambers, William N. and Burnham, Walter Dean (eds) (1967) *The American Party Systems: Stages of Political Development*, New York: Oxford University Press.

Chubb, John E. and Peterson, Paul E. (1985) *The New Direction in American Politics*, Washington, DC: Brookings Institution.

Clark, Peter B. and Wilson, James Q. (1961) 'Incentive systems: A theory of organization', *Administrative Science Quarterly* 6: 129–66.

Clor, Harry M. (1976) 'Woodrow Wilson', in Morton J. Frisch and Richard G. Stevens (eds) *American Political Thought*, New York: Charles Scribner's Sons.

Clubb, Jerome M., Flanigan, William H. and Zingale, Nancy H. (1980) *Partisan Realignment: Voters, Parties, and Government in American History*, Beverly Hills: Sage.

Cole, Donald B. (1984) *Martin Van Buren and the American Party System*, Princeton: Princeton University Press.

Commission on Party Structure and Delegate Selection (1970) *Mandate for Reform*, Washington, DC: Democratic National Committee.

Commons, John R. (1966) 'Introduction', in John R. Commons *et al.*, *History of Labor in the United States*, vol. 1, New York: Augustus M. Kelley. Originally published 1918.

Converse, Philip E. (1976) *The Dynamics of Party Support: Cohort-Analyzing Party Identification*, Beverly Hills: Sage.

Converse, Philip E., Campell, Angus, Miller, Warren E. and Stokes, Donald E. (1961) 'Stability and change in 1960: A reinstating election', *American Political Science Review* 55: 269–80.

Cotter, Cornelius P. and Hennessy, Bernard C. (1964) *Politics without Power: The National Party Committees*, New York: Atherton.

Cotter, Cornelius P. and Bibby, John F. (1980) 'Institutional development of parties and the thesis of party decline', *Political Science Quarterly* 95: 1–28.

Cotter, Cornelius P., Gibson, James L. Bibby, John F. and Huckshorn, Robert J. (1984) *Party Organizations in American Politics*, New York: Praeger.

Crewe, Ivor and Denver, David (eds) (1985) *Electoral Change in Western Democracies: Patterns and Sources of Electoral Volatility*, Beckenham: Croom Helm.

Crotty, William J. (1976) 'Anatomy of a challenge: The Chicago delegates to the Democratic National Convention', in Robert Lee Peabody (ed.) *Cases in American Politics*, New York: Praeger.

_____ (1984) *American Parties in Decline*, 2nd edn, Boston: Little Brown.

_____ (1985) *The Party Game*, New York: W. H. Freeman.

_____ (ed.) (1986) *Political Parties in Local Areas*, Knoxville: University of Tennessee Press.

Cunningham, Noble E., Jr (1957) *The Jeffersonian Republicans: The Formation of Party Organization 1789–1801*, Chapel Hill: The University of North Carolina Press.

Davidson, Roger H. (1988) 'The new centralization in Congress', *Review of Politics* 50: 345–64.

Davis, James W. (1967) *Presidential Primaries: Road to the White House*, New York: Crowell.

Deckard, Barbara (1976) 'Political controversy and congressional voting: The effects of the 1960s on voting patterns in the House of Representatives', *Journal of Politics* 38: 326–45.

De Nitto, Andrew J. and Smithers, William (1972) 'The representativeness of the direct primary: A further test of V. O. Key's thesis', *Polity* 5: 209–24.

Dennis, Jack (1980) 'Changing public support for the American party system', in William J. Crotty (ed.) *Paths to Political Reform*, Lexington, Mass.: D. C. Heath.

―――― (1986) 'Public support for the party system 1964–1984', Paper presented at the American Political Science Association Annual Meeting, Washington, DC, 28–31 August.

Dorsett, Lyle W. (1977) *Franklin D. Roosevelt and the City Bosses*, Port Washington, NY: Kennikat Press.

Dreyer, Edward (1973) 'Change and stability in party identification', *Journal of Politics* 35: 712–22.

Dubois, Philip L. (1988) 'The Illusion of judicial consensus revisited: Partisan conflict on an intermediate state court of appeals', *American Journal of Political Science* 32: 946–67.

Duverger, Maurice (1959) *Political Parties*, 2nd edn trans. Barbara and Robert North, London: Methuen.

Edsall, Thomas B. (1988) 'In US cities, race realigns the parties', *International Herald Tribune*, 4 November: 3.

Edwards, George C. (1984) 'Presidential party leadership in Congress', in Robert Harmel (ed.) *Presidents and their Parties: Leadership or Neglect*, New York: Praeger.

Eidelberg, Paul (1974) *A Discourse on Statesmanship*, Urbana: University of Illinois Press.

Eldersveld, Samuel J. (1964) *Politial Parties: A Behavioural Analysis*, Chicago: Rand McNally.

―――― (1982) *Political Parties in American Society*, New York: Basic Books.

Epstein, Leon D. (1978) 'Political science and presidential nominations', *Political Science Quarterly* 93: 177–96.

―――― (1982) 'Party confederations and political nationalization', *Publius* 12: 70–121.

―――― (1986) *Political Parties in the American Mold*, Madison: University of Wisconsin Press.

―――― (1989) 'Will American parties be privatized?', *Journal of Law and Politics* 5: 239–74.

Erie, Steven P. (1988) *Rainbow's End: Irish- Americans and the Dilemmas of Urban Machine Politics, 1840–1985*, Berkeley and London: University of California Press.

Erikson, Robert S. and Tedin, Kent L. (1981) 'The 1928–1936 partisan realignment: The case for the conversion hypothesis', *American Political Science Review* 75: 951–62.

Fenton, John (1966) *Midwest Politics*, New York: Holt, Rinehart Winston.

―――― (1979) 'Turnout and the two-party vote', *Journal of Politics* 41: 229–34.

Finkel, Steven E. and Scarrow, Howard A. (1985) 'Party identification and party enrolment: The differences and the consequences', *Journal of Politics* 47: 620–42.

Fiorina, Morris P. (1977) *Congress: Keystone of the Washington Establishment*, New Haven, Conn.: Yale University Press.

―――― (1981) *Retrospective Voting in American National Elections*, New Haven, Conn.: Yale University Press.

Fischer, David Hackett (1965) *The Revolution of American Conservatism: The Federalist Party in the Era of Jeffersonian Democracy*, New York: Harper & Row.

Fishel, Jeff (1985) *Presidents and Promises*, Washington, DC: Congressional Quarterly Press.

Foner, Eric (1970) *Free Soil, Free Labor, Free Men: The Ideology of the Republican Party before the Civil War*, New York: Oxford University Press.

Franklin, Charles H. and Jackson, John E. (1983) 'The dynamics of party identification', *American Political Science Review* 77: 957–73.

Galderisi, Peter F. and Ginsberg, Benjamin (1986) 'Primary elections and the evanescence of third party activity in the United States', in Benjamin Ginsberg and Alan Stone (eds) *Do Elections Matter?*, Amonk, NY and London: M. E. Sharpe.

Garrity, Patrick J. (1984) 'Young men in a hurry: Roosevelt, Lodge, and the foundations of twentieth century Republicanism', in Thomas B. Silver and Peter W. Schramm (eds) *Natural Right and Political Right*, Durham: Carolina Academic Press.

Gibson, James L., Cotter, Cornelius P., Bibby, John F. and Huckshorn, Robert J. (1983) 'Assessing party organizational strength', *American Journal of Political Science* 27: 193–222.

_____(1985) 'Whither the local parties: A cross-sectional and longitudinal analysis of the strength of party organization', *American Journal of Political Science* 29: 139–60.

Gibson, James L., Fredreis, John P. and Vertz, Laura L. (1989) 'Party dynamics in the 1980s: Change in county party organizational strength, 1980–1984', *American Journal of Political Science*, 33: 67–90.

Goldberg, Arthur S. (1966) 'Discovering a causal pattern among data on voting behavior', *American Political Science Review* 60: 913–22.

Goldenberg, Edie N. and Traugott, Michael (1984) *Campaigning for Congress*, Washington, DC: Congressional Quarterly Press.

Goldman, Sheldon (1975) 'Voting behavior in the United States Court of Appeals revisited', *American Political Science Review* 69: 491–506.

Goodman, Paul (1967) 'The first American party system', in William Nisbet Chambers and Walter Dean Burnham (eds) *The American Party Systems: Stages of Political Development*, New York: Oxford University Press.

Gosnell, Harold F. (1968) *Machine Politics: Chicago Model*, 2nd edn, Chicago: Chicago University Press.

Grantham, Dewey W. (1988) *The Life and Death of the Solid South: A Political History*, Lexington: University Press of Kentucky.

Greenstein, Fred I. (1970) *The American Party System and the American People*, Englewood Cliffs, NJ: Prentice-Hall.

Greenstone, David J. (1966) 'Party pressure on organized labor in three cities', in M. Kent Jennings and L. Harmon Ziegler (eds) *The Electoral Process*, Englewood Cliffs, NJ: Prentice-Hall.

Handlin, Oscar (1951) *The Uprooted*, New York: Grosset & Dunlap.

Hartz, Louis (1955) *The Liberal Tradition in America: An Interpretation of American Political Thought Since the Revolution*, New York: Harcourt, Brace.

Heclo, Hugh (1978) *A Government of Strangers*, Washington, DC: Brookings Institution.

Herring, Pendleton (1940) *The Politics of Democracy*, New York: W. W. Norton.

Herrnson, Paul S. (1986) 'Do parties make a difference? The role of party organizations in Congressional elections', *Journal of Politics* 48: 589–615

_____ (1988) *Party Campaigning in the 1980's*, Cambridge, Mass.: Harvard University Press.

Hitlin, Robert A. and Jackson, John S. (1979) 'Change and reform in the Democratic party', *Polity* 11: 617–33.

Hoadley, John F. (1986) *Origins of American Political Parties 1789–1803*, Lexington: University Press of Kentucky.

Hofstadter, Richard (1969) *The Idea of a Party System: The Rise of Legitimate Opposition in the United States, 1780–1840*, Berkeley: University of California Press.

Huckshorn, Robert J. (1976) *Party Leadership in the States*, Amherst: University of Massachusetts Press.

Inglehart, Ronald (1977) *The Silent Revolution: Changing Values and Styles Among Western Publics*, Princeton: Princeton University Press.

Jackman, Mary R. and Jackman, Robert W. (1983) *Class Awareness in the United States*, Berkeley: University of California Press.

Jackson, John E. (1975) 'Issues, party choices, and presidential votes', *American Journal of Political Science* 19: 161–85.

Jacobson, Gary C. (1983) *The Politics of Congressional Elections*, Boston: Little, Brown.

_____ (1984) 'Money in the 1980 and 1982 Congressional elections', in Michael J. Malbin (ed.) *Money and Politics in the United States: Financing Elections in the 1980s*, Chatham, NJ: Chatham House.

_____ (1985–6) 'Party organization and distribution of campaign resources: Republicans and Democrats in 1982', *Political Science Quarterly* 100: 603–25.

Jacobson, Gary C. and Kernell, Samuel (1981) *Strategy and Choice in Congressional Elections*, New Haven, Conn.: Yale University Press.

Jaffa, Harry V. (1965) 'The nature and origin of the American party system', in *Equality and Liberty*, New York: Oxford University Press.

_____ (1973) *Crisis of the House Divided: An Interpretation of the Lincoln-Douglas Debates*, Seattle: University of Washington Press.

Jefferson, Thomas (1903–5) *The Writings of Thomas Jefferson*, ed. A. A. Lipscomb and A. E. Bergh, 20 vols, Washington, DC: Memorial Edition.

Jewell, Malcolm E. (1984) *Parties and Primaries: Nominating State Governors*, New York: Praeger.

Jewell, Malcolm E. and Olson, David M. (1978) *American State Political Parties and Elections*, Homewood, Ill.: Dorsey Press.

Jewell, Malcolm E. and Patterson, Samuel C. (1986) *The Legislative Process in the United States*, 4th edn, New York: Random House.

Johnson, Donald Bruce (1982) *National Party Platforms of 1980*, Urbana: University of Illinois Press.

Johnson, Donald Bruce and Porter, Kirk H. (1973) *National Party Platforms 1840–1972*, Urbana: University of Illinois Press.

Johnston, Michael (1979) 'Patrons and clients, jobs and machines: A case study of the uses of patronage', *American Political Science Review* 73: 385–98.

Jones, Ruth S. (1984) 'Financing state elections', in Michael J. Malbin (ed.) *Money and Politics in the United States: Financing Elections in the 1980s*, Chatham, NJ: Chatham House.

Katz, Richard S. (1986) 'Party government: A rationalistic conception', in Francis G. Castles and Rudolf Wildenmann (eds) *Visions and Realities of Party Government*, Berlin and New York: de Gruyter.

Kayden, Xandra and Mahe, Eddie, Jr (1985) *The Party Goes On: The Persistence of the Two-Party System in the United States*, New York: Basic Books.

Kazee, Thomas A. and Thornberry, Mary C. (1990) 'Where's the party? Congressional candidate recruitment and American party organizations', *Western Political Quarterly* 43: 61–80.

Kelley, Stanley, Jr (1960) *Political Campaigning*, Washington, DC: Brookings Institution.

Kernell, Samuel (1977) 'Presidential popularity and negative voting: An alternative explanation of the midterm Congressional decline of the president's party', *American Political Science Review* 71: 44–66.

Kesler, Charles R. (1984) 'Woodrow Wilson and the statesmanship of progress', in Thomas B. Silver and Peter W. Schramm (eds) *Natural Right and Political Right*, Durham: Carolina Academic Press.

Key, V. O. (1955) 'A theory of critical elections', *Journal of Politics* 17: 3–18.

_____ (1956) *American State Politics: An Introduction*, New York: Alfred A. Knopf.

_____ (1959) 'Secular realignment and the party system', *Journal of Politics* 21: 198–210.

_____ (1964) *Politics, Parties and Pressure Groups*, 5th edn, New York: Crowell.

_____ (1966) *The Responsible Electorate: Rationality in Presidential Voting, 1936–1966*, Cambridge, Mass.: Harvard University Press.

Kirkpatrick, Jeane J. (1975) 'Representation in American national conventions: The case of 1972', *British Journal of Political Science* 5: 265–322.

_____ (1976) *The New Presidential Elite: Men and Women in National Politics*, New York: Russell Sage Foundation and the Twentieth Century Fund.

_____ (1978) *Dismantling the Parties: Reflections on Party Reform and Party Decomposition*, Washington, DC: American Enterprise Institute.

Kleppner, Paul *et al.* (1981) *The Evolution of American Electoral Systems*, Westport, Conn.: Greenwood Press.

Kleppner, Paul (1985) *Chicago Divided: The Making of a Black Mayor*, DeKalb, Ill.: Northern Illinois University Press.

Kramer, Gerald H. (1970–71) 'The effect of precinct-level canvassing on voter behavior', *Public Opinion Quarterly* 34: 560–72.

Kritzer, Herbert (1977) 'The representativeness of the 1972 presidential primaries', *Polity* 10: 121–9.

Ladd, Everett Carll, Jr. (1970) *American Political Parties: Social Change and Political Response*, New York: W. W. Norton & Company.

_____ with Hadley, Charles (1975) *Transformations of the American Party System: Political Coalitions from the New Deal to the 1970s*, New York: W. W. Norton & Company.

_____ (1976–77) 'Liberalism upside down: The inversion of the New Deal order', *Political Science Quarterly* 91: 577–600.

_____ (1978) *Where Have All the Voters Gone?*, New York: W. W. Norton & Company.

_____ (1981) 'The brittle mandate: Electoral dealignment and the 1980 presidential election', *Political Science Quarterly* 96: 1–25.

_____ (1989a) 'The 1988 elections: continuation of the post-New Deal system', *Political Science Quarterly* 104: 1–18.

_____ (1989b) 'Like waiting for Godot: The uselessness of *realignment* for understanding change in contemporary American politics', paper presented at the Annual Meeting of the American Political Science Association, Atlanta, 31 August–3 September.

La Palombara, Joseph (1987) *Democracy, Italian Style*, New Haven and London: Yale University Press.

Laslett, John H. M. and Lipset, Seymour Martin (1974) *Failure of a Dream: Essays in the History of American Socialism*, Garden City, NY: Anchor/Doubleday.

Lawson, Kay (1985) 'Challenging regulation of political parties: The California case', *Journal of Law and Politics*, 2: 263–85.

Lehmbruch, Gerhard (1977) 'Liberal corporatism and party government', *Comparative Political Studies* 10: 91–126.

Lemarchand, Rene (1981) 'Comparative political clientelism, structures, process and optic' in S. N. Eisenstadt and Rene Lemarchand, (eds) *Political Clientelism, Patronage, and Development*, Beverly Hills: Sage.

Lengle, James I. (1981) *Representation and Presidential Primaries*, Westport, Conn.: Greenwood Press.

Levitin, Teresa E. and Miller, Warren E. (1979) 'Ideological interpretations of presidential elections', *American Political Science Review* 73: 751–71.

Lipset, Seymour Martin (1967) *The First New Nation*, Garden City, NY: Doubleday.

Lipset, Seymour Martin and Rokkan, Stein (1967) 'Cleavages structures, party systems and voter alignments: An introduction', in Seymour Martin Lipset and Stein Rokkan (eds) *Party Systems and Voter Alignments*, New York: Free Press.

Longley, Charles H. (1980a) 'National party renewal', in Gerald M. Pomper (ed.) *Party Renewal in America*, New York: Praeger.

––––––– (1980b) 'Party nationalization in America', in William J. Crotty (ed.) *Paths to Political Reform*, Lexington, Mass.: D. C. Heath.

Lowi, Theodore J. (1967) 'Machine politics – old and new', *Public Interest* 9: 83–92.

Lubell, Samuel (1965) *The Future of American Politics*, 3rd edn, New York: Harper & Row.

McConnell, Mitch (1987) 'Don't make taxpayers finance campaigns', *The Washington Post National Weekly Edition* 20 July: 29.

McCormick, Richard P. (1967) 'Political development and the second American party system', in William Nisbet Chambers and Walter Dean Burnham (eds) *The American Party Systems: Stages of Political Development*, New York: Oxford University Press.

McKay, David (1989) 'Presidential autonomy in a fragmented polity', in Richard Maidment and John Zvesper (eds) *Reflections on the Constitution: The American Constitution After Two Hundred Years*, Manchester and New York: Manchester University Press.

MacKenzie, Calvin G. (1981) *The Politics of Presidential Appointments*, New York: Free Press.

McNitt, Andrew D. (1980) 'The effect of preprimary endorsement on competition for nomination: An examination of differing nominating systems', *Journal of Politics* 42: 257–66.

McWilliams, Wilson Carey (1989) 'The meaning of the election' in Gerald M. Pomper (ed.) *The Election of 1988*, Chatham, N J: Chatham House.

Madison, James (1900–1910) *The Writings of James Madison*, ed. Gaillard Hunt, 9 vols, New York: Putnam.

Mair, Peter (1984) 'Party politics in contemporary Europe: A challenge to party', *West European Politics* 7: 170–84.

Mann, Thomas E. and Wolfinger, Raymond E. (1980) 'Candidates and parties in Congressional elections', *American Political Science Review* 74: 617–32.

Mansfield, Harvey C., Jr (1965) *Statesmanship and Party Government*, Chicago: University of Chicago Press.

'Marcus Brutus' (1800) *Serious Facts, Opposed to 'Serious Considerations'*, n. p.

Markus, Gregory and Converse, Philip E. (1979) 'A dynamic simultaneous equation of electoral choice', *American Political Science Review* 73: 1055–70.

Marshall, Thomas R. (1980) 'Minnesota: The caucus- convention system' in Gerald M. Pomper (ed.) *Party Renewal in America*, New York: Praeger.

Mayhew, David R. (1986) *Placing Parties in American Politics*, Princeton, NJ.: Princeton University Press.

Mazmanian, Daniel A. (1974) *Third Parties in Presidential Elections*, Washington, DC: Brookings Institution.

Merriam, Charles Edward (1968) *A History of American Political Theories*, New York and London: Johnson Reprint Corporation. Originally published 1903.

Meyers, Marvin (1957) *The Jacksonian Persuasion*, Stanford: Stanford University Press.

Milkis, Sidney M. (1985) 'Franklin D. Roosevelt and the transcendence of partisan politics', *Political Science Quarterly* 100: 479–504.

———— (1987) 'The Presidency, democratic reform, and constitutional change', *PS* 20: 628–36.

Miller, Arthur H., Miller, Warren E., Raine, Alden S. and Brown, Thad H. (1976) 'A majority party in disarray: Policy polarization in the 1972 election', *American Political Science Review* 70: 753–78.

Miller, Penny M., Jewell, Malcolm E. and Sigelman, Lee (1988) 'Divisive primaries and party activists: Kentucky, 1979 and 1983', *Journal of Politics* 50: 459–70.

Monroe, Alan D. (1983) 'American party platforms and public opinion', *American Journal of Political Science* 27: 27–42.

Morehouse, Sarah McCally (1981) *State Politics, Parties and Policy*, New York: Holt, Rinehart & Winston.

Nagel, Stuart (1961) 'Political party affiliation and judges' decisions', *American Political Science Review* 55: 843–50.

Nelson, Michael (1988) 'The president and the court: reinterpreting the court packing episode of 1937', *Political Science Quarterly* 103: 267–94.

Nie, Norman H., Verba, Sidney and Petrocik, John R. (1976) *The Changing American Voter*, Cambridge, Mass.: Harvard University Press.

Norpoth, Helmut and Rusk, Jerrold G. (1982) 'Partisan dealignment in the American electorate: Itemizing the deductions since 1964', *American Political Science Review* 76: 522–37.

Norpoth, Helmut and Kagay, Michael P. (1989) 'Another eight years of Republican rule and still no partisan realignment?', Paper presented at the American Political Science Association Annual Meeting, Atlanta, 31 August–3 September.

Page, Benjamin I. (1978) *Choices and Echoes in Presidential Elections*, Chicago and London: University of Chicago Press.

Page, Benjamin I. and Brody, Richard A. (1972) 'Policy voting and the electoral process: The Vietnam War issue', *American Political Science Review*, 66: 979–95.

Penniman, Howard R. (1984) 'US elections: Really a bargain?' *Public Opinion* June/July: 51–53.

Perlman, Selig (1970) *Theory of the Labor Movement*, New York: Augustus M. Kelley. Originally published 1928.

Petrocik, John R. (1981) *Party Coalitions*, Chicago: University of Chicago Press.

—— (1987) 'The political landscape in 1988', *Public Opinion*, September/October: 41–4.

Petrocik, John R., and Steeper, Frederick T.(1987) 'Voter turnout and electoral preferences: The anomalous Reagan elections', in Kay Lehman Schlozman (ed.) *Elections in America*, Boston: Allen & Unwin.

Phillips, Kevin D. (1970) *The Emerging Republican Majority*, Garden City: Doubleday.

Piereson, James (1982) 'Party government', *The Political Science Reviewer* 6: 2–53.

Polsby, Nelson (1978) 'Presidential cabinet making: Lessons for the political system', *Political Science Quarterly* 93: 15–25.

Polsby, Nelson W. (1983) *Consequences of Party Reform*, New York: Oxford University Press.

Polsby, Nelson W. and Wildavsky, Aaron B. (1976) *Presidential Elections: Strategies of American Electoral Politics*, 4th edn, New York: Charles Scribner's Sons.

Pomper, Gerald M. (1967) 'Classification of presidential elections', *Journal of Politics* 29: 535–66.

—— (1972) 'From confusion to clarity: Issues and American voters, 1956–1968', *American Political Science Review* 66: 415–28.

Pomper, Gerald M. and Lederman, Susan (1980) *Elections in America*, 2nd edn, New York: Longman.

Popkin, Samuel L., Gorman, John W., Phillips, Charles and Smith, Jeffrey A. (1976) 'What have you done for me lately? Toward an investment theory of voting', *American Political Science Review* 70: 779–805.

Powell, G. Bingham, Jr (1980) 'Voting turnout in thirty democracies: Partisan, legal and socio-economic influences', in Richard Rose (ed.) *Electoral Participation: A Comparative Analysis*, Beverly Hills: Sage.

Ranney, Austin (1954) *The Doctrine of Responsible Party Government*, Urbana, Ill.: University of Illinois Press.

—— (1968) 'The representativeness of primary electorates', *Midwest Journal of Political Science* 12: 224–38.

—— (1972) 'Turnout and representation in presidential primary elections', *American Political Science Review* 66: 21–37.

—— (1975) *Curing the Mischiefs of Faction*, Berkeley and London: University of California Press.

—— (1978) 'Political parties: Reform and decline', in Anthony King (ed.) *The New Amerian Political System*, Washington, DC: American Enterprise Institute.

—— (1983) 'The president and his party', in Anthony King (ed.) *Both Ends of the Avenue*, Washington, DC : American Enterprise Institute.

Ranney, Austin and Kendall, Willmoore (1956) *Democracy and the American Party System*, New York: Harcourt, Brace & World.

Re Pass, David E. (1971) 'Issue salience and party choice', *American Political Science Review* 65: 389–400.

Reichley, A. James (1985) 'The rise of national parties', in John E. Chubb and Paul Peterson (eds) *The New Direction in American Politics* Washington, DC: Brookings Institution.

Reilly, Steve (1987) 'Social change and the party system', Paper presented at the UK American Politics Group Annual Conference, University of London, 3–5 January.

Roosevelt, Franklin D. (1932), 'Campaign address on progressive government' (Commonwealth Club Address, San Francisco), in Samuel I. Rosenman (ed.)

Public Papers and Addresses of Franklin D. Roosevelt, 13 vols., New York: Harper & Bros, 1938–50, 1: 742–56.

Rose, Richard (1974) *The Problem of Party Government*, London: Macmillan.

Rosebloom, David Lee (1973) *The Election Men: Professional Campaign Managers and American Democracy*, New York: Quadrangle Books.

Rosenstone, Steven J. and Wolfinger, Raymond E. (1978) 'The effects of registration laws on voter turnout', *American Political Science Review* 72: 22–45.

Rosenstone, Steven J., Behr, Roy L. and Lazarus, Edward H. (1984) *Third Parties in America: Citizen Response to Major Party Failure*, Princeton: Princeton University Press.

Sabato, Larry J. (1981) *The Rise of Political Consultants: New Ways of Winning Elections*, New York: Basic Books.

―――― (1987) 'The attack on PACs', *The Washington Post National Weekly Edition*, 24 August: 29.

Salmore, Stephen A. and Salmore, Barbara G. (1985) *Candidates, Parties and Campaigns: Electoral Politics in America*, Washington, DC: Congressional Quarterly Press.

Samson, Leon (1935) *Toward a United Front*, New York: Farrar & Rinehart.

Sartori, Giovanni (1976) *Parties and Party Systems: A Framework for Analysis*, Cambridge: Cambridge University Press.

Schattschneider, E. E. (1942) *Party Government*, New York: Holt, Rinehart & Winston.

―――― (1960) *The Semi-Sovereign People*, New York: Holt, Rinehart & Winston.

Schlesinger, Joseph (1984) 'On the theory of party organization', *Journal of Politics* 46: 369–400.

Schneider, William (1981) 'The November 4 vote for president: What did it mean?' in Austin Ranney (ed.) *The American Elections of 1980*, Washington, DC: American Enterprise Institute.

―――― (1989) 'JFK's children: The class of '74', *The Atlantic Monthly*, March: 35–58.

Scott, James C. (1969) 'Corruption, machine politics, and political change', *American Political Science Review* 63: 1142–58.

Scott, Ruth K. and Hrebnar, Ronald J., (1979) *Parties in Crisis*, New York: Wiley.

Shafer, Byron E. (1983) *Quiet Revolution: The Struggle for the Democratic Party and the Shaping of Post-Reform Politics*, New York: Russell Sage Foundation.

―――― (1988) *Bifurcated Politics: Evolution and Reform in the National Party Convention*, Cambridge, Mass. and London: Harvard University Press

―――― (1989) 'The election of 1988 and the structure of American politics', *Electoral Studies* 8: 5–21.

Shapiro, Martin (1978) 'The Supreme Court: From Warren to Burger', in Anthony King (ed.) *The New American Political System*, Washington, DC: American Enterprise Institute.

Shefter, Martin (1976) 'The emergence of a political machine: An alternative view', in Willis D. Hawley (ed.) *Theoretical Perspectives on Urban Politics*, Englewood Cliffs, NJ: Prentice-Hall.

―――― (1983) 'Regional receptivity to reform: The legacy of the progressive era', *Political Science Quarterly* 98: 459–83.

Sinclair, Barbara (1977) 'Party realignment and the transformation of the political agenda: The House of Representatives 1925–1938', *American Political Science Review* 71: 940–53.

_____ (1982) *Congressional Realignment 1925–1978*, Austin: University of Texas Press.

Smith, Gordon (1986) *Democracy in Western Germany*, 3rd edn, Aldershot: Gower.

Snowiss, Leo (1966) 'Congressional recruitment and representation', *American Political Science Review* 60: 627–39.

Sombart, Werner (1976) *Why Is There No Socialism in the United States?* trans. Patricia M. Hocking and C. T. Husbands, London and Basingstoke: Macmillan. Originally published 1906.

Sorauf, Frank J. (1963) *Party and Representation: Legislative Politics in Pennsylvania*, New York: Atherton.

Soule, John W. and Clarke, James W. (1970) 'Amateurs and professionals: A study of delegates to the 1968 Democratic convention', *American Political Science Review* 64: 888–98.

Spotts, Frederic and Wieser, Theodore (1986) *Italy: A Difficult Democracy*, Cambridge: Cambridge University Press.

Stave, Bruce (1970) *The New Deal and the Last Hurrah: Pittsburgh Machine Politics*, Pittsburgh: Pittsburgh University Press.

Stokes, Donald E. (1966) 'Some dynamic elements in contests for the presidency', *American Political Science Review* 60: 19–28.

Sundquist, James L. (1973) *Dynamics of the Party System: Alignment and Realignment of Political Parties in the United States*, Washington, DC: Brookings Institution.

_____ (1983) *Dynamics of the Party System: Alignment and Realignment of Political Parties in the United States*, revised edn, Washington, DC: Brookings Institution.

_____ (1988–89) 'Needed: A political theory for the new era of coalition government in the United States', *Political Science Quarterly* 103: 613–36.

Tate, C. Neal (1981) 'Personal attribute models of voting behavior of US Supreme Court Justices: Liberalism in civil liberties and economic decisions, 1946–1978', *American Political Science Review* 75: 355–67.

Thernstrom, Stephan (1970) 'Working class social mobility in industrial America', in Melvin Richter (ed.) *Essays in Theory and History*, Cambridge, Mass.: Harvard University Press.

Tobin, Richard J. and Keynes, Edward J. (1975) 'Institutional differences in the recruitment process: A four-state study', *American Journal of Political Science* 19: 667–82.

Trilling, Richard J. and Campbell, Bruce A. (1980) 'Toward a theory of realignment: An Introduction', in Campbell and Trilling (eds) *Realignment in American Politics: Toward a Theory*, Austin: University of Texas Press.

Tufte, Edward R. (1975) 'Determinants of the outcomes of midterm Congressional elections', *American Political Science Review* 69: 812–26.

Ulmer, Sidney (1962) 'The political party variable in the Michigan Supreme Court', *Journal of Public Law* 11: 352–62.

Van Buren, Martin (1827) Letter to Thomas Ritchie, 13 January, quoted in Ceaser 1979: 160–61.

_____ (1967) *Inquiry into the Origin and Course of Political Parties in the United States*, New York: Augustus M. Kelley. Originally published 1867.

Ware, Alan (1985) *The Breakdown of Democratic Party Organization, 1940–1980*, Oxford: Oxford University Press.

_____ (1988) 'The United States: The disappearance of party', in Alan Ware (ed.)

Political Parties: Electoral Change and Structural Response, Oxford: Basil Blackwell.

Watson, David (1981) *Why Is There No Socialism in the United States?* Winchester: King Alfred's College.

Wattenberg, Ben J. (1988) 'The Curse of Jesse', *The New Republic*, 5 December: 20–21.

Wattenberg, Martin P. (1982) 'Party identification and party images: A comparison of Britain, Canada, Australia and the United States', *Comparative Politics* 15: 23–40.

——— (1986) *The Decline of American Political Parties, 1952-1984*, Cambridge, Mass. and London: Harvard University Press

Weatherman, Donald V. (1982) 'America's rise to a mature party system', Paper presented to the American Political Science Association Annual Meeting, Denver, 2–5 September.

——— (1984) 'From factions to parties: America's partisan education', in Thomas B. Silver and Peter W. Schramm (eds) *Natural Right and Political Right*, Durham: Carolina Academic Press.

Weinstein, James (1967) *The Decline of Socialism in America, 1912–1925*, New York: Monthly Review Press.

Wekkin, Gary D. (1984a) *Democrat versus Democrat: The National Party's Campaign to Close the Wisconsin Primary*, Columbia: University of Missouri Press.

——— (1984b) 'National-state party relations: The Democrats' new federal structure', *Political Science Quarterly* 99: 45–72.

White, John K. (1983) *The Fractured Electorate: Political Parties and Social Change in Southern New England*, Hanover, NH and London: University Press of New England.

Williams, T. Harry (1969) *Huey Long*, London: Thames & Hudson.

Wolfinger, Raymond E. (1972) 'Why political machines have not withered away and other revisionist thoughts', *Journal of Politics* 34: 365–98.

——— (1974) *The Politics of Progress*, Englewood Cliffs, NJ: Prentice-Hall.

Zvesper, John (1977) *Political Philosophy and Rhetoric: A Study of the Origins of American Party Politics*, Cambridge: Cambridge University Press.

——— (1989) 'The American founders and classical political thought', *History of Political Thought* 10: 701–18.

Index